Profit from Gold and Rare Coins Now

by

Donald H. Kagin, Ph.D.

Cover design by Byran

ISBN-10: 1-933990-30-9
ISBN-13: 978-1-933990-30-9

Published by:
Zyrus Press, Inc.
P.O. Box 17810
Irvine, CA 92623

Printed in the United States of America

This book is dedicated to my wife Candace, children Adam, Justin and Jessica, grandchildren Jacob, Aaron, and Isaac, and future generations of collector/investors.

Profit from Gold and Rare Coins Now

by

Donald H. Kagin, Ph.D.

Introduction by
Scott Travers

With tax and estate planning contributions from
D. Larry Crumbley, Ph.D., CPA, CFF

Table of Contents

Introduction by Scott Travers

"Appreciation" is a five-syllable word with big meaning for people who purchase collectible coins. For pure collectors, it describes the enjoyment they get from acquiring these tiny treasures—the pleasure they derive from the beauty and history embodied in many coins and the pride they feel in owning them. For buyers concerned with profit as well as pleasure, "appreciation" takes the form of potential financial gain, and well-chosen coins have risen in value steadily—even sharply—over the years.

Most rare coin investment books and guides provide you with detailed collector history. This book, *Profit from Gold and Rare Coins Now*, instead focuses on the serious investor, not only relating coin investment history but meticulously dissecting the four main factors which come to bear on coin values—supply, demand, timing and true value.

This book is written by one of the most educated, professional numismatists in the world—a highly respected man that I have known for over thirty years: Donald H. Kagin, Ph.D. Dr. Kagin has impressive credentials as a numismatic authority, having received the first Bachelor of Arts degree in Numismatics granted by Northwestern University and the very first Ph.D. He has also served on the board of our umbrella organization, the American Numismatic Association. Clearly, he is the right person at the right time to guide you in not only appreciating coins but in selecting coins for financial appreciation.

In order to profit and understand today's markets, it is important to begin with a historical perspective. Prior to modern times, coin investing was unheard of and coin collecting was largely a pursuit of the wealthy—noblemen and those with wealth who had both time and money to indulge such passions. For that reason, coin collecting came to be known as "The Hobby of Kings." Ironically, the hobby's democratization began in earnest during the Great Depression of the 1930s when many Americans, needing inexpensive forms of diversion, took a fancy to a simple new product called the "penny board." Essentially, this was an 11-by-14-inch piece of thick cardboard, suitable for display, with rows of circular spaces designed to hold cents or other U.S. coins by date and mint mark. It was coin collecting's Johnny Appleseed, planting the seeds that led to the hobby's dramatic flowering several decades later. It was on its way to being "The King of Hobbies."

Dr. Kagin's father, A.M. "Art" Kagin, was an early advocate of these coin boards and coins in general, who started a long career as a coin dealer in 1933. In the early 1950s,

Art Kagin sold more coin books than any other coin dealer, creating and nurturing hundreds of new hobbyists, including his son, Don.

The postwar economic boom after World War II set the stage for coin collecting, and eventually investing, to blossom. Working people found themselves with more free time—not because of massive unemployment, but rather because of shorter workweeks—and also had more disposable money because of rising wages. Millions took up sports and hobbies on which to spend that newfound time and money, and coin collecting soon began to draw attention from many.

The big boom occurred in the 1950s, and again a second surge followed in the 1970s, when coins got an important boost from the U.S. Government's "Great Silver Sale" of old silver dollars found in the Treasury's vaults a decade earlier.

In January 1980, speculative fervor drove the price of gold to about $875 per ounce on the international market—more than twenty-four times its official price of $35 per ounce a decade earlier, and rare coins' value soared even higher. The bullion market crashed, dragging coin prices lower, but the coin market recovered and reached even higher levels, and the coin investment market was now well established.

By any measure, gold and top-quality rare coins have been among the highest-appreciating assets, and Dr. Kagin not only documents this growth but presents specific examples of portfolios that he has recommended to clients with great success.

As one of the few coin dealers with a Certified Financial Planning degree, Dr. Kagin is eminently qualified to give you step-by-step due-diligence questions to ask and answers to expect from your numismatic adviser.

Additionally, he demonstrates that it isn't enough just to buy the right coins through the right adviser: You also must make sure to pay the right price. Deciding when to sell is also crucial, and Dr. Kagin illustrates how you can determine that timing. With many vehicles available to sell investment portfolios, he helps you figure out which mode is best for you, while revealing little-known secrets of the trade.

In this comprehensive "how-to" investment book, you will also learn the latest tax and estate planning implications for coin investing presented and co-authored by tax authority and numismatic specialist Dr. D. Larry Crumbley.

I've known Dr. Don Kagin for over thirty years, as well as his father, A.M. "Art" Kagin, the former "dean of numismatics." Dr. Kagin was tutored well by his father, and is one of the most prominent and most trustworthy coin dealers and numismatic investment advisers in today's marketplace. That is why I believe that if you are considering coin collecting as an investment opportunity, or even a serious hobby, you will ultimately get the fullest possible appreciation of numismatics—especially as a sound investment—by studying and acting upon the sage advice in this great book.

Scott A. Travers, Author

The Coin Collector's Survival Manual

Acknowledgments

The cooperation and support of many people made this book possible. I would like to thank all those who contributed. Among them are Dr. D. Larry Crumbley, who provided most of the tax information in Chapters 11 and 12 and colleague and investment advisor, Scott Travers, who wrote the introduction to this book. Also to David Ganz, Gary Knaus, Brent Johnson, Lawrence Goldberg, the Professional Coin Grading Service (PCGS) and the Numismatic Guaranty Corporation (NGC), who generously provided statistical data and charts.

Greg Galdi, Brent Johnson and Gary Knaus reviewed portions of this manuscript and provided charts and comments; and as she has done for every other one of my books, my sister, Judy, provided many unfiltered comments and suggestions. From my staff I would especially like to thank Kaye Robinson, Lena Taylor, Beth Catcher and Sara Kenworthy for their many hours of creative endeavor, image sourcing and re-writes.

And to those who reviewed this work and added comments, ideas and suggestions that made it better including Kaye Robinson, Meredith Hilton, David McCarthy and Candace Kagin.

Finally I owe a great deal of thanks to my editor, Bruce Porter who devoted far more effort and time than usual in helping me to become a much better communicator.

How to Use this Book

This book does not contain all of the answers. Rather, it is intended as a roadmap, laying bare all the unmarked curves and forks in the road that, ultimately, dictate how and when to invest in gold and rare coins and currency. This volume is an excellent resource that can be drawn upon during each stage of the investment process.

Within various chapters you will find a website address to visit that provides supplemental resources and information useful to making informed decisions. These resources guide the active collector or investor in his or her journey through the numismatic market, but they are not essential to learning how to walk, talk and think like a seasoned numismatic investor. For that, I grant you this book!

Access to the website is free to those that register online at www.goldandrare-coins.net.

To that end, this book is a Living Book: through the website you will receive periodic market updates. If I've done my job—and I think I have—you will not want this book to end with the last chapter. And, so to speak, we will continue on this journey together, online.

Think of this book as boot camp for the numismatic mind. Forget what you think you know about investments. And when you have absorbed every word and set this book down, you will be prepared enough to begin your journey. You will also be armed with this rather essential piece of advice: don't go at it alone; find and always work with a credible, established numismatic investment advisor—preferably one with a good track record!

Good luck and have fun.

Preface: Today's Perfect Storm

Three decades have passed since I wrote *Donald Kagin's Guide to Rare Coin Investments*. Since then the numismatic industry has experienced many exciting changes and advancements.

Independent grading in 1985 was a fledgling idea to standardize what is essentially a subjective art—principally through the American Numismatic Association Certification Service. It wasn't until 1986, however, with the inception of the Professional Coin Grading Service, that the difficult questions of authentication and universally-accepted grading standards were answered. PCGS made rare coins fungible and it has revolutionized the industry.

Today's perfect storm of economic and numismatic factors converging to dramatically raise bullion and rare coin values. (© Kagin's Inc.)

Other significant developments include the ubiquitous Internet. Electronic trading and auction platforms transformed myriad numismatic villages into a veritable metropolis, giving the marketplace a cohesive quality that old-timers would have never dreamed possible. Sites like eBay, Amazon, Certified Coin Exchange and public forums allow collectors and investors to take the pulse of the market with the swift ease of a mouse-click. Modern communications technology is also largely responsible for the terrific influx of people—the next generation of coin collectors—who have taken up the Hobby of Kings.

Financial sectors, including numismatics, are cyclical in nature, of course, with every new cycle presenting a unique set of opportunities. Some price moves are driven by short-term circumstances—a country such as Greece defaulting on their international loans, for instance.

The most dramatic illustration of a rapid shift in price equilibrium for coins occurred in 1989 when New York stock brokerages took a sudden interest. Always eager to put their name on new investment products, their initial foray into numismatics turned out to be a minor disaster. Simply, there wasn't enough of the right type of coins to absorb the big dollars that Wall Street mutual funds brought to the table.

The handwriting on the wall appeared in bold, 72-point type. Money made in a down market spends exactly the same as in a bullish one. If the pop in coins had come as a pleasant surprise, their inevitable collapse came with an engraved warning notification. Getting out of Morgan dollars and other common rare coins proved to be such a heady move that a couple years after I had urged my clients and newsletter readers to sell (months before the crash), I was perhaps too cautious about getting them back into this particular subcategory—despite an ample amount of evidence that generics (readily available rare coins) had bottomed.

Still, the element of unpredictability is the one constant, dreadful, frequently frightful characteristic of every market cycle. Some markets trend with determined pace, as precious metals did from 2000 to mid 2011, before experiencing significant corrections.

Other markets languish for long periods, offering little opportunity to cash out in a reasonable period of time. From 1982 to 1988, coin prices traded within a narrow range. It wasn't long into that cycle before the comfort of price stability began to feel downright boring. There are two basic strategies to take in such an environment. Convinced the market would eventually break to the upside, some slowly accumulated larger positions. More aggressive clients did exactly the opposite. They divested from much of their hard asset portfolio and parked their investment capital elsewhere—mindful that they'd jump back into coins when the market showed signs of life again.

How you approach this type of situation will depend on several factors, which this book examines in great detail.

Timing is the key to solving the dilemma of market cycles. The good news is that numismatics—now into the foreseeable future—points to a once-in-several-decades investment dynamic. *A perfect storm of opportunity.*

The Emerging Perfect Storm of Opportunity

The timing of this book is no accident. Thirty years ago, the first million dollar coin (one of the five known, much- hyped 1913 Liberty nickels) was still a dozen years away. Today, a rare coin—once worth only its face value—has surpassed $10 million! Indeed, the market for the finest numismatic coins and currency is just beginning to take off.

It is one of the most auspicious times in history for an investor to enter the rare coin market—a perfect storm of macro- and micro-economic circumstances simultaneously converging. We are in the beginning stage of the biggest, most robust bull market in investment-quality and legacy—exceptionally rare and important—coins in the history of numismatics. A significant number of socio-economic and numismatic market trends support this conclusion:

According to official documents, the U.S. Mint did not produce any Liberty Head nickels in 1913. A full account of this bizarre minting is recounted in Million Dollar Nickels: Mysteries of the 1913 Liberty Head Nickel Revealed*. (© National Numismatic Collection, National Museum of American History, Smithsonian Institution)*

- A collector resurgence for high-end and very rare coins: After a four-year correction in the numismatic market, followed by a fairly flat year, prices for the best coins—down 15 to 20 percent from their 2008 highs—are beginning to rise again. These are the coins that tend to lead the pricing of the overall market. It's the classic opportunity to "buy low."

- Recent corrections notwithstanding, the last several years have exhibited a renewed interest in commodities: From crude oil to gold and silver—fuelled by fear of a continuing weak dollar, endemic national and unfathomable foreign-national debt—investors are pouring cash into hard assets. This general economic uncertainty carries an air of the "new norm"—as the former PIMCO co-founder Bill Gross calls it—all of which is a textbook environment for a sustained bull market.

Recent economic indicators reflect a business climate that is finally beginning to expand and grow. The Federal Reserve, however, dogged by the memory of a sluggish economy and persistently high unemployment, is only slowly easing up let alone ceasing its ultra-expansionary monetary policy—a policy which ultimately bodes well for tangible assets.

Since 1990, the rare coin market had been almost entirely devoid of investors, as most leaned toward more traditional areas to put their capital. But with surprising willingness, and in greater numbers, these same investors are now diversifying their portfolios with tangible investments. Over the last five years, they have not only put their investment dollars into commodity products, such as Exchange Traded Funds, but also in taking physical delivery of the underlying bullion.

(© Dreamstime, Justforyou)

Most short-term gold speculators—the primary force behind pushing gold to record heights in 2011—have fled the market. Precious metals have plummeted 40 percent from their peak. This is not unusual. Traders who rely on technical indicators describe and forecast these commonplace retracements using Fibonacci numbers.

With the correction out of the way, gold prices are poised for another long-term run. At the very least, the risk/reward ratio is significantly smaller, and, correspondingly, the potential for unheralded appreciation seems almost likely. Having fallen from favor, it's time to unleash your inner-contrarian and start accumulating gold for your portfolio.

- In spite of recent historic gains in the stock market, the latest financial debacle, culminating in 2008, blamed on derivatives but rooted to highly irresponsible subprime loans in the housing market, has left a bad taste in investors' mouths: Financial advisors and investor-savvy individuals continue to look for alternate areas to put their money. Numismatics and precious metals almost always top their choices from which to diversify out of traditional stocks and bonds. Yes, the stock market has bounced back, but no one wants to see their net worth take such a precipitous fall like that again. Is the best time to jump in when the market is at its all time peak?

- Price spikes in the commodities markets, coupled with the almost $18 trillion in government debt putting pressure on Washington D.C. politicians to increase taxes, have forced even the most conservative investors to consider hedging against future monetary inflation: The Chairman of the Federal Reserve Board warned as recently as October 2013 that the risk of inflation outweighed the cost of a stagnate economy, effectively mandating bullish conditions for metals and, by extension, numismatics.

- Pension plan advisors look to pad their performance by including hard assets: Today, pension plans own just 0.3 percent tangible assets such as gold. Increasing this amount to a modest 1 percent would translate to billions of dollars flowing into the buy-side of the gold and silver markets.

Historically, this movement of funds presages a shift in perception. In 1999, crude oil futures threatened to fall below $10 a barrel and now it sits comfortably between $70 to $100—and few doubt that it'll eventually go to $150 and then to $200 a barrel at some point in spite of greater U.S. oil independence. The precious metals markets operate under a similar dynamic. The days of $5 silver are long gone.

Although international political and economic crises have been at a relatively low level, and the financial markets have reflected this relative peace, a new round of simmering political tensions point to business as usual with regard to world history. As recent events have shown, unrest in the Middle East could escalate at any time, possibly creating unimaginable repercussions. This region is only one of several which could spark the world's powder keg.

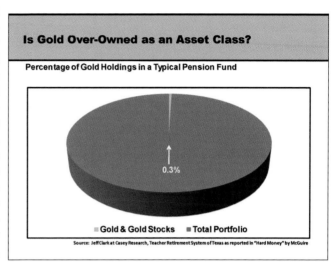

(© Brent Johnson / Santiago Capital)

Not since the inflation-driven 1978 to 1980 coin market have we seen such an opportunity for appreciation. While the latter stage of the Hunt-brothers prodded silver boom was substantial, the upcoming swing of the current bull market stands poised to be potentially even greater in the long run.

Unlike other books, this one is geared toward established investors who, while perhaps new to numismatics, are diversifying their holdings into higher-yielding, non-traditional investments. While still covering the fundamentals in detail, this one focuses on how numismatic portfolios fit into an all-encompassing investment plan.

Most numismatic investment books dwell on the art, beauty, historic and collectible backgrounds concerning numismatics. Often they devote many chapters about coinage terminology, production techniques, artistic iconography, specific types of coins and other areas which—while interesting for collectors—actually have little to do with investing for profit. As the first person in the United States to graduate with a bachelor's degree in Numismatics, and later the first doctorate in this field, I understand the difference between art and collectable appreciation and investing for financial reward.

My aim here, however, is to give you—the sophisticated investor—the information and tools necessary to protect your financial holdings from the unexpected, to identify outstanding buy and sell opportunities, and to leave your progeny a legacy with a minimum of estate tax consequences.

For those wishing for more in-depth information on any more numismatic oriented topic, there are website addresses provided throughout. In conjunction with a special dedicated website, Goldandrarecoins.net, this book also provides more in-depth coverage of many collector oriented topics as well as a selected bibliography to expand your knowledge and promote your interest in this fascinating subject matter.

Through an exclusive arrangement with the University of Rare Coins (UniversityRareCoins.com), you will have access to a wealth of information covering scores of numismatic topics. I encourage you to take advantage of these websites. One link, for example, offers free, limited memberships to the American Numismatic Association (Money.org).

In the grand scheme of things, it isn't important that you rise to my level of passion about rare coins and gold. What is important is that after reading this book you are armed to the teeth with an insider's knowledge of how to make money.

You don't have to be born a blue blood to profit from the nuances that make numismatics the Hobby of Kings. Rather, it is my hope you'll be elevated to that status by following a few simple guidelines—by honing your good instincts with a fundamental base of proven methodologies. With a small amount of due diligence and a smart eye on current events, you'll have the added sense of satisfaction and confidence that comes from profitably navigating the hard asset markets.

Chapter I

Why Invest in Gold and Rare Coins Now

Investors share the same basic objectives of asset preservation and capital appreciation. We'll begin by examining the factors behind the upcoming precious metals bull market. We'll put the fundamentals to the common sense test—is the move supported by supply and demand or by smoke and mirrors? Is the bullion market behaving in the manner we'd expect at this stage?

As of fall of 2014, the stock market is showing signs of slowing its rate of rise and perhaps peaking. Will there be another correction, or have we finally arrived at the big bear turn? How will this influence precious metals in the short term?

What effect will all of this have on numismatics?

From there, we'll isolate different strategies for assembling numismatic portfolios with positive high risk/reward probabilities. Investment decisions typically take the form of comparing alternate paths' advantages and disadvantages. We'll discuss do's and don'ts from both the buy- and sell-side.

Throughout, we'll analyze market behavior. Only instead of wrapping up our hypothetical situations with non-committal advice or vague language, we'll use specific if-then action statements. We'll discuss how to develop good habits and explore various avenues in which to sharpen our trading instincts.

We're going to skip the academic arcane issues usually associated with this genre and go straight to the tricks of the trade. We're going to train our brains to buy low and sell high.

Same Game, Different Rules

Doesn't feel like it's been six years, does it? It doesn't feel like six years since the entire financial system stood at the brink of collapse, because there still remains a palpable pall in the aftermath. It could happen again. Perhaps not as swiftly or deeply as last time, but nonetheless unexpectedly and devastating to many.

Since the '08 financial meltdown, the traditional ground rules for investors have changed. Despite record highs, stocks and real estate are no longer automatic safe havens or no-brainer sure things. The Fed is determined to try and have it both ways. The printing presses are running full bore, and fed funds—the rate at which banks lend each other money—has been kept artificially low in order to stimulate demand. Something's going to have to give.

In the wake of the recession and subsequent government stimulus programs, the markets have been unable to establish sustained periods of positive footing. It's disconcerting. No sooner do traders' spirits rise, when news of a disappointing government statistic or a series of anemic quarterly reports shines a bright light on the economy's blemishes.

A swirling wind storm of uncertainty is blowing through Wall Street and, indeed, on all of Main Street, too. Recent high unemployment, fiscal cliffs, temporary government shutdowns and sovereign debt crises cast doubt on any further substantial moves to the upside. Price to Earnings ratios are already tough to justify.

A lot of money is on the sidelines. It sits idle in the hands of investment advisors who know of few credible alternatives to traditional avenues.

People may well refer to this period in stocks as a bubble. The characteristics of market cycles in a bubble phase are tricky, even for seasoned professionals. It's a nimble trader who can successfully navigate the upcoming volatility that will surely plague the financial markets in the years to come.

It may come in three weeks or three years, but the next big cycle for stocks will most likely be down. For most investors, who are not actively managing their positions on a day-to-day basis, it's an imperative to shift some percentage of those funds into more attractive options.

As an investor, you will want to consider short- as well as long-term planning. If not necessarily on a day-by-day basis, it's important to keep abreast of the market's comings and goings—run through some quick procedure using the corner of your eye to get updated—because market timing is the key to success. Or, if it is on a daily basis, perhaps you'll give *The Wall Street Journal* ten minutes, then read *Coin World* weekly cover to cover—something like that.

To stay current doesn't require an inordinate amount of time. But you don't want to drift away from the action so far that when it becomes time to act that your reflexes are slow. We're going to pick up market timing again in a minute, as that's what this whole book is about, but first let's see how numismatics and precious metals stack up against financial, real estate and other collectible alternatives.

Re-thinking Traditional Wealth Preservation Tools

Traditional wealth preservation vehicles typically include conservative, long-term government and corporate debt instruments. In recent years, however, asset appreciation of triple-A rated bonds have not kept pace with the Consumer Price Index, let alone real inflation. In truth, your wealth is not being preserved at all, but

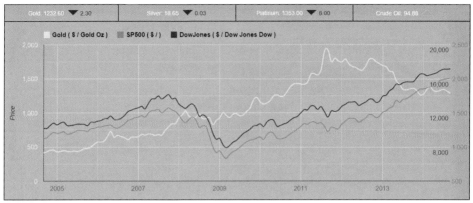

Gold vs. S&P500 vs DOW Chart. Gold is down 40%, while the S&P is at peak levels. (© www.constantgold.com)

is slowly eroding. On paper everything may appear to be shipshape, but the sophisti-cated investor, like yourself, ought to know how to read between the lines.

Conventional savings instruments do not make investment sense for anything other than temporarily parking a chunk of cash. Bank and S&L interest rates are around 1%. The yield on U.S. Treasury 10-year notes hover around 3%. Risk-reward in the bond market, presently, is a long way from ideal. Bond prices and yields are inversely proportional. Logically, there is only one way for bond prices to go in the long term, and, at the risk of stating the obvious, it's never a good idea to buy at the top of the market.

Another traditional safe haven is real estate. While real estate has its tax advan-tages, property values have plummeted from their peak in 2007. Flash-forward to the present, despite pockets of recovery, and wealthy enclaves that had barely registered a blip on the downside, economic projections anticipate an overall slow recovery. It's a buyers' market, and they're being selective about their purchases.

It is a function of the times that we place a premium on liquid investment alter-natives. Real estate, of course, is an asset that cannot be readily converted into cash, especially during a recession. For families in recent years trying to sell their home or investment property, they have had to find out the hard way, experiencing frustration and lowered expectations that comes from waiting for the telephone to ring.

A Portrait of Profit

For those looking for decent returns, say 6% to 8% or better, there are few tra-ditional options left. Erudite investment advisors and pundits can't get a handle on the stock market. The fundamentals are stretched to the limit, and there have been subtle signs it may roll over. The consensus of where the market is going over the next several years is open for debate.

Any mention of good news, say, any tentative agreement between debt-ridden European Union members may bring on celebratory toasts and give stocks a tempo-rary boost. But there is no cause for celebration—it's captain and crew patting each other on the back. *Look how well we're plugging the holes of our sinking ship!* Until the next, inevitable leak sounds the alarm, and then it will be back to manning the pumps.

Europe's economic ship is listing badly. You have to wonder how long they can keep it up before there's a mad scramble for the lifeboats.

Uncertainty creates a skittish atmosphere for long-term investors, which is why price movements have become increasingly choppy. This is your signal, as a forward-thinking investor—now is the time to make a move toward alternative strategies.

The obvious shift is toward hard assets. What, specifically, are our options?

Rarities, including art, antiquities and quality gemstones, are good possibilities. High-end works of art have demonstrated spectacular returns, as mounting popularity shows no signs of abating. A magnificent 1969 triptych, *Three Studies of Lucien Freud*, by the late British painter Francis Bacon sold for a whopping $142 million. A new world record price for a modern painting sold at auction, it shattered the old mark, set by Edvard Munch's *The Scream*, which sold in 2012 for $119 million.

Unfortunately, these collectibles present a number of problems from an investor's standpoint. First, market conditions vary considerably from one area of collectible to another. Antiques, for example, often are literally of unknown worth until offered for sale. Their value may vary from one section of the country to another. The same conditions exist with regards to works of art.

Diamonds and gems are often an excellent source of value but reasonably difficult to sell. (© Ken Brown)

Gems, especially diamonds, are traded at the wholesale level in major markets, such as Antwerp and New York City. But it is a highly specialized trade group and participating in this arena isn't readily feasible even for sophisticated investors let alone for the average man or woman on the street. Never mind too that gemstone prices are notoriously difficult to pinpoint at any given point, which basically translates to the only money to be made in diamonds is as a broker—buying at wholesale and selling at retail.

Although, to be fair, in a mad sort of way, the DeBeers monopoly in the diamond market does set a sturdy floor on price. They're extremely easy to transport and nearly impossible to trace, which is why moneyed criminals like them so much. But the South African mining company controlling price appears keen to keep engagement rings pegged to income levels, severely limiting diamond's upside potential.

Then there are the unusually high commissions typically found in unique collectibles. The difference between what you pay and what you can sell a niche collectible for makes it extremely difficult to make money even in the best of times. If the commission on an object d'art is 30%, it may be many months of favorable winds just to reach the break-even point.

The way the precious metals and rare coin markets can now package its products, with standardized measuring sticks, relatively high liquidity and low mark-ups on transactions makes it the most attractive method in which to diversify out of traditional stocks and bonds.

Check's in the Mail

Part of the fallout from the financial meltdown was a clamor for reform. While some of the new rules and regulations that come from it may end up being helpful staving off future disaster, financial reform will almost certainly have a negative impact on privacy and estate planning.

In an atmosphere in which the U.S. government continues to seek new revenues to keep pace with its expanding budget, estate planning options to legally avoid heavy tax burdens will come under close scrutiny.

Traditional investments' competitive advantages, like capital gains and low estate taxes, are ripe for damaging legislation. As such, they do not warrant the same level of confidence when weighing the various factors that go into your decision-making process. A smart-money investor must know his options, and be savvy enough to think outside of the box.

For many collectors and investors, bottom-line profits are not the only mitigating factor. The challenge of assembling and creating something never before accomplished has entertainment, if not ego, value. A collector's goal could range from acquiring the first or finest set of a type of coins or currency, or owning the most important coin of

Legacy coins, like this 1804 dollar, the "King of U.S. coins", are pedigreed coins that track new a owner's name as part of the pantheon of ownership. Today, coins once part of a great collection, like those of Louis Eliasberg, John Work Garrett and Buddy Epson carry additional premiums because of their provenance. (© National Numismatic Collection, National Museum of American History, Smithsonian Institution)

a series in the finest condition. Making money from your investments need not be a dour sport!

Historically, building a collection of the finest specimens of a particular set of coins, or acquiring great Legacy specimens, yields the highest rate of appreciation relative to other numismatic strategies.

A difficult task, relatively few succeed in acquiring all the items that would constitute a complete collection. Yet, the attempt, in a way, is its own reward—not just from the standpoint of appreciation, but from a perspective of accomplishment, too. Like the angler's trophy catch mounted on a wall, collectors rightfully have the same pride for their most cherished pieces.

New Gold Dream

If you were savvy or lucky enough to purchase traditional-asset vehicles at stock-market lows you may be susceptible to an if-it-ain't-broke-don't-fix-it mentality. The problem with that theory is the sweet bull-market runs of yesteryear are not guarantees of forever. It's time, now, to shift a well thought-out proportion of your portfolio into more attractive opportunities.

Over the last decade—perhaps more importantly, over the last 40 years—two of the best performing asset groups have been precious metals and numismatics. Close scrutiny reveals convincing arguments on two fronts, from both pro and con perspectives.

If your only concern is to be in a good spot from which to throw darts, gold and numismatics are where you want to be while taking blind aim. More than a snide aside, it's an important point of picking winners. Narrowing the field from myriad investment possibilities boils down to an exercise in odds-making. The entire job of a speculator is to take 50-50 propositions and turn those odds to his favor. The probability of picking a winner from an asset class trending higher is far greater than fingering the exception among one rife with losers.

While making the case for diversification, it is important to keep in mind that it's a balanced portfolio we're after. The old adage of *not keeping all your eggs in one basket* is a good one. The point to carry away from this chapter is that stock and bond investments now require highly selective criteria—and not necessarily an occasion to dump your entire net worth on a flyer in Comex gold futures.

One strategy might consist of diversifying paper holdings with physical precious metal assets in order to safeguard against inflation and recessionary cycles. Another might be supplementing your children's college education fund with regular purchases of investment-quality coins. With all of the uncertainties in the marketplace, it's prudent to protect your assets with products that have historical ties to purchasing power.

Government currencies and international stock markets fluctuate with market trends and shifting political climates, whereas precious metals' prices tend to track real wealth. Throughout most of the 20th century, gold produced profits in the worst economic times. During the Great Depression, for instance, gold rose in value by about 75% at the same time the dollar was plummeting.

Savvy investors of the 1930s turned to gold for wealth preservation. Granted, the present-day economic scenario is not identical, but there are enough similarities to indicate that diversification is the smart play. At worst, if prices become stagnant, gold is an insurance policy against financial calamity. In the more likely scenario, gold and rare coin prices continue to move higher.

As such, a thorough understanding of tangible investments—and numismatics in particular—is necessary in order to give yourself the greatest chance for making prudent decisions. These are not formulaic algorithms that you can plug into a computer. It's a sophisticated juggling-act of arranging and rearranging and prioritizing facts, figures, and conjecture that ultimately will determine how well it adds up when it's all said and done.

A surgeon friend of mine once said that he could teach me how to remove an appendix in 15 minutes, but that they go to medical school for seven years so they know what to do if anything goes wrong.

The following chapters are your seven years of medical school—because you're the type of investor who guards against catastrophe, who needs to know the most expedient way to get from point A to point B.

It's to you, I say, welcome to the exciting world of gold and numismatic investing.

Chapter II

Gold Bullion and Pre-1933 Semi-Numismatic Coins

There is no dispute that over the last decade one of the best performing assets has been gold and silver. We will write mainly of the former, but know that most of the advantages and limitations of gold investing are also true for silver.

For those interested specifically in silver, the primary advantage of silver over gold is its demand for industrial purposes. Silver has the highest electrical conductivity of any of the metals, more than copper, which is one reason why in a GFMS Ltd. Report commissioned by the Silver Institute (March 2011), industrial demand in 2015 will be 669.5 million ounces, a 37% increase over 2010.

Silver does have its drawbacks. In bullion form silver, even 90% silver coin bags, can be quite cumbersome, and it is one reason why gold is far more popular with investors. By far the largest global market for over-the-counter gold bullion transactions is in London. According to the London Bullion Market Association (November 2008), average daily volume of gold is 18.3 million ounces, or $13.9 billion, while silver does 107.6 million ounces, or $1.1 billion.

U.S. Mint Platinum Eagles, RCM Palladium Maples, and Swiss Palladium bars have traded actively in the primary and secondary market. Platinum and palladium have even outperformed gold and silver over the past few years, but historically has not had the overall demand from investors as gold.

As an asset class, gold in most all investment forms enjoys similar advantages and limitations:

Advantages:

- Gold metal does not degrade or perish and always retains the value of the alloy. It cannot be created nor destroyed—it survives wars, revolutions, every economic tragedy and boom throughout history. It cannot be diluted by inflation or destroyed by deflation. Gold has been considered a monetary asset for over 2,500 years and has commonly been referred to as a "safe haven" asset.

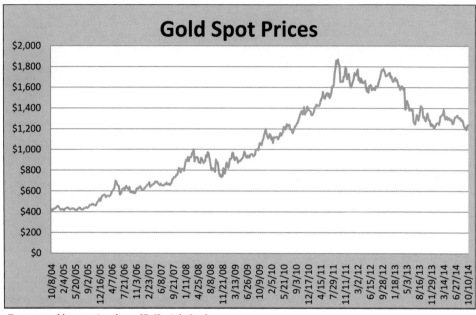

Ten year gold spot price chart. (© Kagin's, Inc.)

- Gold provides safety and protection against a weak dollar and deflation, geopolitical uncertainty, political strife and dislocations in the financial markets. Historically, it has an excellent long-term track record, accumulating over 300% increase in the last ten years. In inflation-adjusted terms, even at $1,300 per ounce, gold is still less than 60% of its peak 1980 levels. It would need to get to $2,250 per ounce just to have the same purchasing power it had 34 years ago. And if inflation was calculated the same way it was back then, the all-time high for gold would be somewhere in the neighborhood of $12,700 per ounce!

- Demand for gold as an investment today is much lower than it was in 1980, meaning that there is considerable room for investor growth. Increasing long-term demand for gold, especially in Asia—principally from India and China in the form of jewelry—continues unabated. This cultural commitment to gold as a store of value provides an underpinning for its value, limiting any substantial long-term, downside risks.

- Gold tends to rise as the U.S. dollar—the world's reserve currency—declines. Considering the dollar, by some estimates, has lost 35% of its purchasing power over the last 10 years, gold will benefit from the buoyancy of restoring historical market equilibrium. While it's possible that the dollar will find its way back to gold, it's far more likely the much smaller gold market makes the jump up.

- Gold provides a hedge against long-term inflation. While inflation has not been a factor in gold's appreciation over the last several years, most economists believe this situation might change if the U.S. government continues its out-of-control spending. Former Federal Reserve Chairman, Ben

Bernanke and, so far, his successor, Janet Yellin, have never kept their bias toward keeping the economy inflated a secret. The Fed has placed its target for inflation at 2% to 2 ½% per year. This effectively means that in 20 years your money will be worth half of what it is today. As the money supply expands here and in debt-ridden, developed-world economies, investors will seek real assets such as gold.

- Gold has always been an international safe haven for capital, especially for central banks in trade-surplus nations.

- A 2010 report by McKinsey & Company on global economic outlook paints a best-case scenario for a six-year horizon for the unwinding of sovereign debt crisis prolonging economic recovery; and reiterated their buy recommendation in precious metals for years to come.

- With gold, there is no default risk.

- There is no upkeep or taxes on appreciation until sold.

- Gold bullion provides good international liquidity.

- Many bullion gold coins can be put into retirement plans.

- While the total supply of gold coming to the market is increasing now (up 8% last year), gold production is down (6.6% per the CPM group, Kitco, Doug Casey Report), and will most likely continue to decrease while gold levels are below $1,200.

- Gold is not subject to the whims of industrial supply and demand trends since industrial demand only accounts for 0.3% of the world's supply.

- Over the last five years gold has performed better than the S&P 500 in spite of the precious metals "meltdown" of 2011-2013 and simultaneous S&P upturn.

Limitations:

- Gold values can be volatile, especially on a short-term basis. Any sustained, fast rise in gold could indicate an incipient bubble and potential plunge. For instance, after hitting record highs in August 2011, by October that year gold lost 12% of its value on favorable economic news. Then again in April 2013 gold plunged 13% to almost below $1,300 per ounce before recovering, and plunged again to below $1,200 on news of the potential end of Monetary Easing in June 2013. Prices could approach $1,100 before moving up for good.

- As with other investments, all profits from precious metals sales must be lawfully reported.

- Gold bullion does not generate revenue, i.e., dividends or interest. In fact, some economists do not recognize gold as being an investment at all, but a store of value which costs more per ounce as the dollar drops in value.

- Gold has little industrial application. Its value is mainly based on its rarity, its use as jewelry, its perception as a store of value, and economic/political uncertainty. Silver, on the other hand, does have significant commercial use, but silver is also subject to industrial fluctuations—although it ought to be noted that industrial demand for silver has been steady for many years.

• Gold is a value, not a price; an insurance policy.

• Some pundits suggest that without inflation or economic fear, gold has limited investment potential—which makes timing extremely important since at some point in the economic cycle there has always been both fear and inflation.

This is why the timing of this book is so important!

Ways to Purchase Gold

Once you have determined you need some gold in your portfolio, you should understand the different avenues for acquiring precious metals and their associated features and benefits, as well as their limitations, so that the right combination fits your particular goals.

There are five primary ways to purchase gold as an asset, excluding jewelry:

• As a security—what are called Exchange Traded Funds—old mining stocks or purchasing units in a gold trading or tangible asset fund.

• Taking a long position in a Comex futures contract.

• In physical bullion form including bullion coins, either by using a third party depository or by taking possession.

• As semi-numismatics, say, pre-1933 U.S. "common" or "generic" gold, and modern gold coins.

• Rare numismatic gold coins.

Purchasing Gold as a Security

For those who are familiar with purchasing stocks, there is an easy way to purchase gold:

Exchange Traded Funds (ETFs): These ETFs purchase gold and offer shares of their holdings on the open market. The most widely held gold ETFs are:

• SPDR Gold Trust (symbol GLD) - Gold Bullion ETF

• ETFs Gold Trust (symbol SGOL) - Gold Bullion ETF

• Sprott Physical Gold Trust (symbol PHYS) - Gold Bullion ETF

• Market Vector Gold Miners (symbol GDX) - Large Miners ETF

• Market Vector Jr. Gold Miners (symbol GDXJ) – Jr. Miners ETF

The following are some of the advantages of purchasing ETFs as well as some of the limitations.

Advantages:

• Transactions are quick and easy.

• You pay low commissions.

- Purchases are marginable.
- You can buy options to limit risk.
- You can receive dividends.
- As in all securities, you can receive almost instant liquidity when you desire to sell.
- You may be able to put shares of stock in your retirement plan.

Limitations:

- You do not have possession of the bullion.
- There are some storage costs.
- Transaction fees, while low, can still be as much as 3%.
- Your bullion holdings are not strictly private; others are privy to your investment.
- There are some reporting requirements.
- Funds are volatile and riskier because they can be bought on margin and that attracts speculative buyers (search the Internet for the unfortunate story on MF Global).
- Interruptions may occur in electronic markets.
- Your bullion assets are neither available nor portable.
- There is little transparency; you really don't know how much bullion the ETF possesses.

Mining stocks are another way to indirectly own gold as a security. Again there are both advantages and limitations for purchasing this type of stock.

The most widely held gold mining stocks are:

- Barrick Gold (symbol ABX) - Largest gold mining company in the world
- Goldcorp, Inc. (symbol GG) - Large gold mining company
- Newmont Mining (symbol NEM) - Large gold mining company

Advantages:

- Like most securities there is an ease of entry.
- You pay low commissions.
- You also get an interest in company assets as well as an indirect investment in the bullion.

Limitations:

- Stocks are affected by production costs and the stock market as much, if not more so, than the price of gold.
- The company may be caught with low reserves at any point in time.
- The value of your asset is subject to the reliance on humans, including labor disputes, not just the commodity.

- Most of these companies are subject to significant volatility from currency changes, etc.
- A government may take over the company (nationalize the mineral or company).
- Corporate taxes can increase.
- The company can go bankrupt.
- The company can "cook the books."
- The company—especially foreign based ones—are often subject to government regulations or other political issues.

Gold bullion such as these one ounce American Gold, Silver Eagles, and Credit Suisse gold bars offer investors attractive advantages with few limitations. (© Dreamstime, Steveheap, Monticello)

Gold Futures

The Commodities Exchange, Inc. (COMEX) was created to allow companies to protect themselves against future price fluctuations by buying futures and options at an established price in the future.

The COMEX provides a platform for buyers and sellers to trade futures in a competitive environment, similar to an auction. Other notable precious metals exchanges include, London Metals Exchange, and "mini"-contracts traded at the Chicago Mercantile Exchange.

For precious metals investors, futures contracts can be a convenient way to take delivery of large quantities since just one COMEX gold contract is 100 ounces. The futures markets also offer investors a tremendous amount of leverage through the use of what is called an "initial margin requirement"—putting a small percentage down, perhaps as low as 5% of the contract value, to control the whole amount—but this is extremely risky.

You are basically gambling that the market will increase by a certain time in the future. If that doesn't happen, you may be out of pocket more than intended. For instance, if you speculate that prices will rise and instead they go down, you would have to cover the loss.

Purchasing Physical Gold Bullion

Physical bullion is a more tangible way to invest in gold and holds additional benefits that help meet the objectives of high net worth investors. There are only two ways in which you can hold physical bullion:

- Vaulted
- Delivered

Vaulted Bullion

Having your bullion held by an outside facility has a good measure of appeal and a few limitations:

Advantages:

- You do not have to take physical delivery.
- You own a store of wealth outside the banking systems and possibly outside the United States (to avoid a 1933-type of confiscation).
- Your risk is mainly just the value of the commodity.
- Your holdings serve as a hedge against the volatility of paper stocks.
- Your bullion can be liquidated or traded while in storage or delivered to you anywhere in the world.

Limitations:

- You will be subject to storage costs.
- You may be assessed a 2% to 5% transaction fee.
- Your holdings are not private.

Delivered Bullion

Taking physical possession of bullion coins, for example American Eagles, South African Krugerrands, and/or Canadian Maple Leafs, offer advantages that uphold in unique situations, like emergencies, retirement plans, as well as a few limitations:

Advantages:

- These pieces are a private source of wealth.
- They are internationally portable.
- In many cases, you can use these coins to make purchases.
- When purchasing some bullion coins there are no reporting requirements.

Limitations:

- Transaction fees run 2% to 5%.

- You probably need to store the coins in privately-owned depositories. Some locations: Delaware, New York, Toronto, Singapore and/or Hong Kong. Alternatively, you can store them in bank safe deposit boxes, home safes or you can even bury them somewhere.

Silver Bullion Coins

For an excellent treatment of what and how to purchase silver bullion-related coins, refer to numismatist Lawrence Goldberg's *What Color Are Your Assets?* (Zyrus Press, 2013). An excerpt is provided at Goldandrarecoins.net.

For up-to-date information on how to purchase/store bullion, contact a representative at one of the bullion storage dealers like Dillongage.com. Another excellent resource not only about gold and gold values but also semi-numismatic coins is by Jeff Garrett and Q. David Bowers' *Gold: Everything You Need to Know to Buy and Sell Today*, (Whitman Publishing).

Purchasing Pre-1933 Semi-Numismatic U.S. Gold Coins

The best way to own gold and to take advantage of the numismatic or collectible feature without having to pay an exorbitant premium over bullion is to purchase limited-quantity, uncirculated pre-1933 U.S. gold coins. Over 75 years old, these coins are limited to a finite supply and have traditionally outperformed strictly bullion-type investments.

While there is no strict definition for generic or semi-numismatic coins, generally the term refers to obsolete and out of circulation U.S. gold coins that are nevertheless obtainable with relative ease—for now—and while they command premiums over their melt value, most of their value is directly derived from the price of gold.

Generic gold coins are a double play: No matter what happens in the rare coin market, these coins will always be worth at a minimum their gold content, but they are poised to benefit from increased collector demand. What is a relatively common coin today may not be 20 or 30 years from now.

It would be difficult to pinpoint a long-term, contemporary timeframe in which semi-numismatic gold performed poorly. Perhaps that doesn't sound like a rousing endorsement, but it is in fact comforting when looking at a worst case scenario. Slow and steady will win this race.

It wasn't too long ago that crude oil traded under $10 a barrel, and in relatively short order, nobody blinks at $100. Now, traders are gearing themselves for the next big jump. Gold prices have shown similar increases and by purchasing the generic U.S. gold coins, you combine that upward potential with a limited downside. That's what I call good risk/reward.

The history they represent—as beautiful works of art—is a strong indication the numismatic component of price will rise with the passage of time. If gold declines in price, the numismatic value of these pieces often cushion the blow due to a healthy market among collectors.

Gold Price on a Historical Basis

2x its previous all time high?

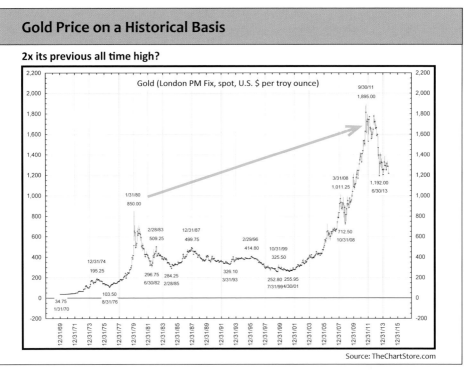

Inflation Adjusted

Inflation weighted...Gold still has a long way to reach its all time high

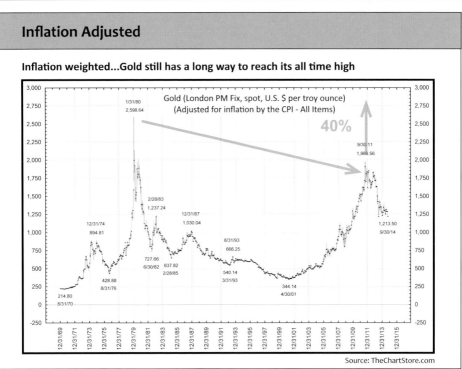

(© Brent Johnson / Santiago Capital)

There are other reasons why pre-1933 United States gold coins have been a better investment than strictly bullion-related gold. Unlike the bullion coins issued today, such as South African Krugerrands, Canadian Maple Leafs or American Eagles, supplies of pre-1933 U.S. gold coins are decreasing.

Although today there might be several thousand pieces of a certain type coin such as the $20 St.-Gaudens in Gem MS-65 condition, it is becoming increasingly difficult to get quick delivery or find premium quality specimens in quantities of even one hundred pieces. Availability becomes even more important in boom periods. As demand increases, people will be bidding for a decreasing supply.

The government traditionally grants special treatment to numismatic coins because for the vast majority of participants, it's a casual, not-to-mention patriotic hobby. One can further imagine the regulatory nightmare of defining which coins go into which taxable category. *Imagine the IRS taxing Aunt Mildred's Statehood quarter collection!* So far, it's a can of worms the government, thankfully, has decided to leave untouched.

In 1933, when Franklin D. Roosevelt called in gold (using the Trading with the Enemy Act of 1917), numismatic coins were exempt. Government attempts to regulate private ownership of gold bullion, such as holding periods and reporting requirements, have almost always exempted numismatic coins. Even so, my father told me stories of how scores of gold coin owners would take their holdings to Europe to be stashed in banks abroad. Clearly they are part of the influx of gold coins returning to the market place in the last several years.

Semi-numismatic coins, generally worth about 15% over their melt value, historically have been subject to favorable tax treatment. Court decisions have favored that such coins can be traded for other numismatic coins as a "like-kind" or "Section 1031" exchange resulting in a non-taxable event.

Until mid-2013, premiums for generic numismatic gold were near their lowest in several years. Even though gold prices stabilized and premiums have almost doubled, they still represent a potential double hedge from bullion appreciation and additional premium increases.

Visualize Success

There are many advantages to semi-numismatic coins, but in the modern era, the superior gold investment play has been in higher quality pieces. Plus or minus, these are pre-1933 U.S. gold coins in Mint State-64 or Mint State-65 (on the Sheldon one to 70-point grading scale).

The supply of gold pieces decreases markedly as the quality rises, especially in these higher grades. Though these coins are still considered semi-numismatic, since compared to truly rare coins they can be obtained fairly easily, these particular grades—MS-64 and MS-65—are scarce compared to bullion gold coins. It's not hard to imagine sometime in the not-so-distant future that convention will drop the "Semi-" qualifier altogether and recognize these coins as rare also. But, for now, it's an opportunity.

Now that gold bullion prices seem to have stabilized in the $1150 to $1300 range, it is unlikely that too many more of these coins will be dumped on the market. Premiums as I predicted have increased, and over time will probably continue to increase until there is another quick run up in gold. In spite of these increased premiums for semi-numismatic coins they are still much lower than they were a decade ago.

While there has been a huge demand over the last several years for bullion gold, demand for relatively common, collectible U.S. gold coins has lagged, causing premiums to hit their lowest percentage in 25 years. Prices for higher grade coins (MS-64 and MS-65) are 35% to 45% below what they were four years ago when gold was at $950 per ounce! From 2012 to 2013, premiums began to rise again as gold values and demand retreated. Why, you may ask, is this phenomenon of extremely low numismatic premiums occurring now?

Increased supply for one. The rapid and dramatic increase in gold prices over the last half dozen years have motivated holders of large quantities of these coins, especially European banks, to sell. Since the confiscation of gold in the U.S. in 1933, millions of dollars of U.S. gold coins have been hoarded abroad. These coins are overwhelmingly raw, which means uncertified by a third-party grading company, like PCGS and NGC.

Major wholesalers in the U.S. of these coins send most of them to PCGS or NGC to be certified. In recent times, approximately 200 to 400 gold $20 Saint-Gaudens get certified as MS-65 per month—thus increasing the supply. It was more than the market has been able to absorb. Wholesalers were forced to offer deals to get rid of them, or lower their bids to cut down their inventories at a time of low demand.

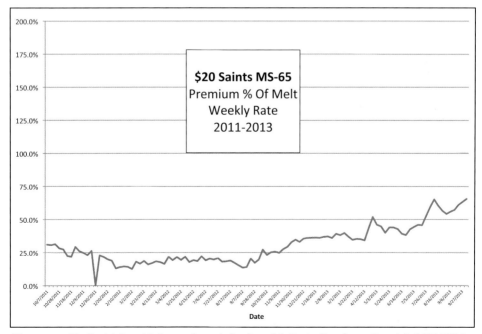

(Chart created by Kagin's Inc with data and permission from Coin Dealer Newsletter, Copyright 2013 CDN Inc. P.O. Box 7939, Torrance, CA 90504 www.greysheet.com)

Until 2013, one could own a U.S. gold coin that hadn't been issued for almost a century in independently-graded Gem quality, hermetically sealed and authenticated, for less than 25% more than a recently minted bullion coin. But when gold values dropped 40% from peak levels in 2011, semi-numismatic coins substantially held their value, dropping only 15% in the same time frame. How? Premium margins over spot gold rose to 65% by November of 2013. If gold were to rise quickly again, premiums could drop that low yet again and create another buying opportunity.

Until recently, basic collector demand has been met by available supply, despite a downturn in the economy, which has meant that most people don't have the same disposable income. They have less money for speculating in gold futures and options. Dealer demand is down because of decrease in demand from speculators above and with premiums so low, there is more money to be made trading rarer, higher premium coins. But the pendulum has now started to swing back as the economy improves.

Other factors have kept premiums artificially low. Although the semi-numismatics we've been talking about are independently certified, not every coin in each grade looks the same. Bottom-of-the-barrel coins have been dragging the market down for "solid-for-the-grade" coins.

Wholesale buyers who buy sight unseen recognize that they may be forced to purchase the worst coins in holders at their bid price. To provide for this contingency, they lower their bids. What that means for you, on the retail level, is to take the time to examine every coin purchased and return those that are not high or solid-for-the-grade.

There are three ways in which know if a coin is solid-for-the-grade:

- A CAC sticker.
- A third-party, probably your dealer, who has a good eye.
- You have a good eye.

You don't need to be able to grade in order to function well comparing coins of the same grade. Truly, it is as simple as referencing other coins of the same grade, then asking yourself: Was it close to the top of the list, or the bottom favorites? Of course, other elements are in play when making buying and selling decisions, too. Perhaps you're buying this coin at a steal of the price. Could be any number of overriding factors.

Coins with green or gold CAC stickers are solid or high for the grade and command premiums. (© Kagins, Inc.)

The largest purchasers of certified MS-64 and MS-65 quality U.S. gold coins are telemarketing firms. Over the last few years, however, these firms have cut back on their purchases. Rumor has it that negative publicity arising from federal, state and government authorities, not to mention bad press from the national media, including certain cable news commentators, have contributed to this cutback.

Timing is Everything

Timing is often overlooked as a key variable when investing in semi-numismatic coins. All things equal for the price of gold, the best time to purchase these coins are when premiums are low.

During rapid swings in the bullion market, premiums for rare coins often get compressed relative to the price of spot gold. A typical semi-numismatic coin such as a generic or *common date* U.S. $20 gold piece in Gem MS-65 condition may have a premium of 100% over its melt content during a stable bullion market. But the premium could fall below 25% in a rapidly rising gold market.

Just such a reduction of premium happened from 2007 until the end of 2012. It came because overall investment attention, especially from non-numismatic sectors of the investment world, focused on buying gold as a financial hedge at the same time the rarity or collector value was ignored.

In 2011, gold skyrocketed. The trajectory of the move couldn't be sustained but you never know where prices may go seeking a new equilibrium.

When my cousin Stan asked for my advice for a long-term move into bullion, despite the probability of a correction, we didn't want to be on the sidelines if prices never came back. Of the total amount he had set aside for his portfolio's gold and numismatic holdings, he put half into $20 gold in MS-63 to MS-65. Premiums over the melt for Stan's semi-numismatic collection were the lowest in memory.

Gold prices did indeed fall back. For Stan, though, his coins' premiums widened substantially, cushioning the price dip. On a day when gold prices were down 13%, $20 St.-Gaudens in MS-63 were practically unchanged, down only about 7%.

The point is this: When examining the different possibilities in a sector, it is better to lean to the strongest in the group. Don't expect the weak market to suddenly become the strongest because its price chart has the most space on top. The strong performers in a group tend to hold up better in down cycles and proportionally better in up swings. That's why they're the strong performers!

Don't allow yourself any mumbo jumbo psychological flights of fancy to ignore this seemingly obvious handicapping trick. You'd be surprised how often I've seen people leave good money on the table by backing a longshot. When you're right, the object is to maximize your return, and when you're wrong to minimize the mistake. Don't make things harder on yourself.

Now, with gold over $700 off its high (a 40% drop), Stan is considering putting the other half of his money into various gold-related plays, buying into weakness, or buying into a bull market correction. It's not easy to buy into weakness; buy into the face of whatever sad story the financial pundits are saying has caused prices to go down. Remind yourself that news stories are often shaped to fit what has just happened. Make a plan and stick to it.

It remains to be seen, of course, how things will pan out for Stan—and for the rest of us, come to think of it. I have to say, though, I'm feeling rather optimistic about our chances. Most of my company's clients are "playing with house money." *As they say—so far so good!*

Chapter III

Rare Coins and Currency

If you're willing to sacrifice potential immediate return and instant liquidity—in the interest of stability and higher long-term appreciation—consider purchasing from the premier area of numismatics that is made up of the most coveted rare coin and currency pieces. And, for at least a certain portion of your portfolio, I'd strongly suggest it.

Perhaps the only reason you wouldn't is if you were adamantly opposed to the extra time and effort putting together a well-thought out collection requires.

For coins, we are talking about the finest specimens, whose rarity command enough of a premium over their metal content that the value of the underlying gold is virtually immaterial. They fall into a narrow category we call *investment-quality* or the narrower yet super rare category we refer to as *Legacy coins.*

The world record for rare coins - $10,016,875 for this Unique Superb Gem Specimen Flowing Hair 1794 Silver Dollar. (© Steven L. Contursi)

Legacy coins and banknotes are high profile pieces that are considered museum-worthy. A sliver of a subset, the most outstanding examples from the world of numismatics—coins and currency that have more in common with fine art than stock certificates—typically brings about the highest returns over time.

By most estimates, investment-quality items represent only 2% to 3% of the entire market. No one person owns hoards of high-quality rare coins or currency, which may be dumped upon the market to significantly alter the value of the group.

This is one big contributing reason to the category's overall price stability. As a group, investment-quality collectors tend to be less skittish than the semi-numismatic crowd.

If someone from the semi-numismatics crowd yells "fire!" there would be a mad rush for the exits. Investment-quality folks, who are quite accustomed to their panic, use those mad rushes out of a market as a buying opportunity, and the same thing goes for the sell-side.

Critical Independent Grading Advances

Some numismatic advantages may not seem like that big of a deal at first glance. For instance, a universally-accepted third-party grading system may sound like simply getting confirmation of what you and your coin dealer already know. Or, it's good news because, although he's a good friend, you wonder if perhaps the proprietor of your local coin shop has a habit of selling at one grade and buying back the same coins at two grades lower—plus his *Blue Book* discount. But what's such a big deal about that?

Turns out, plenty. For better or worse, PCGS and NGC changed the board on which the game is played. Third-party grading has separated numismatics from all other collectible and antique investment sectors. Although every coin is unique, the Sheldon grading scale as applied by experts who are able to describe a coin's condition with near precision accuracy and consistency and back their evaluation with a money guarantee was the catalyst that brought numismatics and rare-coin trading to the masses.

The Sheldon scale is not unlike the grading of securities by firms like Standard & Poor's and Moody's, or that of diamonds by the Gemological Institute Association. With independent sources for grading, PCGS and NGC in particular, a statistical compilation—now with three decades of data—provide benchmark pricing history and makes buying and selling decisions much more transparent and easier to evaluate.

Because of their metallic content and method of manufacture, coins and currency are not easily perishable and can last for years without worry. Of course, how and where one stores uncertified coins can have an adverse effect. That is why grading services seal certified coins in inert, hermetically-sealed, tamper-proof holders that are designed to preserve a coin or banknote's surface from outside chemical exposure. Millions of coins have been preserved this way.

Information Technological Innovations

Also, unlike most other collectibles, prices are posted throughout the trading day. Dealer networks publish bid-ask figures on virtually every type of regularly issued numismatic coin. Weekly industry publications provide similar data. *The Coin Dealer Newsletter* gives weekly and monthly summaries of U.S. coin values, and *The Currency Dealer Newsletter* (originally published by Kagin's in 1978 under the name *The Currency Market Review*) provides monthly compilations of the currency market.

Coin World and *Numismaster* also provide online databases with over a million coin prices. Auction sales records also are available in almost real time. Much of this information is easily accessed on the Internet via industry websites, and the majority of serious collectors subscribe to at least one or two of these publications, including new editions of *The Guide Book of United States Coins* (Referred to as the *Red Book*) (by Whitman Publishing), which comes out usually in the first week of April.

Information on just about any type of coin is easily obtainable. Several online sites offer sales records, reports on market conditions, price guides and investment advice—investment advice you still want to know about, but after reading this book, you'll have an easier time of separating the wheat from the chaff.

The information is out there, and it's important, if for no other reason than to lift the shroud of mystery from the world of numismatic collecting and investing.

For many just getting into rare coins, it has the feel of an exclusive club—one perhaps you're not convinced is worth the effort. Let me assure you that it is most definitely worth it. And what's more, introduce yourself to a few dealers, and, in no time at all, you'll be part of the in-crowd.

The reason bid-ask numbers are available is because much of the trading takes place in public or semi-public forums, where everyone can see the last trade. What that means and why it's a big deal is because for virtually all U.S. rare coins, and a good many foreign, there is near instant *liquidity*. You may think you'll never need to jump in or out of a particular coin, or set of coins, in a big hurry...but chances are there will be a time and place and, in any event, you'll sleep better at night simply knowing you can.

Inexpensive Market Entry

The old paradigm of a 20% spread between wholesale and retail no longer exists among the more credible coin dealers. With pricing information so easily available and transparent, there are few secrets. Savvy investors as well as collectors can verify the value of most any type of regularly traded coin. And for those great rarity and Legacy coins, there are auction records to track what specific coins or banknotes have brought in the past.

Today it's hard to justify more than a 10% markup for rare coins valued at over a few thousand dollars. Investment portfolios of over $100,000 can be negotiated even below that. Your prospects for making money are now significantly improved, especially on a shorter term basis than in the past.

There are other characteristics, what I'd describe as "minor" advantages, to numismatic investing: Coins can be easily and inexpensively stored, transported and insured. A few companies specialize in numismatic insurance, and several others offer options ranging from numismatic-specific riders to comprehensive policies at relatively low rate. Numismatic items are usually not subject to personal property taxes—a decided advantage over, say, real estate. No mortgage broker headaches, closing costs, surprises with the appraisal or other ownership entanglements.

But what makes numismatics unique in the field of financial instruments is how rare coins merge the most attractive elements of the stock market, precious metals and high-end collectibles markets. You could even make the argument that numismatics discards many of the aforementioned most egregious handicaps as well.

A Dwindling Supply

The first and perhaps most important aspect of gaining an understanding of numismatic fundamentals is the realization that supply is finite. True, coins are not a dwindling resource like, say, crude oil, but in a sense it's exactly like crude oil.

Through various forms of attrition, the quantity of rare coins and currency available in the marketplace is *decreasing*. The total amount of coins get reduced by meltdowns, natural disasters, circulation and other non-preventable losses—only what has been put away by collectors will (theoretically) become available in the future. The phenomenon creates a perpetual bullish bias for the rarest specimens.

For all their differences, rare coins still have a lot in common with the collectible market as a whole. So, it's fair to think: If the bull market in coins is for real, we'd expect other areas under the collectibles umbrella to be equally as robust, right?

In fact, this is exactly the collectibles market today. Catch a few episodes of *Antiques Roadshow* and you'll know what I'm saying. It's a healthy environment pretty much across the board. Paintings, in particular, can command millions. The last few years have seen the record price for a painting jump by more than $100 million to $273 million for *The Card Players* by Paul Cézanne in 2011. As magnificent as these paintings are, they are not even the most coveted in the art world. Imagine how much the *Mona Lisa* would go for if it were ever to come on to the market! (*Hint: It'd be in the billion-dollar ballpark.*)

Indeed, the numismatic market often resists recessions and depressions. During a "slow" period between 1975 and 1977, only a small percentage of investment-grade coins declined in value. During the recession of 1980 to 1983 there were substantial increases in value of a number of numismatic coins, such as silver dollars, in spite of the overall downturn. In the last quarter of 1983, when gold values dropped 25%, falling below $370 per ounce, retail prices for investment-quality coins actually increased. When virtually all collectibles plummeted during the financial meltdown of 2008 to 2010, top rarities fell a mere 15%.

Many common coins did drop by as much as 50%, but the correction was far less precipitous than the bloodbath in the housing market. In most circumstances, high-quality rare coins and currency provide a low risk/high profit potential over the long term. As with most investments, the greater the risk, the greater the reward. While there is risk involved in purchasing rare coins, they can be reduced to acceptable levels. After analyzing a half-century of volatile economic data, a few things have become clear. Rare coins are an outstanding store of value, and in most cases, exceptional performers.

On the demand side, collector interest has risen steadily since the early 1960s. By the '80s, long before Tom Cruise found Scientology and "neoliberalism" wasn't a pejorative term, numismatics moved into the investment big leagues. From the handful of collectors at the turn of the 20th century who would correspond personally with the director of the U.S. Mint, perhaps as much as 10 million more people took up the "hobby."

It was a time when the industry experienced growing pains. Wall Street's attempt to package rare coins into mutual funds with prospectuses their clients could understand was a spectacular failure. Fledgling grading firms, PCGS and NGC, would come under close scrutiny by the Federal Trade Commission and other government regulatory bodies. But the public's fascination with numismatics continued to grow.

A decade later collector interest surged again with the advent of the U.S. Mint-sponsored State Quarter program, and again with the Presidential Dollar and the National Park Quarters programs in the new millennium. In 2012, the U.S. Mint estimated the number of collectors at an astounding 130 to 140 million.

A 1933 $20 Saint-Gaudens brought $7.59 million at auction in 2002. It is the only specimen of this date legally available to collectors. Today that coin would easily surpass $10 million and perhaps even $12 million. (© National Numismatic Collection, National Museum of American History, Smithsonian Institution)

We still refer to coin collecting as a hobby, but its popularity is well beyond those handful of guys who fly remote-control airplanes at the park on Saturday mornings. Serious collectors, as judged by those reading the largest weekly industry magazine, *Coin World*, is at 285,000—a subscription base that continues to climb at a time when most print publications are struggling.

Investor demand, relative to their collector brethren, is more cyclical but can have just as great an impact on coin prices. Pure investors are interested in asset preservation and appreciation, and therefore their trading activities are concentrated on the best performing rare coins. Besides individual investors, this sector includes financial advisors, broker dealers, rare coin investment houses and telemarketers. Investors pour into precious metals and numismatics when there's a perception of high inflation or great economic uncertainty.

In 2011, Steve Contursi and Don Kagin handled the sale of the unique Punch-On-Breast 1787 Brasher Doubloon—often referred to as the "most important American coin"—for $7.2 million, the second highest-for-the-time price realized for a numismatic piece. (© Kagin's, Inc.)

Presently, the stock market has shown strength, but when things turn over in equities you probably won't see investors shift their capital into a very unattractive bond market. It will go into precious metals, rare coins and other commodity ventures—and it's probably around this time you can expect another big leg of gold's bull run.

While numismatic coin and currency values are cyclical in nature, usually six to seven years, prices have been increasing over the long term for more than 80 years. A technical stock analyst might describe the price movement using a moving average and note that it has one of the steepest slopes of any investment sector. During the Great Depression, top-quality, rare coins and currency, although more difficult to sell, lost little or no value. During the severe recession of 2008 to 2010, which is still dragging the present-day economy down, finer rare coins and currency lost no more than 15% of the 100% return earned over the previous decade. In the long term, values have been increasing at a rate of 8% to 11% annually (see Case Studies in the appendix).

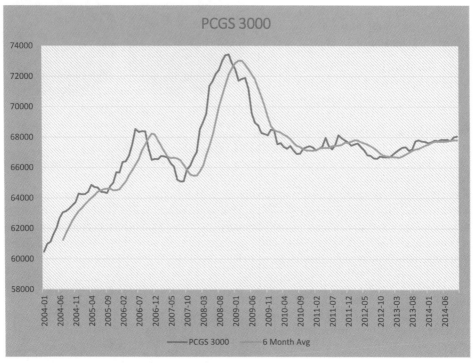

Professional Coin Grading Service compilation of 3,000 rare coin values. (© PCGS)

Assembling a Manicured Collection

In this age of planned obsolescence, more and more of us are beginning to realize that over a long period of time it pays to buy the best quality available. Prices have soared on high-quality materials ordinarily reserved for the super wealthy. Not only was there a new world record for a price paid for a coin just last year in 2013, but the sheer number of coins that are being bought and sold for over a $1 million is surprising—even from where I'm sitting, as president of a company that brokers these deals.

Nevertheless, I'd have to admit, the real action in numismatics takes place with the group of coins in the tier below. These are coins that numismatists still keep detailed provenance records of—but they don't necessarily require an oil sheik's bank account to be the successful bidder.

Recent years have seen record prices for the top 1% of coins as compared to an overall market that has been rather stagnant. Investment-grade and Legacy coin sales occur almost exclusively through private transactions or through large auction houses like Stack's Bowers or Heritage.

Reputable companies that counsel investors and collectors on rare coins and currency almost always urge investing in the highest grades available. As self-serving as that may sound to the cynic, it doesn't mean the advice is wrong. These are the coins the money players are searching for today, and the same folks who will be pushing up the price of your prized coins should they come back on to the market however many days or years from now.

A curious incentive to own fine quality recently came down the pike when the two major grading houses initiated Registry Sets. In 2001, collectors began to register their collections with the grading services to publicize them. But what started out as a novelty has grown and now there are friendly competitions among collectors for the finest quality sets. I can't speak for everybody, of course, but I don't believe many of us in the business anticipated the popularity or corresponding impact it would have. No question, though, the vanity entertainment of Registry Sets have pushed prices higher for the types of coins you're likely to find in these top collections.

Auctions are an excellent way to establish the retail value of numismatic material. For a handful of notable auction houses, large collections up for sale may bring in more than $30 million. However, after putting up a Legacy coin for auction, a collector may expect to wait three to four months to find the right buyer. Rounding up those potential buyers is how auction houses earn their commissions. (© Kagin's Inc.)

Perhaps from a sheer dynamic point of view, investors who are purchasing rare coins and currency for appreciation and who demand only the finest, top-quality numismatic specimens are coming into the marketplace in ever-increasing numbers. And the rate of entry of investors looking to bid on Legacy coins is substantially higher than that.

Legacy coins are the best of the best. They come with the highest grade, pedigree and rarity, and that usually translates into outstanding ROI performances. They are extremely rare, if not unique, have a significant place in United States history and may have touched the hands of important historical personalities. A good portion of Legacy coins are impounded in museums, but there are still brilliant specimens in private hands, and from time to time they come onto the market.

The Legacy collection, illustrated on the following page, represents 54 highly prized coins in the world of numismatics. In 1983, Kagin's assembled and sold this offering of legacy coins, and since then we've been tracking its performance. Over a 30-year period, the portfolio has appreciated over four times its original value.

Notably, the 1927-D Double Eagle saw an appreciation of 500% and the Uncirculated 1795 Capped Bust Eagle was up 400%. Commonly referred to as "America's Most Beautiful Coin," the 1907 Ultra-High Relief Double Eagle increased by an astonishing 733%.

Description	Grade	1983 Value*	2013 Value*	Growth $	Growth (%)	Avg. Annual Growth (%)
EXCEPTIONAL 1852-C GOLD DOLLAR	MS-63	$5,250	$20,000	$14,750	281%	10%
CHOICE PROOF 1858 GOLD DOLLAR	PF-65	$15,000	$37,500	$22,500	150%	6%
CHOICE PROOF 1861 GOLD DOLLAR	PF-65	$9,000	$15,000	$6,000	67%	2%
RARE PROOFLIKE 1875 GOLD DOLLAR	MS-60	$11,500	$17,500	$6,000	52%	2%
RARE 1798 QUARTER EAGLE	AU-50	$11,750	$40,000	$28,250	240%	9%
EXCEEDINGLY RARE PROOF 1829 QUARTER EAGLE	PF-63	$37,500	$200,000	$162,500	433%	16%
EXCEEDINGLY RARE PROOF 1831 QUARTER EAGLE	PF-63	$50,000	$85,000	$35,000	70%	3%
MAGNIFICENT PROOF 1833 QUARTER EAGLE	PF-65	$70,000	$175,000	$105,000	150%	6%
CHOICE PROOF 1881 QUARTER EAGLE	PF-65	$12,500	$40,000	$27,500	220%	8%
CHOICE PROOF 1885 QUARTER EAGLE	PF-65	$12,500	$27,500	$15,000	120%	4%
CHOICE 1854-D $3 GOLD	EF-45	$18,000	$50,000	$32,000	178%	7%
CHOICE PROOF 1862 $3 GOLD	PF-63/65	$17,500	$40,000	$22,500	129%	5%
CHOICE PROOF 1888 $3 GOLD	PF-63	$12,500	$17,500	$5,000	40%	1%
POPULAR PROOF 1879 FLOWING HAIR $4 GOLD STELLA	PF-60	$26,500	$115,000	$88,500	334%	12%
SELECT UNCIRCULATED 1800 HALF EAGLE	MS-63	$17,500	$35,000	$17,500	100%	4%
SUPERB AND VERY RARE 1825/1 HALF EAGLE	MS-65	$75,000	$300,000	$225,000	300%	11%
1825 OVER 4 U.S. HALF EAGLE ONE OF ONLY TWO PIECES KNOWN	VF-25obv EF-45rev	$200,000	$850,000	$650,000	325%	12%
SUPERB FINEST KNOWN 1831 LARGE D HALF EAGLE	MS-67	$65,000	$300,000	$235,000	362%	13%
ATTRACTIVE 1834 NO MOTTO HALF EAGLE	MS-60/63	$4,995	$7,500	$2,505	50%	2%
POSSIBLY FINEST KNOWN 1843-O HALF EAGLE	MS-63	$8,500	$65,000	$56,500	665%	25%
CHOICE PROOF 1862 HALF EAGLE	PF-63	$17,500	$65,000	$47,500	271%	10%
CHOICE PROOF 1863 HALF EAGLE	PF-63	$20,000	$75,000	$55,000	275%	10%
PROOF 1870 HALF EAGLE	PF-63	$15,000	$50,000	$35,000	233%	9%
CHOICE PROOF 1893 HALF EAGLE	PF-65	$12,500	$75,000	$62,500	500%	19%
GEM PROOF 1915 HALF EAGLE	PF-67	$16,000	$75,000	$59,000	369%	14%
EXCEPTIONAL UNCIRCULATED 1795 EAGLE	MS-63	$55,000	$350,000	$295,000	536%	20%
CHOICE UNCIRCULATED 1799 EAGLE	MS-63/65	$24,000	$50,000	$26,000	108%	4%
MINT STATE 1799 EAGLE	MS-60	$14,500	$45,000	$30,500	210%	8%
BEAUTIFUL CHOICE 1800 EAGLE	MS-63/65	$32,500	$165,000	$132,500	408%	15%
PROOFLIKE 1801 EAGLE	MS-63	$28,000	$140,000	$112,000	400%	15%
CHOICE UNCIRCULATED 1803 EAGLE	MS-63/65	$37,500	$80,000	$42,500	113%	4%
EXCEEDINGLY RARE PROOF 1846 EAGLE	PR-63	$62,500	$350,000	$287,500	460%	17%
GEM MATTE PROOF 1912 EAGLE	PR-67	$27,500	$100,000	$72,500	264%	10%
EXCEEDINGLY RARE CHOICE PROOF 1861 DOUBLE EAGLE	PR-63/65	$72,500	$150,000	$77,500	107%	4%
CHOICE PROOF 1866 DOUBLE EAGLE WITH MOTTO VARIETY	PR-63	$36,000	$75,000	$39,000	108%	4%
CHOICE PROOF 1878 DOUBLE EAGLE	PR-63/65	$36,000	$65,000	$29,000	81%	3%
CHOICE PROOF 1881 DOUBLE EAGLE	PR-63/65	$40,000	$65,000	$25,000	63%	2%
CHOICE PROOF 1882 DOUBLE EAGLE	PR-63	$45,000	$65,000	$20,000	44%	2%
FAMOUS 1883 DOUBLE EAGLE CHOICE PROOF	PR-65	$90,000	$250,000	$160,000	178%	7%
SELECT PROOF 1886 DOUBLE EAGLE	PR-63	$37,500	$60,000	$22,500	60%	2%
EXTREMELY RARE MCMVII (1907) $20 GOLD "ULTRA HIGH RELIEF" BY AUGUSTUS ST. GAUDENS "AMERICA'S MOST BEAUTIFUL COIN"	PR-67	$240,000	$2,500,000	$2,260,000	942%	59%
CHOICE UNCIRCULATED MCMVII HIGH RELIEF ST. GAUDENS DOUBLE EAGLE	MS-65	$25,000	$57,500	$32,500	130%	5%
MCMVII (1907) HIGH RELIEF SAINT-GAUDENS DOUBLE EAGLE GEM PROOF WITH LETTER FROM THE WHITE HOUSE	PF-67	$55,000	$275,000	$220,000	400%	15%
CHOICE MATTE PROOF 1908 DOUBLE EAGLE	PF-65	$37,500	$86,000	$48,500	129%	5%
GEM PROOF 1909 DOUBLE EAGLE	PF-67	$42,500	$200,000	$157,500	371%	14%
CHOICE PROOF 1912 DOUBLE EAGLE	PF-65	$32,500	$80,000	$47,500	146%	5%
THE FABULOUS 1927-D DOUBLE EAGLE CHOICE BRILLIANT UNCIRCULATED PROBABLY THE FINEST KNOWN SPECIMEN	MS-65	$250,000	$1,900,000	$1,650,000	660%	24%
RARE 1929 DOUBLE EAGLE	AU-55	$8,500	$27,500	$19,000	224%	8%
ELUSIVE 1931-D DOUBLE EAGLE	AU-55	$15,000	$35,000	$20,000	133%	5%
ATTRACTIVE $5 1849 NORRIS, GREG, NORRIS	EF-40	$5,500	$17,500	$12,000	218%	8%
$10 1849 MINERS BANK	AU-50	$16,000	$65,000	$49,000	306%	11%
POPULAR $50 1851 R.E. HUMBERT "SLUG"	AU-55	$32,500	$100,000	$67,500	208%	8%
1855 KELLOGG & CO. $50 GOLD PIECE	PR-63	$225,000	$550,000	$325,000	144%	5%
POPULAR WASS, MOLITOR & CO. $50	F-15	$15,000	$30,000	$15,000	100%	4%
TOTAL		**$2,399,995**	**$10,711,000**	**$5,811,005**	**346%**	**11%**

A complete list of Kagin's Inc. Classic Gold Rarities Offering. (Table created by Kagin's Inc. with data and permission from Coin Dealer Newsletter, and Whitman Publishing, LLC.)

A Private Source of Wealth

Perhaps as important as any of the above, collectors and investors appreciate that rare coins and currency are a private source of wealth. They remain one of the few investments that you can legally accumulate and liquidate privately.

Sharpe Ratios of Various Investment Portfolios
Ratios are Based on Excess Returns (Returns Above 1 Month CD's)

Percentage of Each Investment in Portfolios

Portfolios	Portfolio #	S&P 500	DJIA	Moody's 30 Year Corporate Aaa	10 Year Treasury Bill	3 Month T Bill (Cash Equivalent)	PCGS 3000	Gold Bullion	SHARPE RATIOS
43 Years - 1970-2012	1	30%	30%	20%	10%	10%			0.020
43 Years - 1970-2012	2	27%	27%	18%	8%	10%	10%		0.096
43 Years - 1970-2012	3	27%	27%	18%	8%	10%	5%	5%	0.093
20 Years - 1993-2012	4	30%	30%	20%	10%	10%			0.223
20 Years - 1993-2012	5	27%	27%	18%	8%	10%	10%		0.182
20 Years - 1993-2012	6	27%	27%	18%	8%	10%	5%	5%	0.189
10 Years - 2003-2012	7	30%	30%	20%	10%	10%			0.258
10 Years - 2003-2012	8	27%	27%	18%	8%	10%	10%		0.262
10 Years - 2003-2012	9	27%	27%	18%	8%	10%	5%	5%	0.481
5 Years - 2008-2012	10	30%	30%	20%	10%	10%			0.140
5 Years - 2008-2012	11	27%	27%	18%	8%	10%	10%		0.140
5 Years - 2008-2012	12	27%	27%	18%	8%	10%	5%	5%	0.210

Prepared by Gary Knaus, Eligius Investments, LLC
2/26/13

(© Gary Knaus / Eligius Investments)

When President Roosevelt confiscated gold in 1933, rare coins were exempt and owners were able to retain their collections. They are not on the U.S. Patriot Act list of reportable items and are not subject to governmental regulation in the manner of stocks, bonds and money markets, nor are 1099 reports needed for the sale of coins. (You are required to report capital gains and should consult your accountant). Social Security numbers are never requested unless large cash purchases are made, and no records are sent to governmental agencies. Outside of your professional dealer, no one needs to know what you own or where it is kept.

Of course, a big reason people collect coins is for its aesthetics. Coins reflect an intriguing part of history. If art objects could speak, rare coins would tell you about the founders of our nation, the likes of George Washington and pioneers like Brigham Young, and countless other stories and events and people that are portrayed through coin and banknote history. Could be the Roman coin in your collection was used by Julius Caesar, or the Spanish gold Doubloon and silver Pieces of Eight were hijacked on the high seas by Sir Francis Drake. All very exciting.

Beautiful coin designs of the ancient Greek diesinker Kimon are among the finest portraitures in history. The $20 1907 Ultra-High Relief, sculptor Augustus Saint-Gaudens' masterwork of design, is perhaps the most recognizable obverse in numismatics. Or, a personal favorite, the Proof $50 1851 U.S. Assay Office Augustus Humbert slug. Slang for "hunk of metal", this particular slug is a unique, octagonal-shaped coin that became the primary medium of monetary exchange in California during the Gold Rush. We'll come back to this subject in detail later.

INTERNAL RATES OF RETURNS AND SHARPE RATIOS										By: Gary Knaus		
Various Investment Portfolios over 40, 20, 10, 5 and 3 Years										Eligius Investments, LLC		
Sharpe Ratios Based on Excess Returns												
2/26/13					Percentage of Each Investment in Portfolios							
(End of Year) Portfolios	Portfolio #	S&P 500	DJIA	Moody's 30 Year Corporate Aaa	10 Year Treasury Bill	3 Month T Bill (Cash Equivalent)	Gold Bullion	PCGS 3000	Key Dates & Rarities	Mint State Rare Gold	SHARPE RATIOS	IRR
40 Years - 1973-2012	1	30%	30%	20%	10%	10%					(0.1000)	5.59%
40 Years - 1973-2012	2	27%	27%	18%	8%	10%	10%				0.050	6.25%
40 Years - 1973-2012	3	27%	27%	18%	8%	10%		10%			0.060	6.29%
40 Years - 1973-2012	4	27%	27%	18%	8%	10%			10%		0.137	5.89%
40 Years - 1973-2012	5	27%	27%	18%	8%	10%				10%	0.091	6.58%
40 Years - 1973-2012	6	24%	24%	16%	8%	8%	5%	5%	5%	5%	0.119	6.85%
20 Years - 1993-2012	7	30%	30%	20%	10%	10%					0.223	5.24%
20 Years - 1993-2012	8	27%	27%	18%	8%	10%	10%				0.284	5.69%
20 Years - 1993-2012	9	27%	27%	18%	8%	10%		10%			0.182	4.74%
20 Years - 1993-2012	10	27%	27%	18%	8%	10%			10%		0.253	5.39%
20 Years - 1993-2012	11	27%	27%	18%	8%	10%				10%	0.193	4.84%
20 Years - 1993-2012	12	24%	24%	16%	8%	8%	5%	5%	5%	5%	0.237	5.10%
10 Years - 2003-2012	13	30%	30%	20%	10%	10%					0.026	4.26%
10 Years - 2003-2012	14	27%	27%	18%	8%	10%	10%				0.393	5.59%
10 Years - 2003-2012	15	27%	27%	18%	8%	10%		10%			0.262	4.10%
10 Years - 2003-2012	16	27%	27%	18%	8%	10%			10%		0.293	4.59%
10 Years - 2003-2012	17	27%	27%	18%	8%	10%				10%	0.282	4.30%
10 Years - 2003-2012	18	24%	24%	16%	8%	8%	5%	5%	5%	5%	0.385	5.02%
5 Years - 2008-2012	19	30%	30%	20%	10%	10%					0.140	1.85%
5 Years - 2008-2012	20	27%	27%	18%	8%	10%	10%				0.237	3.19%
5 Years - 2008-2012	21	27%	27%	18%	8%	10%		10%			0.140	1.81%
5 Years - 2008-2012	22	27%	27%	18%	8%	10%			10%		0.144	1.86%
5 Years - 2008-2012	23	27%	27%	18%	8%	10%				10%	0.131	1.70%
5 Years - 2008-2012	24	24%	24%	16%	8%	8%	5%	5%	5%	5%	0.197	2.40%
3 Years - 2010-2012	25	30%	30%	20%	10%	10%					1.810	6.66%
3 Years - 2010-2012	26	27%	27%	18%	8%	10%	10%				1.880	7.49%
3 Years - 2010-2012	27	27%	27%	18%	8%	10%		10%			1.830	5.92%
3 Years - 2010-2012	28	27%	27%	18%	8%	10%			10%		1.784	5.93%
3 Years - 2010-2012	29	27%	27%	18%	8%	10%				10%	1.738	5.74%
3 Years - 2010-2012	30	24%	24%	16%	8%	8%	5%	5%	5%	5%	1.830	5.88%

Technical analysis by Gary Knaus of Eligius Investments graphically illustrates how inclusion of rare coins in a portfolio of traditional investments proportionately reduces overall risks. (© Gary Knaus / Eligius Investments)

Every coin tells a story—a sort of document of its time. It's this romantic element in conjunction with the nuances of a physical specimen that elevate a relatively simple industrial die-stamping process into High Art. Art and history form the foundation of not only the "Hobby of Kings," but also the king of investments—numismatics.

Be Patient

A new client asked me to sell a rare gem proof gold piece that he'd purchased the previous year to "test the market." I had to tell him that's not how it works. Coin prices do not rise and fall in a straight line. When they are truly rare, they don't trade every day or even every month. A prized coin may linger at some theoretical value for a couple of years until another one sells and then the value could jump by, say, 30%.

Another friend of mine, Ken, is a successful investment advisor, despite his reluctance to recommend gold or rare coins for his clients: If it's not an income-producing asset, it's not a worthy investment. True, you don't receive dividends from holding rare coins—so there isn't going to be an income stream. He has a point. Numismatics does have its limitations.

Of course, it's not a good point in the long run. Pros rarely think that way. Nor do they usually buy or sell based on some tax advantage. Those things are talking points

1) Obverse of the Ionia Striated Stater ~
675 B.C., the first coin of the Western world.
(© Kagin's, Inc.)

2) Obverse of the Lydia Kroisos Stater ~550 B.C.,
the first gold coin. (© Kagin's, Inc.)

3) Obverse and reverse of the Syracuse Decadrachm
ca ~400-395 B.C., the first commemorative coin.
(©Kagin's, Inc.)

4) Obverse and reverse of the 1851 Unique
Proof-64 Augustus Humbert U.S. Assay Office
$50 slug, one of the most
important Gold Rush coins.
(© PCGS)

5) Obverse and reverse of the 1907 $20 Ultra-High
Relief Proof-69, America's most beautiful coin.
(© Stack's Bowers)

6) Obverse and reverse of the Ide Mar
(Ides of March) Denarius, the only "dated" ancient
coin and only coin commemorating a murder –
that of Julius Caesar.
(© Kagin's, Inc.)

7) Obverse and reverse of the first and
finest 1794 Silver Dollar PCGS Specimen-66.
(© Steven L. Contursi)

8) Obverse and reverse of the Unique 1783 Quint,
the first American coin.
(© Heritage Auctions, Inc.)

for neophytes. Most stockbrokers actually believe that. Truth is, it's much simpler than that: You buy when the risk/reward numbers appear to be in your favor. You'll risk $1 for $5 or more. This way if you're right half the time, you'll come out smelling like roses.

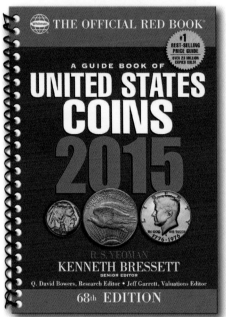

Cover of the 68th edition of A Guide Book of United States Coins 2015. The "Red Book" has been the reigning #1 best-seller for decades. Virtually every professional and collector have the latest edition in their library. The author's father, A.M. Kagin, was a contributor for over 50 years and the author himself, for over 40 years. (©Whitman Publishing, LLC)

What I tell my clients in this situation is that no one investment vehicle is likely to cover every personal need. That's why it's important to have a balanced portfolio. While this book focuses on numismatics, it ought to be made obvious that I'm not advocating putting your entire savings into a million-dollar coin—or into any one or two places for that matter. The possibility of being dead wrong always exists and that's why we spread out our investment wagers, we don't put all of our eggs in one basket, and we count on statistical probabilities to take us through our retirement years.

But, yes, there are some limitations that can't be talked around. The difference between wholesale and retail is higher than the usual financial investments. Plus or minus, numismatic spreads for large transactions is 5%- 10% for most investment quality rare coins and up to 20% for small transactions. Additionally, there is a 5% to 10% fee when you sell your coins. The spread needs to be covered before you can net any profit, which, to be frank, is why it often takes a couple of years just to reach a breakeven point.

There are no substantial tax shelters in numismatics. You can put American gold and silver eagles and a few other bullion coins in retirement plans, but collectible-grade coins have been excluded from retirement plans since 1981.

Despite a universal acceptance of PCGS and NGC decrees, grading is as much an art as it is a science—it's subjective, graders are human and they make mistakes. Even when graded correctly, there is variation within the grade. It's an opportunity for a sharp eye, but for most people it's a flaw in the system that coin dealers don't usually like to talk about.

I remember years ago watching a demonstration hosted by PCGS founder and president, David Hall by "The Expert", a computer programed to grade generic coins. Well, at least that was its mission. It failed. Mainly because there isn't enough programing code to substitute for subjectivity. How do you quantify beauty? Anyway, my hat's off to David for trying. He certainly has not been afraid of trying and funding new innovations. After all, that's how PCGS was born.

But every coin is distinct and I doubt that I will live to see a machine that can distinguish every nuance of each coin. What I tell my clients is that it's important to distinguish original, exceptional specimens from the average or low-end for the grade coins. No two coins are the same, and it is essential that you purchase the coin and not the holder. Ideally you should learn how to grade coins, but in the meantime, do yourself a favor and seek the advice of a professional, especially when you're first starting out. Coin dealers love to talk about coins, so pick their brain while you're at it.

Market timing can be problematic. You can buy the right coin at the wrong time. The coin market is a cyclical one—it has peaks, plateaus and valleys. If you purchase coins at the peak of that particular series cycle, you may have to wait five or more years before you can realize satisfactory profits. While rare coins are an excellent inflation hedge, like most investment sectors, they don't perform well in a recessionary environment.

The year 2014 represents late Stage One. Price trends are slightly on the rise and a bit higher than the 2012 cyclical bottom. Though numismatic values are not expected to decrease, it may be a slow and steady climb before we see the acceleration of higher prices that marks the beginning of Stage Two.

Still, a meandering gold price hasn't meant there wasn't some terrific opportunities within the overall market. Case in point, I'm happy to report that notwithstanding the Saddle Ridge Hoard Treasure sale, Pioneer gold has made noteworthy gains and long dormant clients have been slowly returning to their favorite hobby.

Now, even if you pick the right time to purchase coins, you still may have to wait to acquire the right one. At approximately $40 billion annually, investment-grade coins represent perhaps only 2% to 3% of the whole. Not much in the grand scheme of things.

The small pool of available coins makes finding quality specimens at reasonable prices a difficult and sometimes arduous tasks. This goes for dealers, too. Multi-million dollar orders for top-quality coins and notes may take weeks or months to properly fill—especially during a slow period when prices are soft and owners are reluctant to sell.

But if you work with the right dealer and have some patience, your endeavors will be rewarded. Be deliberate about your choices, no need to rush into anything. On the other hand, when the time comes to pull the trigger, don't hesitate. Pull it.

"Make a plan and stick to it." "Slow and steady wins the race." These chunks of wisdom ought to make intuitive sense to you. It's how you got through grad school, or built your business, or raised your family, or anything else truly worthwhile in your life. Apply the same principles to numismatic investing and your success is all but assured.

Chapter IV

Demand & Supply

As sharpening your forecasting skills is the main objective of this book, it seems practical to examine the factors that cause coin values to fluctuate. While myriad events with an infinite number of permutations and computations ultimately converge to bring together the highest bid and the lowest offer, fundamental analysis of the gold and numismatic markets begins with supply and demand—the same as for the vast majority of products and services in our quasi-free market system.

Nowadays, there is considerable overlap among the three basic coin buyer types—dealers, investors, collectors. In order to quantify their impact, we'll examine individually what motivates their decisions to buy. Although the typical rare coin enthusiast is a mix between the two, it's convenient to examine "collector" and "investor" behavioral tendencies separately.

Collectors constitute the backbone of consistent, unshakeable demand for rare coins and banknotes. As an investor, it is perhaps only necessary to see how this collector-base acts as a floor on price. Still, a closer look provides insight to price movement, which in turn ought to improve our entry-and-exit techniques.

Collectors are a sizeable subset of the overall marketplace. They can be counted upon to step into a falling market without fear or greed. Coin collectors, relative to spot or futures gold traders, provide a cushion-like effect in correction phases of the numismatic cycle. Whereas price to an investor is the alpha and omega, price to a collector is down on his list of priorities.

As a rule, collectors are determined, they want what they want; they're patient, and they have all the time in the world. Ironically, these characteristics give the average collector an edge over the average investor when it comes to market timing.

Most self-proclaimed "investors" I've come across are in a big hurry. A big hurry that gets them nowhere fast.

Demand Variables

Taking account that price elasticity is inversely proportional to rarity, prices for both bullion and rare coins operate under and are affected by the same economic influences. Of the two sides that determine price, demand is by far more dynamic. Supply is not going to change for 99% of the investment-quality rare coins and currency. It is for these reasons, we assert that numismatics is a demand-driven marketplace.

From a macroeconomic perspective, elements that influence purchasing decisions include disposable income, interest rates, inflation, money supply and the strength of the dollar. From a microeconomic perspective, any number of things can influence buy and sell decision-making.

There's not much we can do about macro factors, other than identify a given situation, then formulate a price expectation based on it. For micro factors, simply, we look to keep our emotions in check while remaining as objective as humanly possible.

Rare coin collectors, in their most romantic incarnation, form the foundation of the numismatic industry. Commemorative coinage was often used by visiting dignitaries—quite literally, the hobby of kings, queens and noblemen. In the United States, collecting coins has been a popular hobby, well, since before there were Thirteen Colonies.

For our purposes, it is enough to begin the discussion circa the 1960s. America's middle class began participating in the hobby in droves. Coin collecting has expanded by such a degree that we still call it a "hobby" only as a wink and a nod to the past.

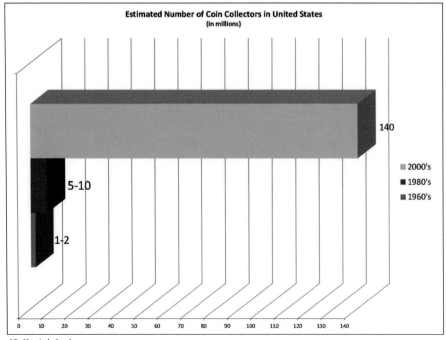

(© Kagin's Inc)

It hasn't grown to match the trading volume at the New York Stock Exchange, nor will it ever. That said, numismatic trading commands a rather respectable slice of the investment pie chart. And, for the only pie chart that truly matters, long-term ROI, numismatics owns it.

Demand Personalities

Most professional numismatists function as intermediaries between buyers and sellers, usually purchasing coins on behalf of their clients. Others buy for their own inventory and hold on to merchandise until they have the right buyer.

Although there is overlap, coin dealers fall into one of three categories:

Wholesalers primarily make their income by selling numismatic specimens to other professional numismatists. Most wholesalers cater to fewer than a dozen retail clients. Each month, a wholesaler will travel to two or three major trade shows.

They'll participate in auctions in order to obtain a sufficient quantity of inventory. Usually a wholesaler will specialize in one or a few specific fields of numismatics. By doing so, he can target the dealers who will pay top dollar for his efforts.

Wholesalers generally depend on other dealers as a source of buyers for their inventory. Any event that causes regular buyers to slow or halt their usual buying pace will have a ripple effect across the industry. For example, a precipitous drop in the price of gold bullion would inhibit the cash flow of **bullion dealers**, who would then be reluctant to buy coins from other wholesalers.

If this hypothetical situation were prolonged, the wholesaler may be forced to sell his coins at lower prices in order to generate cash flow. Coin dealers typically keep their ears to the ground and eyes peeled so they can be the first to take advantage of the weak link in the herd.

Another subset of professional numismatists are bullion dealers, who buy and sell precious metals, often in large quantities, and semi-numismatic coins. Since it takes considerable capital to conduct this scale of operation, there are only a few firms that can consistently serve the market.

Because this type of business generates substantial cash flow, bullion dealers are often in a position to take advantage of large, rare coin buying opportunities. They also are a good source for quick cash if dealers or collectors need to sell material quickly.

Their rare coin buying habits are volatile. They could sell their often substantial holdings at any time to generate cash, and thus are sort of a wild card in the rare coin markets.

Another subset of dealers is those who are also active collectors, sometimes called "vest pocket" dealers. Most dealers today started in the business as collectors and have retained and nurished their collecting interests. My father entered the coin business in 1933 to support his collecting habit. Just like avid acquirers of other collectibles, most collectors take pride in ownership and aim to create the best collection they can that is representative of their specialties.

Retail Dealers are by far the most numerous of professional numismatists. Retailers act as conduits between the seller and the end consumer. These dealers cater to the collector, the investor, other dealers and telemarketers. While retailers often purchase for their own inventory, most of their activity is dictated by the demand from their clientele.

Retail dealers' purchasing habits are usually motivated by their clients' needs and what is offered to them from new and existing clientele. In addition to selling coins from a brick and mortar location, some of these dealers also publish price lists, run advertisements in trade journals, or offer their inventory online. Although large in number—perhaps several thousand across the country—the retail coin dealer usually is not a high volume buyer of investment-quality coins.

Coin shows are a major activity for retail and wholesale dealers. By attending shows, dealers are able to showcase their inventory and personally connect with the buyer. This photo is of Don Kagin at his booth at a popular show in Long Beach, CA, showing historically important pieces to California Governor Jerry Brown and others. (© Kagin's, Inc.)

A small subset of retail dealers consist of telemarketing firms. **Telemarketers** stimulate demand for "limited edition" coins through newsletters, national advertisements, endorsements, televised sales, like on the Home Shopping Network, and telephone cold-calling campaigns.

Although telemarketers claim to be selling rare coins, most of their products are modern or common coins with mass appeal and availability.

Less than a hundred retail dealers in the entire industry have the capital, expertise and experience to buy and sell the finest and rarest investment-quality coins and paper currency. As a relatively small clique within the realm of professional numismatists, investment-quality retail dealers drive the market for top-tier coins, which includes Legacy varieties.

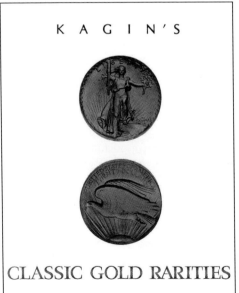

Front cover of Kagin's 1983 publication of Classic Gold Rarities. (© Kagin's, Inc.)

Total Collector Marketplace

In the 1980s, the man on the street became more sophisticated with his invest-ments. With the advent of discount stockbrokerages, financial news networks and other DIY tools, by the time the new millennium came around, the U.S. Mint had estimated there were 140 million people who collect rare coins and currency.

That number counts Aunt Mildred's State quarter collection begun in 1999 and school children who collect Kennedy half dollars. In reality, there is probably about a million serious collectors, and fewer yet avid collectors with the finan-cial means to compete for top-tier coins and artifacts.

Investor Demand

By far, investor demand will have the greatest impact on the very rare numis-matic market over the next decade. While their numbers are low now, they have been slowly increasing over the last four years. There are a number of factors contributing to and reinforcing this rise in investor demand for numismatics.

One of many national news articles highlighting the 7.2 million sale of the Unique Brasher Doubloon in 2011. *(Wall St. Image © Dreamstime, Stuart Monk)*

The real estate and economic crisis of 2007–2010 caused traditional investing vehicles to fail. Housing and stock market values plummeted, causing millions of Americans, at all income levels, to seek strong and safe investment alternatives. For many, there already is that historic, instinctive attraction to precious metals. With such desire for hard assets like gold and silver, interest in rare coins and currency is obviously (if indirectly) intensified.

In spite of recent upticks in our economy, economic uncertainty is still prevalent throughout the world. Investors are looking for safe havens for their assets. Gold and to some extent silver, has been the commodity of choice over the last several years. And many investors are now looking favorably at the long-term track record of the finest numismatic properties that are just beginning to diversify in this area.

Foreign (especially Asian) demand for precious metals has increased almost each year for the last decade, and is expected to continue. In a recent Bonhams auction of 27 high-end US gold coins, two thirds of the successful buyers were offshore purchas-ers! We expect this trend to continue.

Current laws now allow many bullion coins to be placed into retirement plans. With talk of new legislation that will allow investors to once again place rare coins and currency in their individual retirement accounts, the effect on the numismatic market could result in significant appreciation.

The solid track record of investment quality coins and currency is the focus for most investors investigating this field. Their potential substantial buying power will be targeted towards top-end material. With only 2% – 3% of available rare coins qualifying as investment grade, and less than 1% as Legacy coins, demand will only get more intense. This can only bode well for future appreciation for the finest numismatic properties.

Investors and their counselors won't be able to ignore for long the substantial benefits of diversifying their portfolios into gold and rare coins.

Together, the pool of numismatic dealers, investors and collectors continues to grow at a pace that will inevitably create more upward pressure on prices.

Supply Variables

Any discussion on rare coins and currency warrants an in-depth explanation of how the word "rare" is defined in the business. It is overused, often *misused*, when referencing collectible coins and currency.

Misleading advertisements abound from this or that dealer or shady infomercial spokesperson who claims to specialize in rare coins. You will either need to partner with a reputable dealer or get super thoughtful about your investments on your own. Preferably, both.

You see, the way an investor makes money in stocks, bonds, commodities, numismatics…God forbid, chinchilla farms, whatever…is by uncovering *hidden value*.

What is rare? Within the pantheon of rare coins and currency, there are different levels of rarity. How do we measure it and how do we apply those boundaries to the decision-making process?

For high-net-worth investors who strive for top-quality pieces in their numismatic portfolio, gauging rarity is a particularly vital concept. These are the coins that tend to have the highest return on investment, but because thousands of dollars may separate the same coin a grade apart, there are a few things you should know about rarity in order to avoid common pitfalls.

A certified grade, of course, is a sort of shorthand for describing the condition of a coin. The supply or rarity of a coin or banknote is directly related to its grade. Grading is the quantification of the physical condition of a coin or its degree of wear and circulation. Grades are quantified by both objective—wear, marks, scratches—and a more subjective observation of the aesthetic appeal of a coin or banknote—for example, color, luster or "wow" effect.

Population numbers become more important as a coin moves higher on the grading scale. As a consequence, a coin's price is influenced by small changes. This is especially true for the rarer coins.

Before we launch into an in-depth analysis of these factors, let us take a look at the general breakdown of how the blanket term "rare" is applied across the numismatic board.

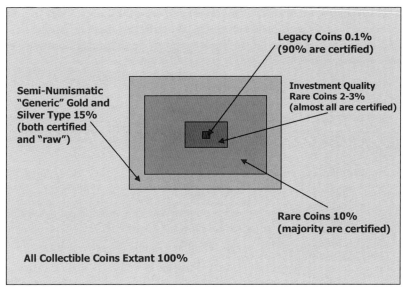

Terms such as "investment quality" and "rare" can be widely misinterpreted. This chart demonstrates the approximate allocation of different levels of rarity. (© Kagin's, Inc.)

The consequence of a loose interpretation of "rare" results in a broad range of investing possibilities and risk/reward levels. For our purposes, we're primarily interested in the serious money level of investing, which involves the subsets of rarities that includes Legacy and investment-grade coins and banknotes.

The Morgan Dollar is one of the most popular coins in numismatics. Morgans provide a great example of how within the same series of coins, values can vary drastically based on a number of factors including the year, condition (grade) and mintmark. The three coins above are each in Mint State condition. The first is an 1880-S; with 8.9 million minted, it is currently worth $175. The second coin, an 1889-CC, has a mintage of 350,000, and it is worth $325,000. The last is an 1893-S; there were only 100,000 minted, and it will run you about $650,000 on today's market landscape. (© Kagin's, Inc.)

Market Dynamics

Philanthropic collectors and investors may donate their coin collections to foundations, museums, universities or charitable organizations. In return, if they're smart, they receive money-saving tax write-offs.

We're going to spend more time concentrating on how to live out your retirement years in luxury or leave your kids a terrific inheritance—but, either way, we need to get there first!

"Market supply" is defined as the number of coins and banknotes that are currently available for trade on the open market. It does not include those numismatic items held by institutions and museums. It's a number that under ordinary circumstances diminishes slowly over time.

Investment-grade numismatic coins are a product of low population availability, relatively high grade and aesthetics for the series, type and date. Whereas Legacy coins require more of a shot-in-the-dark, to qualify for the category, investment-grade specimens need to generate sufficient turnover, which allows for regular-interval price inspections.

It's by monitoring price action that one gets a sense of the numismatic market's ebb and flow—a crucial element when timing your actual buys and sells.

Moving forward, I'll be more specific identifying the specific coins we're talking about, but for the time being suffice to say they are the ones that generate media buzz whenever there's a change in the fundamentals or a surprising auction result.

Essentially, what we'll be doing is learning how to compare and contrast mintage and population figures with the pricing of a coin in its various grades. The object of the exercise, naturally, is to identify the undervalued ones.

The Sheldon Rarity Scale	
Rating	Number Extant
R1	Over 1,250
R2	501-250
R3	201-500
R4	76-200
R5	31-75
R6	13-30
Low R7	10-12
R7	7-9
High R7	4-6
R8	2-3
Unique	1

The Sheldon Rarity Scale is the industry standard scale for identifying how many specimens in a category remain in existence. It was originally developed in the late 1950s by famed numismatist Dr. William Herbert Sheldon for large cent varieties, in particular. Later, it was adopted for general use in most categories of numismatics.

Or, conversely, to identify those overvalued coins of the same type in your collection that you'd consider parting with.

The original supply of a coin or banknote is the total number struck or printed in a calendar year at a specific mint. Official mintage figures are a matter of public record—published and verifiable. Years of scholarly research and review of these records bring virtual exactitude to original supply data.

An exception occurs with coins and currency with mintage figures that are not precisely known. This happens when a mint stamps the same date for multiple strikes, on different occasions, in multi-year time spans. Doesn't happen often, only with certain coins, and some of us have this angle figured out, too. However, in the grand scheme of things, this is an exception not worth getting into a lather over.

A coin is considered "rare" when it has a low original mintage relative to the same coin with a different date, mintmark, or in some cases type and variety. Numismatists will sometimes compare the supply numbers of different coins, but, truthfully, there's no useful information to be had there. It's apples and oranges.

For example, according to PCGS, there are 123 MS-60 or better 1893-S Morgan dollars; compare that to the one or two known examples of Mint State 1842-D half eagles. Which is worth $50,000, and which a cool half-million?

Numismatic experts almost always endorse a coin with a low mintage. Be cautious, however, of firms touting "limited editions." The implication is a relatively low population, but the phrase is actually meaningless. Limited editions are limited to the orders a mint or distributor receives.

It's limited as to how many commemorative Lady Diana dinner plates they can sell—see what I'm saying?

Coins and notes that are newly issued or minted, obviously, are going to warrant high grades. It does not follow that because they have high grades—or limited mintage!—that they are also rare.

On the retail numismatic market, these coins are probably only worth their precious metal content, which is certainly less than your original purchase price. Brokers sell these coins by marking-up the purchase price considerably and touting the "limited," or "just found" marketing angle.

Limited edition government issues that sport a FIRST DAY OF ISSUE tag from one of the grading firms may be a great marketing tactic for the grading firms. Early buyers and promoters who paid a premium for the privilege to have a meaningless phrase stamped onto the holder notes will also benefit from the frenzy of idiots. What these Johnny-on-the-spot dealers do is send them out to be graded in hopes of MS-70 awards, which they will then sell individually for three or four times each one's retail U.S. Mint price.

This game has gained tremendous popularity in the last few years and will probably continue for a short time longer—until a new promotional game comes about. This is not any game I'd be interested in playing.

Modern limited edition coins are newly minted and overwhelmingly in excellent condition. Despite a MS-69 grade for 5 oz. National Park quarter pictured above, it and others like it do not ordinarily carry any numismatic premium to speak of. Demand never exceeds supply, and the initial retail price will likely never be topped in subsequent trading. These modern coins may be fun to collect, but they hold marginal investment promise. (© Kagin's, Inc.)

Neither should you. In the game of Hearts, unless you have a handful of spades, you do not want to be the sucker who ends up with the sloughed off Queen of Spades. Promotional hyperbole is not something that ought to trip you up.

Upon a new issue's release, its price on the secondary market may bounce around for a few weeks, but, sooner or later—probably sooner—the coin's price will fall back to its natural premium over spot, and it's a boring trading market after that.

Prices don't move and why should they? You'll be a grown-up and not fall for any this malarkey?

Although, to be fair, those late-night, overpriced shopping network State quarter collections do make fine holiday gifts. But here, just now, we're talking about real money, we're talking about your investments—not a modern set of quarters or commemoratives. The U.S. Mint is really the only entity that makes out on these deals.

You're too smart not to see through infomercial companies' thin veil of legitimacy, hello! Enough said. No need to speak of the Coin Hucksters again.

Insider's tip:

Mintage figures are easily obtainable from various publications, but they are often unreliable indicators of a coin's true rarity. If a mint melts a significant portion of a production run before going into circulation, the remaining specimens would be much rarer than indicated.

Many Ways to Count the Vote

"Population," or the actual real-life supply, is defined for any given coin or banknote as the total number extant—the total number of like items that currently, physically still exist. It is a combination of all specimens in the private domain, plus those in public institutions, such as those collections housed at museums and university libraries. If your town supports a coin club collection, well, we count those, too.

"Certified population" is the cumulative amount of coins that have been independently certified by either PCGS or NGC. There are notable grading services for currency—Professional Currency Grading Service and Paper Money Guaranty—run by PCGS (but now under new ownership) and NGC, respectively.

Certified population numbers can include second-tier grading firms, such as American Numismatic Association Certification Service and International Coin Grading. However, without a trading platform it's hard to gauge these numbers.

A CAC sticker is another matter entirely, but we'll get to that in a later chapter.

Back to population: PCGS or NGC certification involves authentication of a specimen by experts at one of those two grading companies. These highly trained and experienced graders, usually in groups of three, independently examine, then caucus to reach a final decision on grade. Certified coins are hermetically sealed in an official, tamper-proof holder, assigned a unique barcode identification number, and then added to the population census.

Certified population censuses are updated monthly, although some specialized series such as Pioneer gold and Pattern coins are updated only quarterly. Some numismatists, or companies like Kagin's, keep their own private census for the areas in which they specialize. Knowing the correct statistics are a dealer's edge going into private sale negotiations or narrowing down a top-bid amount at an auction.

Population reports can be further broken down to a coin's issue, date, variety and grade. These reports do not indicate market availability. An 1840 Dahlonega quarter eagle, for instance, is rare in all grades—it may be years before the one or two known examples in Uncirculated come up for sale.

In one case, Kagin's was privy to an unpublicized collection of high quality raw specimens that, if graded and added to the certified pop censuses, would radically alter collectors' perception of that type's rarity. Subsequently, we quietly advised our clients to unload that particular category of rarities.

You may think that's the end of the story. But staying on top of the market, or having a trusted dealer to do so on your behalf, is the gift that keeps on giving. Those high quality raw coins did in fact leak on to the market, keeping a lid on prices. The coin's underwhelming performance had media pundits scratching their heads.

Since that time, I've noticed the population numbers slowly start to rise. I have a number in my head. When the population reports fully realize the addition of the private collection, and, let's say, I see that coin swinging in the wind at some low, depressed price—I'll once again think of it as a buying-opportunity candidate.

PCGS Population Report

Return to Population Report

Print | Expand all Varities

Type 1, High Relief, MS

PCGS No	Description	Desig	P/AG	G	VG	F	VF	EF	AU	MS/PR	Total
Total		MS	1	2	3	6	46	77	725	3,833	4,691
9135	1907 $20 High Relief-Wire Edge	MS	1	2	2	5	36	63	643	3,281	4,031
9136	1907 $20 High Relief-Flat Edge	MS			1	1	10	14	82	552	660

Type 2, No Motto, MS

PCGS No	Description	Desig	P/AG	G	VG	F	VF	EF	AU	MS/PR	Total
Total		MS			2	2	5	32	2,212	133,541	135,791
9141	1907 $20 Saint	MS			1	1	4	5	506	13,552	14,067
9142	1908 $20 No Motto	MS					1	16	1,464	115,666	117,146
9143	1908-D $20 No Motto	MS			1	1		11	242	4,323	4,578

Type 3, With Motto, MS

PCGS No	Description	Desig	P/AG	G	VG	F	VF	EF	AU	MS/PR	Total
Total		MS	4	2	3	7	93	309	15,171	689,953	703,514
9147	1908 $20 Motto	MS					1	5	193	2,010	2,209
9148	1908-D $20 Motto	MS					1	1	264	2,627	2,893
9149	1908-S $20	MS				1	22	56	208	160	447
9150	1909 $20	MS					3	14	337	1,719	2,074
9151	1909/8 $20	MS			1	1	17	53	669	1,320	2,058
9152	1909-D $20	MS					8	27	205	456	693
9153	1909-S $20	MS					3	11	333	5,919	6,266
9154	1910 $20	MS					2	5	349	6,388	6,743
9155	1910-D $20	MS					2	5	356	6,008	6,369
9156	1910-S $20	MS	1		1	2	14	30	588	3,935	4,571
9157	1911 $20	MS						6	386	2,121	2,512
9158	1911-D $20	MS					1	7	560	10,294	10,859
PCGS No	Description	Desig	P/AG	G	VG	F	VF	EF	AU	MS/PR	Total
9159	1911-S $20	MS		1			3	13	252	4,324	4,592
9160	1912 $20	MS					1	5	384	3,115	3,504
9161	1913 $20	MS				1			405	2,198	2,604
9162	1913-D $20	MS	1				2	8	320	3,942	4,273
9163	1913-S $20	MS					2	9	205	1,571	1,787
9164	1914 $20	MS					2	1	177	1,842	2,022
9165	1914-D $20	MS			1		2	3	333	6,364	6,704
9166	1914-S $20	MS						8	512	17,699	18,217
9167	1915 $20	MS					1	1	308	1,688	1,997
9168	1915-S $20	MS						3	306	12,874	13,183
9169	1916-S $20	MS					1	2	180	4,450	4,632
9170	1920 $20	MS						2	223	5,514	5,739
9171	1920-S $20 100 to 150 known	MS					1	5	32	51	88
9172	1921 $20 About 150 known	MS						1	47	45	93
9173	1922 $20	MS				1		3	1,150	36,636	37,789
9174	1922-S $20	MS							89	1,098	1,186
9175	1923 $20	MS							362	21,092	21,454
9176	1923-D $20	MS						1	53	8,253	8,306
9177	1924 $20	MS						2	1,928	260,098	262,026
9178	1924-D $20	MS						1	92	542	635
9179	1924-S $20	MS							66	395	461
9180	1925 $20	MS							474	43,866	44,340

Population reports are censuses of a particular grading company's certified coins and currency. Those statistics are compiled by dealer firms and various numismatic publication sources. You can usually find what you're looking for online free of charge. (© PCGS)

Let's Do It Again

Dealers, investors and collectors frequently imagine this or that coin ought to be a higher grade. True enough—among professionals and seasoned collectors, resubmissions are fairly common occurrences.

Regrading can put the same coin into the population a second or even multiple times, as the certification process is repeated and the specimen is assigned a new ID number, added to the census and etcetera. It skews the report, proffering more certified pieces than there actually are.

Investors can avoid mistakes by analyzing the numbers with a numismatic expert who knows the market well enough to be able to compensate for inaccuracies in the population reports—or until you get the hang of it yourself.

First generation PCGS holders and grading tags. Grading tags are inserted into coin holders for identification purposes as well as grade assignments. When coins are removed from their holders for re-grading, these tags need to be returned to the grading service in order to keep the census accurate. For more information, read about upgrading and grading arbitrage in this chapter. (© Kagin's, Inc.)

There's no magic to it, but it does require a heaping teaspoon of experience. Regardless, when making big decisions, it's my feeling that a second opinion is never a bad idea. As a matter of habit, I always consult with a trusted colleague before big money handshakes. Once or twice, it's kept my butt out of the proverbial sling.

Inexpensive specimens are the least likely candidates for regrading. In a nutshell, those types apt to be resubmitted are coins of a certain grade, population number and depressed price, which takes a giant leap in price at one grade higher.

A friend of mine once resubmitted a coin that came back a grade lower. Oh boy, the look on the poor man's face! I thought the guy was going to have a heart attack. Yes, resubmissions can work both ways. If you're lucky, you'll never learn a thing about grading—you'll accept PCGS and NGC verdicts as law of the land—and never have to cross a situation like this.

I kid—but, frankly, there's more good advice there than may initially meet the eye. It will be more than enough—we'll discuss it shortly—for you to be able to choose "solid-for-the-grade" specimens with your purchases.

You have enough on your plate to worry about without grappling with the possibility of certification foul-ups, or otherwise lapses of good judgment. Seriously, PCGS and NGC grading errors are too infrequent to start biting your fingernails over.

Argh! There's always at least one overachiever in the group, right? OK, we'll talk about grading for another few minutes, but then that's it.

Insider's tip:

A common mistake novice numismatists and investors make when selecting coins, is to select items based on grading rarity. While selecting a coin with only grading rarity may bring small, short-term gains and may be a rewarding prospect to the numismatic equivalent of the day trader, serious investors need to be very cautious if they want to see maximum returns. The savvy numismatic investor understands why it is imperative to analyze not only grading rarity but also mintage rarity and the number of items extant.

Think Outside the Box, Inside the Box
& Everywhere In-between

I went at this section at length hoping that you'll have caught on to the Hidden Value in the story. Yes, of course, it's the coin-grade category with the inflated population numbers.

It's a category that I look upon favorably, figuring there have been many attempts to regrade these certain coin categories to the higher grade and substantially higher price that comes with it.

There are times when I'm able to confirm an educated guess about who's been resubmitting their inventories, to call out those foolish dealers or investors who're jacking the numbers all up. I will sometimes interrogate my dealer colleagues and harangue them until they cough up the truth.

Truthfully, it doesn't bother me a bit. To the contrary. They don't necessarily think of it, but they've just handed me the inside track to a skewed population report. Thanks!

Liar, Liar, Pants on Fire

There are several categories regarding population, variety and grade that cannot possibly be true. I happen to know for a fact there are stats for specific coin categories published by grading firms or a certain few dealers that are complete hogwash.

This is not as unusual as you may imagine. When a monthly population report jumps for a particular scarce coin in the same grade by an inordinately high amount, I know the population increase is imaginary. There always seems to be a stat printed somewhere that gives those of us in-the-know a big belly laugh.

One dealer, who has an excellent eye for standardized grades, sent the same coin in on seven different occasions to one service and three times to another until he got the desired result. He was convinced the coin was at the top of its grade and that chances were good he'd eventually get the bump.

After all, he reasoned, the coin was worth $5,000 more a grade higher, so it was worth the risk to accumulate grading fees and shipping charges on the chance of getting the upgrade. In this particular instance it worked, but you can see how fine a line it is. It took a trained expert 10 attempts to put-one-over on the modern grading system.

One more note of interest is that PCGS and NCG in their early years had a tendency to grade on the conservative side. Dealers and collectors are aware of this, which is why you see so few of the old holders around these days. A large percentage of them were broken out and regraded.

Holder designs have changed over the years, and it's easy to determine the approximate year a certified specimen was graded by the look of the holder. The green, first generation PCGS slabbed coins were more conservatively graded than the later blue, second-generation slabs.

NGC followed a similar path, and the old holders with the plain text print are often good candidates for a higher grade by today's standards.

You can look up a certified coin's record by going to the appropriate services' website and typing in the ID number. To be fair, both PCGS and NGC have been consistent right out of the gate. Somehow, both companies see virtually eye-to-eye on how grades should be applied.

It's a given there's going to be an exception to the rule, but push comes to shove, I'd have to say that I trust the grading firms to get it right. It's not a perfect system, but what is? I'm inclined to think it's about as good as it can be.

No Two Coins the Same

I trust certified slabs have been fairly and accurately graded. My mindset on the subject reminds me of how I used to balance my checkbook at the end of every month. After 20 years of spot on monthly bank statements, I've since replaced my printer-roll calculator for a cursory scan of our personal-banking transaction summaries. Takes 20 seconds to pull one up online. If a PCGS or NCG slab reads MS-64, the coin is a Mint State-64 on the Sheldon scale and that's pretty much the end of it.

The trick about selecting the best specimen within a particular grade involves examining several relevant specimens, comparing prices and eye appeal, and choosing the one with the best combination of those factors.

Some collectors lean toward blast white specimens over toned ones or vice versa. That's fine. In a choice between two similar coins with a negligible price differential, I tell my clients that it's OK—just this one time!—to forget about which one is technically the better buy and to pick the one that puts the biggest smile on their face.

Of all the recommendations I've put down in this book, this is the one piece of advice that I'm 100% confident about. Collecting coins is a heck of a lot of fun, and it's not a crime to keep within those historical periods or particular coin designs that give you a thrill. If you're into 19th-century U.S. gold coins, there's no need to fret about the recent rise in ancient Chinese coins.

Insider's tip:

Independent or third-party grading revolutionized the numismatic market when it adopted a standardized system to assign levels of wear and imperfection to coins. It also allows for a public census of each coin that is graded or certified. Once a coin is assigned a grade, it becomes certified and listed at that grade.

This census is called a population report, as related earlier in this chapter as it pertains to supply. Third-party graded coins also provides more security to owners, as each coin that is graded is sealed into a hard plastic archival encasing—called a holder or "slab"—and on its tag is assigned a unique identification number and barcode.

Finally, independent grading has created a new aspect to the numismatic market called grading rarity, which we discuss in depth below.

The independent standardized grading, especially for more common coins, provides some degree of fungibility to the industry since theoretically the same dated coins in a similarly graded holder are valued the same and therefore exchangeable sight unseen.

As this chapter reveals, however, the theory is often different than the reality in that the population reports are flawed and there are other factors to consider.

There's money to be made in virtually every area of numismatics, and it's smart to focus your attention on coins that make your eyes light up.

This applies to the investor, too. I have yet to encounter anyone that has no interest in the coins whatsoever. Mr. Spock could probably buy and sell numismatics without passion or prejudice, but I doubt you can. Or, what I mean to say is, why bother trying?

I beg you not to bother with an attempt to track the entire World Coin market. There are simply too many coin types to follow to get an accurate handle on future price movement for all of them. You'd be a juggler with at least one too many balls in the air. Your enthusiasm for one or two niche categories is guaranteed to produce better bottom-line results.

For me, I enjoy Old West folklore, and, although not strictly limited to this area, Kagin's and KaginAmericana auction house specialize with collectibles circa the California Gold Rush.

Ask us about how a 1343 Edward III Florin went for $6.8 million and we'd probably have to look it up just like you. Ask us about the Carson City mint and we're liable to tell you an amusing anecdote in which an institution known for its short-run of Morgan silver dollars and valuable gold eagles proffers a measly silver dime as its most highly regarded artifact.

Pull up a chair because we've got a lot more just like it.

Those Pesky Serial Numbers

This $10 1863 Legal Tender Note has a unique serial # so would be difficult to sell.

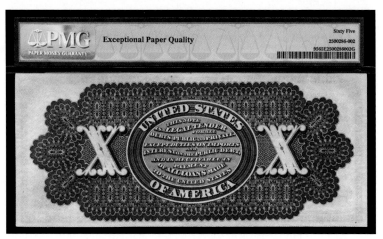

The unique barcode on the back of the hermetically sealed certified $10 1863 Legal Tender Note makes it easy to identify (© Kagin's, Inc.)

With paper currency, there are few resubmissions, or reholdering attempts, since once a serial number is recorded in the population report as existing in one grade, PCGS and PMG (a division of NGC) are reluctant to regrade the note, much less award it a higher mark. It's very much in the same vein of how judges don't make it a habit of turning over other judges' legal decisions.

It would have to be a terribly botched examination for me to recommend reholdering certified paper to one of my clients. It has happened, though. And, in the one instance I'm thinking of, it worked out. That was one time in 20-some odd years—you can do the math. For more on history and an expanded discussion of coin grading and population reports, please visit Goldandrarecoins.net.

(© Kagins, Inc.)

One of the most common Pioneer gold coins is an 1853 United States Assay Office $20 gold 900 thous fine. In the late 1980s, this coin in Gem condition (MS-65) was considered a great rarity and valued at over $125,000. Since then a number of these coins have been assigned the same grade and today, a quarter century later, they are still worth $100,000 to $125,000—a poor showing over a period when most nearby coin categories more than doubled in value.

In the case of the 1853 $20 Assay Office of Gold piece used in the example above, an expert will know there is another variety of this coin. The .884 fine variety does not share the same grading misfortune. With only about 20 extant in all grades combined, this is truly a rarity.

During the same period of the late 1980s, this variety was valued in AU-50 at $15,000. Recently one of these coins realized $47,500 in auction. Although the grade isn't particularly high on the Sheldon Scale, AU-50 is a high grade for the variety, which makes it a relative grading rarity.

A popular coin, the 1853 $20 U.S. Assay Office of Gold piece comes in two varieties: a 900 thousandth fine (above left) and an 884 thou fine (above right). (© Kagin's, Inc.)

Insider's tip:

Since the advent of Registry Sets, even more emphasis and demand has been focused on the finest graded numismatic items.

Having the finest graded piece in the finest graded set for the series, as defined by either PCGS or NGC, can greatly enhance that coin's value and, in some cases, disproportionately.

But again, beware of finest known designations which may be timely—finest at that point in time—but probably are not timeless—a coin likely to be relegated to a second or even third best grade at some point in the near future as more become graded.

PCGS Set Registry Collections

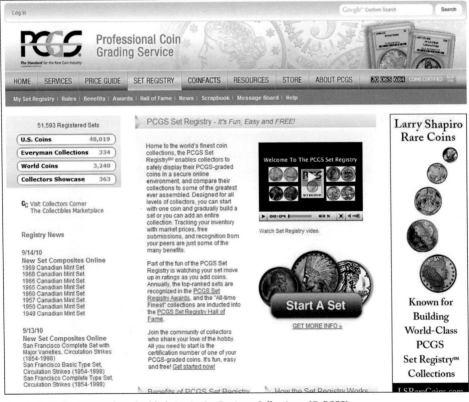

A page from the PCGS website highlighting its Set Registry Collections. (© PCGS)

The Numismatic Grading Scale

Prefix	Numerical Grade	Description
MS	60–70	Mint State (Uncirculated)
AU	50, 53, 55, 58	About Uncirculated
XF	40, 45	Extremely Fine
VF	20, 25, 30, 35	Very Fine
F	12, 15	Fine
VG	8, 10	Very Good
G	4, 6	Good
AG	3	About Good
FA	2	Fair
PR	1	Poor

Grading is done on a standardized numerical scale from 1 to 70, with 70 being the highest grade assigned.

Chapter V

The Investment Track Record

Investment-quality rare coins and currency represent proven, outstanding long-term, high-yield, low-risk investment vehicles. During the economic crisis of 2008 to 2010, investment-quality coins and currency, with few exceptions, held their real-dollar value better than traditional investments. Incredibly, the rarest and finest Legacy items continued to set record prices when sold both privately and at auction.

44 Year Performance Chart - Market performance from 1970-2014. High quality coins and stocks had the highest returns over the past three decades, despite the strong performance of gold over the past nine years. (© Gary Knaus / Eligius Investments)

Numismatic materials have appreciated cyclically at increasingly higher levels—and this pattern continues today. Virtually all markets are cyclical, including the rare coin market. We're going to come back to market cycles shortly, but for the moment I'd like to illustrate how recurring patterns and cycles can assist a trader's forecasting accuracy.

In 1977, Ned Johnson, III, Chairman and Chief Executive Officer of Fidelity Investments, was one of the principal investors in a limited partnership that invested in rare U.S. coins. The portfolio was purchased for less than $360,000. In 1980 the portfolio was sold for $2.15 million, creating a profit of more than 500%. This example is far from unique. Of course, not every investor can be so fortunate in their timing. But with a good understanding of previous market cycles and professional help, you can maximize your investment potential.

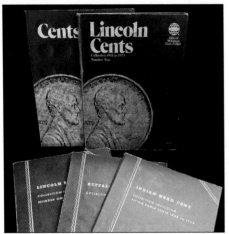

Whitman coin collecting books from 1940s – 1980s. (© Kagin's Inc. with Permission Whitman Publishing, LLC)

Coin collecting has been a popular diversion for the past 2,500 years, and there is every reason to believe that it will continue to be popular long after present forms of money have been replaced by chips of plastic, computers, the Internet and virtual bit coins.

Understanding what makes coins valuable and why people have collected them ever since they were first introduced into commerce, will help an investor such as yourself to see how rare coin investments, relatively speaking, are low-risk, high-yield assets.

By and large, coins and banknotes are not a necessity of life. You cannot eat them, nor do they provide shelter. Yet they are always in demand because money in any form is still money. Coins, especially, have a certain charm that makes them highly desirable as collectibles. Traditionally, coins and banknotes have been collected for their beauty and artistry, rarity and variety, and historical appeal.

The story of numismatics and those who collected coins through the last two and a half millennium is fascinating and informative, rich with interesting personalities, incidence and romance. It is not, however, imperative to know this history to be a successful numismatic investor. It is enough to know there has been a long tradition of collecting coins and this provides the underpinning of constant demand and consequent secondary market for these historic artifacts.

Early Stages of Numismatic Investing

Relatively little attention was paid to numismatics as an investment until the mid-1930s, when it was realized that rare coins and currency held their values better than almost any other tangible asset. Also during this period the relative strength of rare coins and currency as a store of value became increasingly evident.

When the stock market crashed in 1929 pulling down other investments, to a certain extent, coins held their values.

Spurred by the popular commemorative coinage series, coin values rose dramatically in the mid-1930s. The rapidly increasing demand initiated by the newly created collectors filling out their "penny boards" rapidly depleted available inventories and forced a continuing rise in values. Collectors and dealers alike realized handsome profits.

Another jump in value occurred during World War II when many people received substantial increases in income. This increase in wealth enabled collectors to invest more in pursuit of their favorite hobby.

Following World War II, another rise occurred with the reintegration into society of the returning soldiers, who renewed their interest in numismatics. Many devoted some of their savings or bonuses accumulated in the service toward acquiring wanted coins.

A.M. "Art" Kagin in uniform during World War II. (© Kagin's, Inc.)

My father, A.M. "Art" Kagin, recounted how he and my uncle Paul locked up their coins and currency when they went to war. When they returned, their inventory essentially doubled in value. This appreciation was due in part to the post-war inflationary boom and partly as a result of the introduction of R.S. Yeoman's *A Guidebook of United States Coins* in 1948. The *Red Book* has since introduced hundreds of thousands to the fascinating world of collectible U.S. coins.

Similarly, an April 27, 1953 *Life Magazine* article highlighting the only time someone—Louis Eliasberg, Sr.—assembled a complete set of U.S. copper, nickel, silver and gold coins, created a sensation. According to his son, Richard, his father received and responded to over 10,000 letters. It was the second most popular article *Life Magazine* had ever written.

The First Rare Coin Investment Market: Boom and Bust 1963-1965

Potential investors began to flock to coin shows when rare coins entered a new bull market in 1956 and 1957. The introduction in 1960 of the weekly magazine, *Coin World*, allowed anyone to compare coin prices on a weekly basis. Within four years, circulation had climbed to 175,000.

Rare coins and currency were now recognized not only as the Hobby of Kings, but also as potentially an excellent long-term investment. Since that time, there have been five major boom periods in numismatic investment history: 1963 to 1964, 1973 to 1974, 1978 to 1980, 1989 to 1990, 2002 to mid-2007. Each of these periods significantly altered the face of business, but more importantly, confirmed the investment potential of numismatics.

The coin boom of 1963 brought record prices and an active coin market, as evidenced in this contemporary Kagin's advertisement.

The 1963 to 1964 "coin boom" was kick-started by the U.S. Treasury's release of scarce silver dollars dating back to 1878, and with the introduction of a nationwide numismatic teletype system.

Many coin dealers and speculators entered the market without any previous numismatic experience. These opportunists promoted various items without regard to their true rarity. The items they chose were the most easily marketable material, such as rolls and bags of similar coins, proof sets and commemoratives.

This influx of capital from unknowledgeable individuals in turn led to massive speculation and price increases of more than 10% per month. I remember watching the Kagin teletype clattering away constantly with offers to buy and sell hundreds and thousands of proof and mint sets and original rolls of coins as well as seeing two- to four-page, full color ads from such colorful sounding dealers like "Shotgun" Slade.

Predictably, the market eventually crashed with some speculative items dropping a whopping 70% to 80%. When the market declined rapidly in 1964, the carpetbaggers and their clients were literally left holding the bag.

The Next Two Cycles: 1965-1978

Values again slowly but steadily increased from 1965 until 1972, when the devaluation of the dollar prompted the beginning of a new boom period in numismatics.

Remarkably we are experiencing some of these same consequences of a weak dollar 40 years later.

During the '65 to '72 period of growing inflation, the increasing number of collectors and dealers and the general public's desire to own silver and gold culminated in a blending of collector and investor interest, which gave birth to the pure investor.

Silver (1964), Silver/Clad (1965-1970) and Clad Kennedy halves (1971-today) (© Kagin's, Inc.)

The market once again reached a plateau in 1974, and subsequently several of the items that were overly promoted, such as proof and mint sets, rolls and commemoratives, went through what we dealers are fond of euphemistically calling an "adjustment period"—or a significant drop in value.

For another four years prices remained stable. By 1978 the economy and coin market began rising again and by the end of that year, the coin market was heating up again.

The Hyper Boom and Bust: 1978-1982

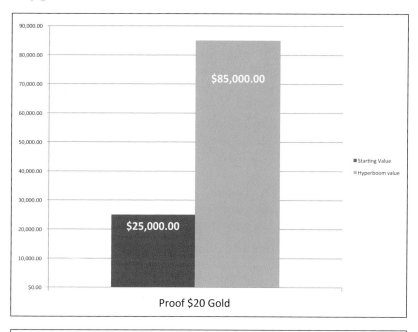

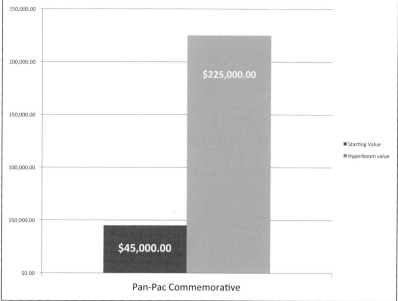

Rarities saw dramatic increases in value during the hyper boom of 1978-1980. (Graphs created by Kagin's Inc. with data and permission from Whitman Publishing, LLC)

The third and probably most important boom period occurred from 1978 until the spring of 1980. Four basic factors contributed to this boom period:

- The concurrent positive media coverage of the bullion and rare coin market.
- The advent of sustained double-digit inflation.
- United States government approval of the placement of rare coins and other collectibles into retirement plans, pension funds and other tax advantaged plans. This development consequently led a number of individuals and corporations with IRA, Keogh and pension plans to place rare coins into tax-deferred retirement accounts. Indeed, Kagin's Numismatic Services was the first numismatic firm approved by the IRS as a custodian for IRAs and Keogh plans, and we ended up administering almost $2 million worth of coins and currency.
- The suitability of rare coins as an investment encouraged money managers and financial planners to look at alternative investments in the wake of the relatively low performance of traditional investments.

During the 1978 to 1980 boom and hyper-boom period, top-quality coins were heavily promoted. By mid-1979 tremendous increases in the price of bullion and the resultant injection of bullion-related money into the rare coin market caused prices to shoot up dramatically and decreased the overall market supply.

Higher ticket rarities and proof gold coins dramatically surged in value as speculators seemingly clamored to buy any coin in top-quality condition, regardless of the price. In just a few months, gem-quality proof $20 gold pieces increased in price from $25,000 to $85,000. Panama-Pacific gold and silver commemorative sets rose in value from $45,000 to $225,000.

Naturally, the market could not sustain these prices since the collector had been left on the sidelines months earlier, frustrated by the rapidly increasing cost for desired items. In February 1980, my father and I recognized that the market was becoming overheated, and we issued a "sell" advice to our clients and began liquidating items which had appreciated too far, too fast.

When the market hit its auction peak at the Johns Hopkins University's Garrett II sale by Bowers and Merena (then owned by General Mills) in November of 1979, I made a note in my auction catalog: "This market is ridiculous. There will be a crash soon." I didn't bid on a single item that day. Weeks later, the market did indeed come to a screeching halt, and most series of coins fell precipitously during the next several months. I now wish in 20/20 hindsight that we had sold more inventory faster, but no one could predict how quickly prices would fall.

In April of 1980 and for two years thereafter, the market went through a "readjustment" period. Prices dropped by almost 50% from their peaks. Several negative factors combined to cause this about-face. Foremost was that the Federal Reserve kept raising prime interest rates to curb spending until it hit an incredible 21.5%. Virtually all commodities were adversely affected.

The staggering drop in precious metals' values caught many rare coin and bullion dealers by surprise. Called upon to raise cash quickly to cover leveraged positions and faced with a lack of cash, dealers halted their buying activities and began selling. Speculators had long left for greener pastures, and suddenly there was nobody on the buy-side. The market plunged.

Throughout the second half of 1980 and most of 1981, prices continued to fall. Bankruptcies, cutbacks and mergers were at their highest level in numismatic history. During the last quarter of 1981, however, collectors began to reenter the marketplace via auctions. The number of collectors and the amounts they were willing to spend slowly, but steadily increased through the rest of 1981 and 1982, and coin values slowed their descent.

The summer of 1982 marked the low point of this coin cycle. During this time investors with staying power could have made their biggest profits; however, few investors reentered the market until much later. It is interesting to note, even after the readjustment of April 1981 to August 1982, prices remained over 100% higher than in the winter of 1978 to 1979.

A New Cycle Begins: 1982-1991

At the end of August 1982, a new cycle began, and the coin market turned up once again. What made this boom different from the others was its long-lasting effects. The movement of financial planners, pension fund managers, retirement planners and others into the rare coin market continued unabated in recessionary as well as inflationary times. Likewise, the media outlets wrote about numismatics as a viable investment alternative.

Financial gurus were popular as people turned to them for investment advice. Unfortunately the Tax Reform Act of 1986 significantly altered the financial planning industry, and most of them ceased offering rare coins.

Independent grading firms such as these have revolutionized the numismatic industry.

That same year the numismatic industry saw the establishment of the Professional Coin Grading Service and a year later, the Numismatic Guaranty Corporation. Staffed with world-class professional numismatists, and backed by a grading guarantee, these companies standardized coin grading and provided authentication services. From this they began building an international population census.

Coins, and in 2004, banknotes graded by either PCGS or NGC were accepted by the numismatic community and general public. Hermetically encased in tamper-proof holders, certified coins and banknotes number almost 50 million individual items today.

By early 1989, numismatics was fast becoming a media darling. With good press from national magazines, television and radio programs, and the developments of independent grading, rare coins and currency came back into the investment spotlight. Wall Street firms Merrill Lynch and Lehman Brothers christened numismatic funds.

Meanwhile, there was rumored to be a big money player coming on to the scene—an Iranian investor with $30 million burning a hole in his pocket. Unfortunately for him, most of his investments were concentrated in relatively common generic gold, and when the market turned down his inexperience almost cost him the entire amount.

A rule for which there are no exceptions is not to risk more than 10% of your capital on any one idea. That way, it would take 10 losers in a row for you to go belly up. Everybody goes through a slump here and there, but I've never come close to striking out 10 times in a row, and neither should you. Ten winners in a row, yes; three or four losers in a row, possibly—but it would take a combination of extraordinarily bad luck, bad timing, bad everything for 10 disasters to come one after another.

It's not easy to bite the bullet and take a loss, but it's precisely this type of discipline that separates pros from neophytes. If it's any consolation, I can tell you that it's been my experience that my best trades—whether we're talking gold, numismatics, stocks, real estate, antiques, whatever—tend to work straight away. So if it's not working, just dump it and move on.

Gold prices on the rise. (© Dreamstime, Justforyou)

Recession and the New Millennium: 1991 to 2008

The next decade turned moribund for the rare coin market, reaching a low point with the recession of 2001 to 2002 and the horrible tragedies of the events on 9/11. Finally, early in the new millennium the nation experienced an improved economy, thanks to a combination of easy credit, low interest rates, rising gold prices and the effects of a real estate boom. Correspondingly, the coin market made a long steady rise until the real estate and financial crashes of 2007 and 2008, respectively.

Recession and Renewal: 2008-2014

The economic crisis of 2008 resulted in another general decline in the numismatic market. As with virtually all collectibles at the time, rare coin prices dropped as much as 50% for generic coins. Only the very finest and rarest coins retained most, approximately 85%, of their values.

By 2012, the sustained collapse of the real estate market and the shaky economy made many financial advisors and investors reconsider their traditional investment portfolios. The Federal Reserve's policy of continued low interest rates, stimulus money and quantitative easing coupled with seemingly intractable huge deficits considerably weakened the U.S. dollar.

Gold prices soared to an all time high approaching $2,000 an ounce before it gradually retrenched to the $1,550 level. A short-term plunge in April 2013 to below the $1,350 level demonstrated the short-term volatility of bullion. This anomaly was caused by a combination of interrelated factors:

- China's report that their economic growth slowed unexpectedly.
- A slowdown in Asian (China and India) physical gold purchases.
- The proposal in mid-April 2013 that Cyprus sell some of its gold reserves to support its banks and the potential for other nations such as Spain and Italy to do the same.
- A general notion that the U.S. economy as a whole is becoming stable and that it will expand more quickly than expected.
- The notion that Euro-zone debt crisis has stabilized.
- Partisan furor in Washington has died down.
- Report that wholesale prices fell in March and coupled with the Federal Reserve easing off their stimulus program, the notion that there may not be much inflation in the short run.
- Automatic stop-loss sell orders triggered when gold fell from support levels.
- A panic to cover short positions or just to get out of bullion holdings.
- A general exit of bullion speculators from the market.

Another plunge occurred in June 2013 as the Federal Reserve declared they were taking their foot off the gas pedal of their monetary easing policy. Gold retreated briefly to under $1,200 per ounce, rallied in 2013, then retreated again below $1170. There appears to be strong support in this price range. More volatility may be in store, but the long-term trend inevitably will take us to record highs.

Volatility aside, tangible assets have received positive press over the last few years as alternative investments. Considering the recent retrenchment in gold values, the timing couldn't be better. This is your price dip. Right now is your best opportunity to get into the bull market before gold prices make a run for higher ground.

During the last two years, new investor groups and investment funds have entered the rare coin and currency market. This phenomenon has not been seen since the market boom of 1989 to 1990. Increased demand, coupled with an extremely limited market supply of high-end rarities have begun to drive prices up once again.

By early 2013, a number of the best rare coins and currency specimens, including the record-breaking $10 million 1794 Silver Dollar, have surpassed their 2007 peaks. There have been world-record prices for three U.S. banknotes. In September 2013, Bonhams auction house conducted a U.S. Proof gold sale of 27 Legacy-type coins struck between 1836 and 1915. The sale, which took place during a relatively quiet time in the rare coin investment cycle, smashed all expectations.

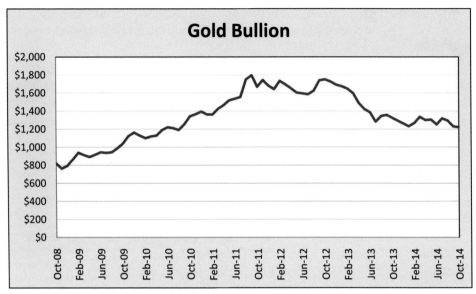

Gold Bullion Chart. A weakened dollar caused gold prices to soar over the last 72 months. (© Kagin's, Inc.)

One pattern gold coin, an 1880 coiled hair $4 gold piece brought an astonishing $2.5 million—more than doubling its presale estimate. World records were set for virtually every coin. Bonhams' Director of Rare Coins and Medals, Paul Song, pointed out that "probably more than 75% of the sale was bought directly by collectors." Paul went on to say that most of those buyers were not the typical coin buyers but were from the fine art, jewelry and collectibles fields. Presumably looking for solid overall value. We believe this trend will continue.

Overall Performance Record of Numismatics: 1970-2014

A recent study, conducted on behalf of the Joint Committee on Taxation of the House and Senate, revealed what savvy numismatic investors already know: U.S. rare coins produced better investment returns than other financial sectors, including gold bullion. The study was conducted by Raymond E. Lombra, professor of economics at Penn State University, and provides a comparison of the performance of gold and rare gold coins. Originally, the report was conducted in the 1990s and was recently updated in 2014. Its findings are telling:

- Rare coins are a better inflation hedge than gold, treasury bonds and traditional stocks.
- Rare coins can produce significant profits even during periods when the price of gold is falling.
- The average annual return on key date coins and rarities was almost double the return on gold.

In 2010, a year of severe economic turmoil, rare coins outperformed the stock market and gold. The Dow was down 33.8% and S&P by 38.5%; gold, on the other

Table 2

Investment Returns, Risk and Timing

A Long Term View: 35 Years, 1979-2013

	Average Annual % Return	Years Pos	Years Neg	Best Year % Return	Worst Year % Return	Standard Deviation
Gold	5.7	21	14	100.2	-28.9	15.6
Stocks	13.0	29	6	36.8	-37.3	13.0
3 Month T-bill	5.1	35	0	14.3	0.02	2.4
Treasury Bond	8.4	29	6	34.8	-9.3	8.3
Coins (all types MS65)	12.2	22	13	198.8	-40.6	21.1
Coins (gold type- MS63-65)	10.4	23	12	198.8	-42.7	20.1

2

Source: R L Associates, Penn State University

Table 3

Market Timing

1979–2013, Average Rate of Return

	Stocks	Treasury Bonds	Coins MS65	Coins MS63-65	Gold Bullion
Best 3 Years	34.1	29.5	107.4	101.3	53.0
Worst 3 Years	-23.4	-8.5	-27.9	-34.7	-27.1
Other 29 Years	14.6	8.0	6.5	5.6	4.3
Total 35 Years	13.0	8.4	12.2	10.4	5.7

3

Source: R L Associates, Penn State University

Over the long run, investment quality rare coins have kept pace with the stock market even when accounting for the latter's recent peak performance, but when timing is factored in, coins have been the superior performance. (© Raymond Lombra)

hand, was up 6%. Rare coins performed even better, up 14%. A 2004 study by the Chief Investment Officer for G.E. Private Asset Management, Inc. concluded that rare coin returns have been highly attractive since 1941.

It's highly unlikely that gold will return to its pre-recession lows. In the short-term, we can expect prices to be fairly volatile. A one-week period in September 2011 saw the price of gold take a 20% nosedive while the stock market fluctuated wildly.

Not so with rare coins. From 2011 to 2014, prices for investment-quality coins rose steadily, albeit slowly. For five specific case studies please visit Goldandrarecoins. net. Portfolios showcased boast an annual appreciation of 8% to 12% over the last 14 years, which included a lengthy recession. The usual disclaimers are in effect: Past performance is not a guarantee of how the next 14 years will go, etcetera and so on. But all the signs are pointing to higher prices. Much higher.

Chapter VI

Market Timing and the Numismatic Price Cycle

If it's supply and demand that determines price for goods and services, it's market timing that determines whether the difference between the sale price and buy price is a red number or a black one. Just like traditional investments. Timing is everything.

Or, it's almost everything, I should say. Not necessarily the end of the world. If your timing is off—you buy the right coin at the wrong price—it may be an additional 12 months or so before it turns profitable, but it all starts with buying the right coin.

Good market timing can sure make your life a whole lot easier, though. Often it feels as if there's a fine line between success and failure. Good timing will radically skew the odds in our favor.

What we're going to do is describe long-term numismatic price behavior from different perspectives, using different pricing models. Our job is to identify the theoretical model that best describes and anticipates the coin price in question. It could be one model is good about forecasting short-term moves, and another timing tool good about long-term moves.

Timing as applied to numismatic investing means comprehending not just broad market cycles, but the intricacies associated with a particular coin series. This includes tracking a series types, key dates, mintmarks and varieties. A particular coin series may experience price gains for reasons extrinsic to those that affect the macro collectible coin market. Sharp investors will be on the lookout for niche areas and subsets of the rare coin group that will outperform the overall market. Perhaps even appreciate in the midst of a down cycle.

The ability to identify undervalued specimens is what separates experts from a sales person. An intimate knowledge for a niche selection of coins or notes will provide the basis for making most of your buy and sell decisions, and this is largely training your intuition with years of experience. But there are also general timing principles universal to every coin type and series, and that's what we're going to take a closer look at in this chapter.

Of course, there are no crystal balls, no magic spells that can be cast to accurately forecast the low tick on a stock, rare coins or any other investment vehicle for that matter. The best we can hope to do is identify particular market behaviors that have abnormally high tendencies to follow with specific up or down moves. To that end, let's look at the factors to consider when pulling the trigger on buy or sell situations.

> **Insider's tip:**
>
> *Pricing guides cannot foresee what a rare coin or currency collector will pay for an item a collector has been waiting years to acquire. For particularly rare items, when the speed of the sale is not an issue, I often offer the piece at an appropriately strong price. For particularly rare items there is almost always someone someone willing to pay top price! (Hint: Don't be this guy.)*

Drive for Show, Putt for Dough

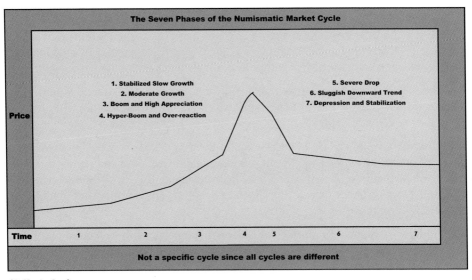

(© *Kagin, Inc.*)

Market timing essentially involves identifying the correct phase in the cyclical market and coordinating buy and sell points such that we minimize our risk on the downside and maximize our profit on the upside. To accomplish that may involve buying into weakness or watching and waiting and jumping onto a price breakout—a strong move above a previously stubborn resistance level.

We're going to explore factors that affect short-term price movements in a minute. However, if we know, say, 10 or 20 years down the road that gold will be significantly higher, what does it matter how or when we buy?

That's a fair point. As strategies go, simply having the wind at your back vastly increases your odds of reaching El Dorado. If you're happy with sailing on autopilot, it's steady as she blows!

Why leave good money on the table, though? What if the effects of poor timing had a more profound impact on your trading results? What if the effects of poor timing meant that a hearty five-year bull move was not enough to get you into positive territory? You'd be stuck in that position for a long time. You'll ride the swing down, then, yes, up again. Only now it's nine years later.

For me the answer is simple. We leave enough things in this world to chance. Yes, absolutely, I'm going to arrange all the pieces on the board in such a way that I give myself the highest probability for successful outcomes.

Nevertheless, if your only takeaway from this book is that it's a good time to get into precious metals and rare coins, I'd say you've only just begun to appreciate this field.

To be perfectly frank, though, you're still well ahead in the game.

Contrary to Popular Belief

At a minimum, we can't imagine any scenario in which it's OK that we willingly allow ourselves to get ripped off.

If this self-defense mechanism is a trigger that factors into your investor thought-making process, congratulations and read on, you're already thinking like a contrarian. But before we get to that, it's worthwhile to define exactly what we mean by "contrarian."

In its strictest sense it means to act, mindlessly, in opposition of popular opinion. The objectionable part here, is the word "mindlessly." We do not wish to be the contrarian investor who steps out of his gold position at the first signs of healthy confidence with market participants. We'd end up missing the last eight years of the bull market or some such.

It's a tool and like any other indicator it's not infallible. It can be extremely useful, too. What we're really talking about is learning how to read investment information with impartiality. It's a little like asking an avid Democrat to be self-aware enough of his own prejudices to be able to take the spin out of MSNBC news reporting. (Or an avid Republican viewer of Fox News, if you prefer.) Being an effective contrarian has a lot to do with the ability to separate the shades of grey for any given situation.

To be able to examine investment opportunities objectively, you have to be aware of the things that may cloud your judgment. It could be, say, that you know you're liable to get caught up in the electricity of a live auction environment and that you have had a tendency to overpay for pieces in this manner.

So you make an adjustment. You come in late with a top bid one time and let the cards fall where they may, or perhaps you withdraw from buying in auction settings altogether—but it's all part of what we mean by contrarian.

Yet, the definition of "contrarian" we're after isn't necessarily so esoteric. It also includes a healthy dose of simply being able to act in a contrarian manner. The key word here is "act," and it's easier said than done. When it seems as if everybody is riding high on a bullish cycle phase, this is when it may all come crashing down. The market likes to move where it can do the most amount of damage.

It is human nature to be optimistic about one's investments and rather easy to hang on to them long past their due date. Before you know it, you have to alter your entire investment capital game plan because you missed a cycle high, and the next one may not come for another six years.

In one application of utilizing contrarian concepts, there are several variations of consumer confidence barometers. For the stock market, I like to know about short interest. The commodities markets, which includes gold and silver futures contracts, provide a monthly Commitments of Traders report.

This branch of investing is called "technical" analysis, and for the most part all of my technical analysis is aimed toward figuring out what the smart money players are doing. For commodities, like gold, smart money is usually the commercial interests.

Confidence numbers, you will notice, usually trade within some definable band, and the highs and lows of these bands often are strikingly close to important price-cycle highs and lows.

The Consumer Confidence Index (Year 1985 = 100), for instance, tends to move between 140 on the high side and 60 on the low side. When consumer confidence is high it may be a good time to sell.

If you're selling into strength, you're the one with the upper hand going into any negotiations. Likewise, the opposite for identifying buy opportunities.

Contrarian actions pass the common sense test. The indicator is supported by concrete empirical data, and it is within this narrow framework we're exactly fine with the classical definition of "contrarian."

I thought it was Bernard Beruch who said, "Buy when there's blood in the streets," but the saying actually goes back an 18th-century banker of the British Rothschild family. In any event, this is what it means to be a contrarian.

Most investors wait until a financial crisis is already upon them before reacting. Why, you ask? I'm not a psychologist, but, in my experience, few are willing to go out on a limb and boldly act upon their convictions. People, by nature, crave the comfort and support of their actions by seeing that others are acting in a similar fashion.

Unfortunately, the most attractive opportunities are not made readily available on an open-ended basis. It's "monkey see, monkey do"—the annualized returns of the man-on-the-street standing as a pitiful testament to the effectiveness of running with the herd as an investment strategy.

By the time most people work up the courage to join, the opportunity is lost; or worse, they find themselves buying at the top of the market. For water buffalo and gazelle on the Serengeti, the herd mentality makes absolute sense. Wall Street, however, is a different kind of jungle, and it takes a contrarian approach to be successful here. The same is true for numismatics and every avenue of the financial world that dares for more than the return on a 90-day T-bill.

To act in a contrarian manner often boils down to being able to put in a buy order in what may appear to be an avalanche of sellers. Again, not as easy as it sounds. It's a lot like being the first fireman who goes into a burning house. So make a note, this is my one important caveat on the subject, my not-so contrarian advice: Don't be the first guy who goes through the door—the house is burning for crying out loud!

Although, if you could, say, be the third or fourth fireman who goes through the door…as soon as you're sure the roof isn't going to cave in…maybe rescue a baby and time your exit to coincide with the TV news vans.

Contrarian indicators are useful for giving you a heads up when cycle forces are about to change, but don't take the concept to the extreme and risk being the first guy who goes into a burning building. Let's instead be that fourth guy—the hero fireman with his picture in the newspaper. Then, it'll be our secret that numismatic investing isn't all that dangerous for the likes of us.

Insider's tip:

It may not be necessary for you to compile, compare and contrast Commitments of Traders stats, but it is advisable to have some specific gauges that you can measure, some barometers that you can compare and contrast, because this is a tricky concept in which your brain is liable to twist to suit an emotionally desired outcome. You may get the bright idea to stamp OK on an overly risky play by calling it a contrarian move. Let's not do that.

New Car Smell Comes From an Aerosol Canister

If you go to a Ford dealership, any day of the week I imagine, and ask a salesman what kind of car he recommends, chances are good it'll be a Ford. If you call a stockbroker, chances are good he's got just the mutual fund for you. So, I worry, as I write this book, I'll be perceived as the numismatics broker who's got just the coin for you!

This seems like the appropriate place to stop, and let it be known, from time to time, I'm also the rare coin salesman who advises his clients not to buy. Incidentally, that is the kind of straight talk you want from a coin dealer. If your dealer is a "Yes Man", has never pulled back on your investment reins, he is either dishonest or dimwitted—neither of which are character traits I'd think you'd want from your numismatic advisor.

The last monster coin boom was in the late '70s, early '80s. Speculators, inexperienced investment counselors and their clients jumped with the same reckless abandon of children doing cannonballs at a crowded, public swimming pool.

Prices soared. The last frenzied increase took place from January through April of 1980. It so happens that one of my best contrarian indicators is one that you likely cannot recreate easily for yourself—but I mention it, anyway.

When phones in our offices are constantly ringing, and we're opening an unusual number of new accounts, I know things are reaching a fevered pitch. By February the phones were ringing off the hook, and that's when we started advising our clients to sell. I like this story because it was an unusual time. As quickly as prices had doubled, they came back down in a freefall.

The sell advice in this newsletter is very uncommon in the numismatic industry. A good advisor will provide both buy and sell advice. (© Kagin's, Inc.)

About a year later, clients were purchasing coins identical or similar to the ones they had just sold, and I thought to myself: This is what it must feel like to be a day trader!

The story illustrates another point. Although the price bounces you'll be looking for will be far smaller in magnitude, it's in a period of heavy flux in which you want to be making the bulk of your transactions.

You're going to buy into weakness, or, at least, buy with prices moving sideways. We want to buy into weakness; we want to sell into strength.

It's perhaps not as easy to get a sense of the ebb and flow of price movement with numismatics as it is with, say, stocks. Numismatics does not have the volume of activity, therefore, coins do not come with daily price charts, stochastics, and other technical talking points the stock boys have.

Rare coins and currency actually do have the same rhythm to their price movement—it's just that you can't see it. As I say, though, these price bubbles are opportune times for making transactions.

Numismatic Market Cycles

Earlier we mentioned cycles, and now is a good time for us to take a closer look as to what they're all about. I've been in this business for 46 years, and, I suppose, I think to describe price patterns with cycles is useful in the same way Eskimos find it useful to have 50 words to describe snow.

If your life and livelihood depend upon snow, it's helpful to have 50 descriptors in which to make sure everybody is on the same page!

Yes, I'm aware that technical analysis is somewhat akin to reading tea leaves. Stare at it long enough and you're bound to see Elvis, the Mother Mary, or some price direction and action you secretly hope takes ahold of the market.

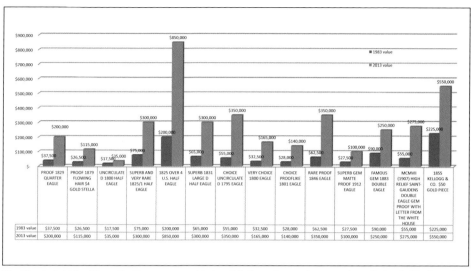

	PROOF 1829 QUARTER EAGLE	PROOF 1879 FLOWING HAIR $4 GOLD STELLA	UNCIRCULATE D 1800 HALF EAGLE	SUPERB AND VERY RARE 1825/1 HALF EAGLE	1825 OVER 4 U.S. HALF EAGLE	SUPERB 1831 LARGE D HALF EAGLE	CHOICE UNCIRCULATE D 1795 EAGLE	VERY CHOICE 1800 EAGLE	CHOICE PROOFLIKE 1801 EAGLE	RARE PROOF 1846 EAGLE	SUPERB GEM MATTE PROOF 1912 EAGLE	FAMOUS GEM 1883 DOUBLE EAGLE	MCMVII (1907) HIGH RELIEF SAINT-GAUDENS DOUBLE EAGLE GEM PROOF WITH LETTER FROM THE WHITE HOUSE	1855 KELLOGG & CO. $50 GOLD PIECE
1983 value	$37,500	$26,500	$17,500	$75,000	$200,000	$65,000	$55,000	$32,500	$28,000	$62,500	$27,500	$90,000	$55,000	$225,000
2013 value	$200,000	$115,000	$35,000	$300,000	$850,000	$300,000	$350,000	$165,000	$140,000	$350,000	$100,000	$250,000	$275,000	$550,000

The Classic Gold Rarities collection was assembled mainly from the purchases made at the Louis Eliasberg Auction. The entire offering included over fifty of the finest and rarest coins extant. This chart shows a sampling of the performance of those rarities. Overall, the collection appreciated over $5.8 million or 346% between 1983 and 2013. See Case Study II for a complete listing. (© Kagin's, Inc.)

Although I think of myself as a fundamentals value investor, naming the specific stages of the boom and bust cycle gives us a sense of where we are in the process, and from there we can set our expectations for what we think should happen.

A lot of what we're doing here is comparing what we think should happen versus what actually transpires—and to that end, cataloging the numismatic market cycle is a particularly useful tool.

There are seven specific phases of the numismatic market cycle:

- Stabilized slow growth
- Moderate growth
- Boom and high appreciation
- Hyper-boom and overreaction
- Severe drop
- Sluggish downward trend
- Depression and stabilization

A full cycle usually takes about six to seven years to complete. Obviously, no cycle repeats itself exactly. The current cycle will probably last much longer than most.

What follows is a more in-depth breakdown of the stages of a numismatic price cycle, but, keep in mind, this analysis is based on historic averages and weighted market trends, which never repeat themselves exactly.

The importance of this analysis is not so much that we're able to call the precise time when a peak will be reached, but so we are not caught unaware of what is hap-

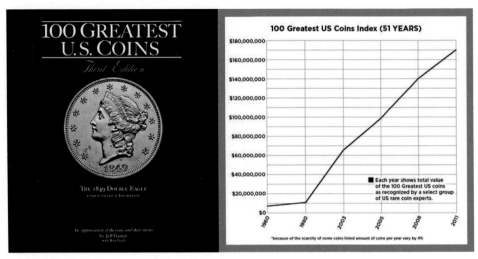

100 Greatest U.S. Coins (© Karl Newman and Whitman Publishing, LLC)

pening within the marketplace. Then we can then effectively plan ahead, maximizing our opportunities to post profits.

Ideally, for coins that interest you, you'll never be taken aback by a shocking quote or an outrageous auction result. Rare coins are your business, now. What you ought to notice, as the weeks and months go by, is that your price anticipation and forecasting keeps improving.

Stabilized, slow, upward growth is the beginning of Stage One of a rare coin market cycle. It is characterized by an overall confidence in numismatic values from a collector's point of view. In spite of the fact that Stage One provides the best opportunity for long-term profits, few investors will take the opportunity to accumulate these severely discounted specimens until the second or third phase.

The collector-to-investor ratio in Stage One is between 1,000 to 1 and 50 to 1. Some of the economic characteristics of this phase include a steady and relatively low rate of inflation, or at least a general perception that this is the case.

Stage One is characterized by economic recovery from a recession in conjunction with stable bullion prices.

In the past, overall market trends usually lead the general economy by approximately six months to a year. Top-quality rare coins, along with the super rare Legacy coins, can be expected to rise in value at approximately 3% to 5% annually. Then stretches those gains to 10% or more before finally transitioning into Stage Two.

Since September 2011, we have been in Stage One. As this book goes to press, I would look for us to be moving into Stage Two somewhere around the end of 2015.

By the time Stage Two rolls around, we'll know for sure we're in a bull market. In Stage Two, we'll expect periods of moderate appreciation, say, 5% to 10% annually for investment-grades, and more like 10% to 15% for Legacy specimens.

During this phase, collectors become investors, investors become collectors, and new participants enter the market as an alternative to unattractive stock and bond markets. The overall collector-to-investor ratio declines from 50 to 1 to, perhaps, 20 to 1—although this decline is hard to judge since the demarcation between collectors and investors is becoming increasingly difficult to make.

Stage Three is characterized by the smell of economic prosperity in the air. An increase of investor presence and an upswing in collector's buying activities bringing scores of new dealers to the market on their behalf, where they aggressively fight for quality material.

Neophyte dealers hang shingles on their storefronts, some calling themselves "investment advisors." With demand at these levels increasing and no changes in supply, quality investment-grade material becomes scarce. Look for investment-quality to appreciate by 10% to 20% on an annualized basis.

The hyper-boom of Stage Four is an overreaction to a series of unusual economic and market occurrences. Every other TV commercial is an offer to buy gold. And, I'm bound to get a call from a distant relative asking how much she can get for the family silverware.

Fear and panic among investors who're late for the party and do not wish to be left behind again push prices to rise inordinately. Long-term collectors, frustrated at rapidly higher prices, drop out of the market. Or, they sell for large profits to get rich quick speculators—who may get poor by the time it's all said and done.

On the business side, Stage Four is characterized by dealers pouring profits from their bullion trading into rare coins, which at this time are much more stable than spot gold and silver prices. Still, demand for high quality coins is far greater than available supply, and frustrated investors and wholesalers who under-bid at auctions raise their offers in an effort to stay ahead of the curve. Prices seemingly rise day after day, week after week, month after month.

Relatively high inflation rates and an inflation to interest-rate ratio greater than 2 to 1 fuels the market during this phase. It's an exciting time to be in the business. The economy is either expanding from an economic boom, panicking from international monetary crises, or possibly both.

Precious metal prices are soaring to staggering new levels. You scratch your head and wonder how long can this go on! Unfortunately, turns out this period is short-lived, and it's played out and over within three to six months.

Stage Five marks the beginning of the bust half of the cycle. Historically, gravity is a killer. Bear markets are usually much faster and more severe relative to the climb up.

The collapse's predominant characteristic is highly volatile price swings. Prices are all over the board, but if you look very close the tops are often identifiable by a price spike. Sometimes you'll see a "double top," or perhaps your other technical analyst friend will be muttering the lingo, phrases like "island reversal."

Speculators end up leaving the market and selling off their holdings, more than likely at a loss. It's worth noting that since we are often trying to figure out where the smart money is going, that this particular group is a terrific contrarian indicator. Definitely not smart money.

Since speculators are dropping out and there are no collectors to speak of on the buy-side either, dealers follow suit. They cut back or stop buying altogether, too.

Some dealers are forced to sell inventory as a result of their own speculation. It's easy to get caught up in the frenzy. For us, however, it's time to relax. We're mostly out of the market by now. We've been selling our holdings into the strength of the previous stage (at least I hope we were smart enough to do that).

Tangible assets also drop in value. Investors sell. Suddenly, it looks as if everybody wants out at the same time—right now. Prices tumble. It is musical chairs—if you can't find a chair it is not going to be a pretty picture.

The market is prescient and pretty soon we'll start to see various government and private reports confirm that whatever was before is no longer. We now know why prices have turned.

You'll read news headlines of government officials explaining the various ways in which they intend to keep inflation under control. Or, how they're going to keep interest rates from spiraling out of control.

Precious metal prices fall fast and with it comes the end of the economic boom.

A sluggish downward trend defines Stage Six, following the big sell-off as dealers and investors find themselves squeezed by a lack of cash flow to offset high overhead costs. Few dealers, collectors or investors are willing to buy at this stage. During this period of falling precious metal prices and running inflation rates, a general malaise pervades the marketplace.

The final stage of the numismatic market cycle is characterized by a deepening depression. The coin market bottom may be subject to overreaction. Stage Seven is earmarked for slow and meandering price movement.

A rash of bankruptcies and layoffs occur as the need for cash among dealers and investors force drastic reductions in overhead and inventory.

Your eyes should begin to light up as you take note of the terrific bargains that await. We're going to start the seven-phase numismatic cycle again shortly.

Collectors begin to reenter the market, and the ratio of collectors to investors balloons to 50 to one. Maybe higher. New investors are practically non-existent. Except for you and me, that is. We begin buying. Perhaps slowly at first. We recognize that this is our "blood in the streets" moment, and soon we're buying like madmen again.

The seven stages outlined are approximations only. No two historic scenarios are ever exactly the same. The numismatic cycle model ought to give you clues as to what lies ahead—no more and no less than that. Use it accordingly.

Today's Perfect Storm

Successful rare coin investing is a function not only of buying the right coins at the right price, but buying them at the right time. Timing is important.

The year 2014 represents the right combination of macroeconomic scenarios of low interest rates, potential for international sovereign debt crises, a relatively weak greenback, and the beginning stages of economic growth and higher employment numbers.

Combined with a hyper-expansionary Federal Reserve monetary policy, impending inflation and overall uncertainty—let us make note of the beginning stages of a coin-collecting resurgence.

Soon, we'll witness record prices for Legacy coins. Followed closely by strong investment-grade specimens. The current stage, the latter half of Stage One, marks the best time to purchase rare coins in 35 years. A veritable perfect storm for investment opportunities.

This 1876-CC 20¢ coin is currently worth $460,000.00 and is considered a Legacy coin. (© Kagin's, Inc.)

Chapter VII

Finding Hidden Values

As a result of experience and research, a seasoned collector or professional is frequently able to uncover value in a rare coin that is not readily apparent. To realize a coin's potential sometimes calls for specialized knowledge that is beyond the scope of this book. Nevertheless, there are certain general principals to help an experienced buyer to gain an edge. I call this recognizing a coin's potential for maximizing value, or uncovering its hidden value.

For instance, a numismatist might purchase a numismatic collection based on the coins apparent rarity and condition. But upon a detailed analysis of the individual specimens, it often happens that the items contain additional not-so-apparent value. These may include discovering that a coin is a better (rarer) date than originally thought. (Remember, mintage figures alone do not tell the whole population story of a coin or notes true rarity.)

Supply + Demand + Potential = TRUE VALUE

Further research could uncover an important pedigree, which would increase collectors' desire for such an item and therefore its value to them.

A coin may have surface dirt rather than circulation wear obscuring hidden original lustre, which would give the item a higher grade and value designation. Such was the case with the Saddle Ridge Hoard Treasure.

When my associate David McCarthy was first shown one of the recovered coins, it was covered with muddy gravel, rust and surface dirt. He wasn't thinking about Saddle Ridge as the greatest buried treasure find in the U.S.—that's not in his job description. David did recognize the original mint bloom of the surface peeking through, though.

David has considerable experience with numismatics. He knew he could expose the Saddle Ridge coins' hidden value beneath the debris. After several months of painstaking restoration, several millions of dollars' worth of added value was bestowed to the 1,427 coins.

1883-S $20 before conservation   **The same 1883-S $20, conserved**

This $20 1888-S coin from the Saddle Ridge Hoard Treasure contained much surface gunk obtained over 120 years of burial in a metal can. Professional conservation revealed the hidden pristine original surfaces and exposed significant hidden value.

Proof's in the Pudding

Another tool an investor and his numismatic advisor can use to uncover hidden value is by applying an analysis of a rare coin's investment history to determine which numismatic items in which ideal condition have represented the best-performing investment. This research does not necessarily mean that the coin will be either the finest graded or the rarest coin in a particular series.

This advice may seem counterintuitive, especially after hearing from almost every other numismatic investment advisor that you should buy only the finest and rarest coins. But what you almost never hear is that some of these coins, despite fitting the criteria, do not have the best investment track record. Why?

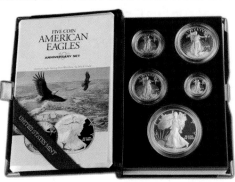 

Modern coins like this proof gold set of American Eagles and this set of Foreign Proof coins are often referred to as rare because of their "limited edition" and "high grade." However, these coins are not in high demand on the secondary market, and their mintage is high enough to meet modern collector demands. These factors do not provide a true value to investors. (Photos © Kagin's, Inc.)

Actually, there could be a number of reasons. Some coins or notes are so rare that they do not come on the market often enough to gauge their value. While you can try to develop a theoretical value based on comparable rarities, value is really just educated guessing, especially if the comparable coin is from a different series and therefore corresponds to a different level of demand.

Fully fourteen coins from the Saddle Ridge Hoard Treasure were the finest known example of that date and mintmark. How does one value a coin that has never been known in that condition? David and I spent many hours analyzing price history for the same coin in lower conditions, similar rarities in the same type of coins, and other value matrix to determine what a fair value would be for both buyer and seller. It wasn't easy, and I'm sure it wasn't perfect, but with our several decades of experience, it probably was reasonably fair. This is not an exact science.

After a coin has been off the market for a few decades, it is hard to jump a coin's value from $50,000 to $1,000,000, even if it is theoretically worth it. Nevertheless, one coin recently did just that. A Legacy coin, the unique 1783 Nova Constellatio Silver Pattern Quint—the first coin to be struck after the Revolutionary War—sold in auction in November 1979 for $55,000. It next sold 34 years later in April 2013 for $1,175,000—a 2,000% appreciation or 59% on an annualized basis. No one could really predict this actual price, but it was experienced professionals who were both the buyers and under bidders. They understood the hidden value of this first attempt at coinage in the fledgling United States.

Add It Up

Another important factor in selecting numismatic material with true value is quantifying a particular coin or series investment potential by using the results from the historical performance analysis and projecting their future appreciation. This process necessarily means predicting future demand. Of course, no one can be certain of what the future holds, but a careful analysis of past performance, coupled with an understanding of why certain series of numismatics and particular dates within a series performed better than others, can help you, the investor, project which investment-quality coins will likely perform the best.

Who will desire what is a good question to ponder. In every previous modern-era bull market, Legacy coins have enjoyed the most interest and demand from investors. There are no reasons to think this situation will change.

As a matter of fact, since 2010 the greatest demand for rare coins has been for those which are traditionally the most desirable. They include the following specimens, which have realized record prices in a down market:

- The unique Punch-On-Breast Brasher Doubloon: America's first gold and most important coin.
- The Ides of March ancient coin commemorating the assassination of Julius Caesar.
- The Stater of Lydia: The first gold coin in the Western World.
- The silver-centered cent—the first United States experimental, or Pattern coin.

In December 2011, Don Kagin and colleague Steve Contursi sold the Unique 1787 Ephraim Brasher Punch-On-Breast Doubloon for $7.4 million to a Wall Street investment group. Don and Steve Contursi had purchased it for $2.9 million in 2005. (© Kagin's, Inc.)

Lydia Kroisos Gold Stater (© Kagin's, Inc.)

This 1792 Silver Center Cent Pattern, an example of the first coin to be struck at the Philadelphia Mint, is valued at $1 million by numismatic experts in the definitive price guide, A Guide Book of U.S. Coins. In April 2012, it sold at auction for $1.15 million. (© Heritage Auctions, Inc.)

The first and finest known specimen of the 1794 Silver Dollar was the first silver dollar struck by the United States Mint and the first coin to reach $10 million. (© Steven L. Contursi)

This 1783 Nova Constellatio Silver Pattern Quint was the first coin of the American Confederation and the finest decimal coin. It appreciated over 2,000% when it sold for $1,175,000 or just under 60% per annum from 1979 until 2013. (© Heritage Auctions, Inc.)

The characteristics that all these coins have in common is that they are all historically truly rare, have a great story to tell, are interesting to look at, and the demand for them has always exceeded the supply. These characteristics are the mark of true value, and it is no coincidence that Kagin's, Inc. has bought or sold four of these six coins in the last three years.

The Elevator Pitch

Any discussion of numismatic pricing that doesn't include a word on the valuation of the history/backstory of the coins or banknotes in question would be incomplete. This is the fundamental difference between a generic commodity, like gold, and a collectible.

For generic commodities, take gold once again, it doesn't matter so much whether it's stamped by PAMP or NTR Metals or into modern U.S. Mint American Eagles—it's gold, it's gold, it's gold. Numismatics falls into the collectibles category precisely because the artistry of individual specimens and their stories are the primary determinants of price.

As part of its definition, the word "collectible" assumes rarity will be a major component in the calculation. There's a limited amount of the item. We could be talking about one of the 12,367 No Motto 1907 High Relief St.-Gaudens that will run you about $10,000 in mediocre condition but might only cost you $20,000 in Mint State—a difference that could easily widen in the years to come.

We could be talking about one of the 1,120 known three-dollar Dahlonega gold pieces, of which each of the 45 or so in Mint State will go for about $125,000. We could be talking one of three Lamborghini 2014 Veneno supercars—cars that look like spaceships, travel almost as fast and will set you back a cool $3.9 million; or we could be talking about the Millennium Star—a 203 carat pear-shaped white diamond insured for £100,000,000.

Notable collectibles invariably come with fascinating backstories, the degree to which is a matter of taste. In the case of Lamborghinis, it is not so much the allure of a historical era, as it is with numismatics, but rather the company's storied history—the Italian sports car enthusiast who wasn't happy with the work of Enzo Ferrari so he started building his own.

If you are unimpressed that Lamborghinis are custom built by hand, don't care that production series are named after famous bulls, perhaps it's the sparkle of freakishly large diamonds that put a twinkle in your eye. In the case of the Millennium Star, the now celebrated robbery attempt at London's Millennium Dome in 2000—foiled by Scotland Yard's Flying Squad—has surely added to the estimated $750 million that it would go for should De Beer's ever decide to part with it.

Of course, rarity alone isn't the deciding factor when it comes to hanging a price tag on an object. There's good reason Aunt Millie's oil painting wasn't able to sell at her garage sale—five bucks is five bucks. Still, I invite you to take a second look. There's also a pretty good chance that Aunt Millie's disaster-on-canvas comes with a beautiful old frame. Frames are expensive.

A Character Study

Every backstory then is clearly not created equal. Prices for collectibles are largely based on desirability, which is a subjective matter and difficult to quantify. If you're asking me why the 1907 No Motto St.-Gaudens runs about $20,000 instead of

$120,000, the answer is I don't know. But, I can tell you that in the context of other coins with a similar pedigree, the number makes sense.

It's our job to find Hidden Value within the context of coins with established track records of price history. We look at coins with similar ratios of conditions and we see that desirable U.S. coins in Mint State may run 10 times as much as poor quality ones. In this case, my conclusion is that there may be hidden value with the top-end St.-Gaudens. Maybe not $120,000, but all things being equal, I could see the 1907 No Mottos fetching $40,000 maybe $50,000.

It's important to develop a sense of what drives collectors interested in 19th- and early 20th-century coins to buy. Every subset of coins will have their own historical backdrop in which we attempt to gauge toward estimating future price movement. Collectors of Roman coinage are perhaps drawn by the allure of Cleopatra and Mark Antony or by the Romans influence over early British history. Collectors of Chinese coinage are often part of the new middle class there or are drawn by the mysteries of the Far East.

Since neither of those branches of numismatics are a specialty of mine, what I'd like to do is to return to 19th-century U.S. coins and currency—which are specialties—and walk us through the timeline from the perspective of an investor hunting for hidden values. The idea being, if your area of interest is Roman, Chinese or British that you'll be able to extrapolate the concepts here to the historical era.

American Graffiti

Managing a national currency is no easy undertaking. The ruble has been Russia's currency for 500 years, but in all instances dollars are strongly preferred. Soft currencies, like the ruble, are usually fixed at some unreasonable exchange rate, such that hard currency countries, like the U.S., are unwilling to accept it. The practice translates into good business for trade brokers, but otherwise it hangs over these countries' heads like dark storm clouds.

It's easy to sit and second guess the Russian Federation's monetary policies from here, though. Consider, however, the political backlash if President Putin merely suggested a free market float for the ruble—that's right, it's just not going to happen. Lately, the Russians are showing cold-war enthusiasm for another boxing match with the West—but that's neither here, nor there. Point is, the Russians are not alone on this—all governments play politics.

From a historian's standpoint, from the standpoint of a coin collector, there is no government politics more fascinating than the first 100 years or so of the United States of America. In many ways, the evolution of the dollar is emblematic of the country as a whole. Once the training wheels came off, the country's bicycle zigzagged wobbly for quite some time. Never mind the pundits, who're sure to point out it remains a work in progress.

In the same manner that some modern nations, like Zimbabwe, are compelled to forgo their own currency, usually in favor of the dollar, the United States' monetary policy and implementation of a currency came piecemeal, mostly through trial and error. Regarding the two main schools of thought—Alexander Hamilton's Federalist side pushing for a central bank and Thomas Jefferson's Republicans' championing states' rights—the political factions spent a good deal of their time dismantling each other's efforts.

Early American politicians borrowed when and where they saw fit, as with The Bank of the United States being fashioned after the Bank of England, but for the most part they figured it out as they went. Since its congressional charter in 1785, the development of a robust U.S. dollar was anything but a foregone conclusion.

The events that transpired during this period of history were the catalysts propelling the country and the rest of the world into the Modern Age. Nineteenth-century U.S. coins, the gold varieties in particular, are magnificent artifacts of the most exciting time in world history.

I say "most exciting time" with some conviction—it's more than a subjective opinion. If we compare price and population among the branches of numismatics, what we find is a collective body of coins in greater demand relative to the other segments of the market. Sure, certain British coins, say, command huge sums at auction—but the U.S. coin market is by far the largest trading pool where numismatic investment dollars are concerned.

To illustrate, an exceptional Lydia stater, one of the earliest known coins manufactured specifically for commerce—dating back to the 7th-century B.C. and made of "white" gold (a gold/silver combination called electrum) no less—sold for a modest $7,250 at a recent auction (Heritage 2014). A lovely specimen of the world's first gold coin, the Lydia lion and bull stater struck by King Croesus around 550 B.C. can be had for under $10,000, which seems like an incredible bargain—but that's the market.

Other than superstar specimens, foreign coins do not enjoy nearly the same demand or liquidity and, as a consequence, comparables usually trade at a hefty discount relative to their U.S. counterparts. (Incidentally, Ancients is one branch of numismatics that you'll want to be on-guard for forgeries—at least more so than usual. A modern foundry could easily replicate most types, and sophisticated examination techniques are required for authentication.)

Liquidity will be a salient talking point as we look at various subsections of 19th-century U.S. coins and banknotes. As a rule, we want to put our investment dollars in coin types with high demand and enough supply, more or less, to keep pace. Or, at least hold out the possibility that one will come on to the market before the Chicago Cubs win a World Series.

Collectors like to assemble sets of coins with a theme. Take Type sets for example. Since 1796 there have been six types of quarters: Draped Bust, Capped Bust, Liberty Seated, Barber, Standing Liberty and Washington.

Collectors may go after the coins that make up a series, say, Indian Head half eagles, coins in production from 1908 to 1929. After completing a set without regard to mintmarks, a collector might then widen his net to include Philadelphia, Denver, New Orleans and San Francisco Mint origins.

This kind of self-imposed challenge is an aspect of collecting that makes it such a kick.

Later in the chapter, we'll return to this subject and expand the possibilities to include or exclude distinctions like variety. But to wrap up my thought, investors are not likely to collect Capped Head half eagles by series because there are only three 1822s known to exist, and therefore it would be extremely unlikely—even if the million-dollar plus price tags were not an obstacle—a person would be able to complete the set. When the Eliasberg/Pogue specimen is sold by Stack's Bowers in the next two years, several underbidders will be disappointed.

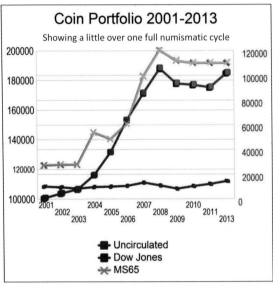

This chart tracks the price appreciation for 10 Ultra-Rare or Legacy Coins clearly demonstrating their superior track record to other subsets of Rare Coins. (© David Gantz)

But what about these Legacy pieces? You've heard me trumpet the appreciation potential of Legacy coins, but now I'm saying it's better to be in markets with enough supply that a collector can reasonably expect a dozen or ten dozen to change hands during a calendar year. How do we reconcile this? My response is...yes, both concepts have merit. How you divide your priorities is another one of those personal preferences.

As a rule of thumb, you can expect the liquidity of an item to decrease as you move up the rarity ladder. This trade-off ought to make intuitive sense. If there are more of a given item, you would expect them to trade more often.

The flipside is that top-tier and Legacy coins have better historical rates of return—and nothing in the cards to suggest the coming years will be any different. I say that as a collector you ought to focus on markets with liquidity, but not so much relative to Legacy wares, but rather to comparative markets. Say, from an investor's point of view, it's better to collect U.S. coins than South American ones.

Although there's no rule that says you can't collect South American currency for pleasure and collect U.S. coins for profit. Of course, most of you, if the percentages hold, collect U.S. pieces for pleasure and profit.

The reason I bring this up again now is because that's what we'll be discussing in the context of this chapter—how, for instance, the upside potential of Pioneer gold is stronger than Type I U.S. gold dollars—but the trade-off is the buying and selling Pioneer gold presents more difficulties. They come on to the market far less frequently, and sellers have to be equally patient waiting for serious buyers.

With regard to the various branches and specialties in numismatics, it's my opinion that some avenues are definitely preferable to others. But for 19th-century U.S. coins and banknotes, it is not so much that one segment has an absolute edge over another, but rather it is an exercise of evaluating advantages and disadvantages and choosing the segment that best suits your investment objectives.

Not Worth a Continental

The American Revolution—I think its import gets taken for granted or forgotten altogether—took eight years of hard fighting. The weapons were crude and inaccurate by modern standards, but so too were medical practices, and a flesh wound often turned into a slow and miserable death.

It should perhaps be called the First World War. By 1778, it was no longer a private matter between His Majesty King George and the Thirteen Colonies. France, Netherlands and Spain took the opportunity to side with the Patriots, though it would be more accurate to say those countries took the opportunity to side against Great Britain.

The French, it must be said, went above and beyond the call. Recent years, the last ten or so, France has developed a public relations conundrum with the States, periodically cropping up in clubhouse locker rooms as the punch-line for jokes; in some quarters there is real vitriol. The French, you see, have become reluctant to back our play with various U.S. military incursions.

$5 February 17, 1776 FR.CC21 front. This popular Continental Currency bill was designed by Ben Franklin. (© Kagin's Inc.)

I let friends and acquaintances' snide remarks slide, but I don't join the sabre rattling. France spent so much money on the American Revolution, their country went into recession. A recession that led to another rebellion—the French Revolution. You could say Louis XVI and Marie Antoinette gave their lives for the United States of America.

Without the French, there is no hope of defeating the lobsterbacks. There is no birth of a nation. No nothing.

The British, you'll recall, were the most powerful nation on the planet. In the 19th and 20th centuries, the sun never set on the British Empire. (The phrase originally referred to the Spanish Empire of the 16th and 17th centuries.) Not long after a Brown Bess fired its first grape shot, the British Army dumped an enormous amount of counterfeit Continental currency onto the colonies.

They were winning most of the musket battles, but their most important early victory was a clever act of economic warfare. By 1780, Continentals were 1/40th of face value, and a year after that they'd be worth more as leggings for the Colonial troops at Valley Forge than as money. The British had the colonies on the ropes.

While counterfeiting for personal gain traces back to the earliest known currencies, this is believed to be the first time it was used as a tactic to undermine the enemy. Its success didn't go unnoticed, and counterfeiting—both as an offensive tactic and as a defensive measure—has played a part in just about every war since.

Famously, the most ambitious was Operation Bernhard—codename for the Nazi plot that used prisoners from concentration camps to forge £5, £10, £20 and £50 paper in order to destabilize Great Britain. The fake £135 million worth of pound notes are said to have been nearly indistinguishable from the real thing. The counterfeiters were all set to turn their attention to the dollar when in February of 1945 production was shut down due to the advancing Allied armies.

Many like to collect counterfeits, especially those of the Confederacy during the Civil War. However, as with error coins or banknotes, for an investor, counterfeits present a number of problems. This goes to the point we mentioned earlier. There are so few of them and they trade so irregularly that it's difficult to get a fix on pricing. For large runs, like those Nazi British pounds, even if you could tell them apart, a high population number summarily kills their collectability.

Or, it could be that I don't fancy counterfeit numismatics because I imagine there's something inherently wrong about knowingly purchasing a fake. The exceptions I have is for counterfeit Continentals, Pioneer Gold, and Fractional Currency. From a historical perspective, the British forgeries are a valuable document of the times, and the fact that there are fewer of them make them quite collectible.

The Gold Rushes

There are two primary reasons the United States was able to become the world's superpower before its bicentennial. The Declaration of Independence, the United States Constitution, which set the framework for the federal government, ratified in 1788, and subsequent Bill of Rights, the first ten amendments to the Constitution that guarantees certain personal freedoms, ratified in 1791, created a supreme law of the land unlike any before or any since.

All good intentions aside, though, the U.S. is blessed with an abundance of natural resources—the richest on the planet. It's this combination of vast resources and free market enterprise that provided a young United States with a juggernaut economy seemingly overnight. Success, as you might expect, came part and parcel with magnificent growing pains.

In the aftermath of the collapsed Continental currency, President George Washington put Secretary of the Treasury Alexander Hamilton in charge of creating a new national currency—the U.S. dollar. Still stinging from runaway inflation, delegates at the then-capital Philadelphia Constitutional Convention in 1787 included a gold and silver clause, which prohibited individual States from issuing their own bills of credit, among other safeguards.

The Coinage Act of 1792 gave rise to the country's first mint. The Philadelphia Mint was authorized to convert anyone's precious metals into standard coinage without seigniorage (face value minus the cost of making the physical specimen) charges beyond the cost of production.

Starting from scratch, it's easy to see how there was not enough U.S. coin and currency to go around. Indeed, the Spanish pillar dollar and other foreign currencies were legal tender until 1857. It was convenient then, when, in 1802, a shiny-metallic yellow 17-pound stone that had been used as a doorstop for several years turned out to be near solid gold—the country's first documented discovery of gold.

A jeweler asked John Reed to name his price. Reed asked and received $3.50, about a week's wages for the common working man but only about 1/1000th of the "rock's" true value. He wised up soon enough. The Reed Gold Mine of Midland, North Carolina, was the first mining operation of its kind in the U.S. Not long after, one of his slaves found a 28-pound yellow doorstop, and John Reed died a wealthy man.

Today, some 3.7 million Americans work in the mining industry, and it's estimated another 20 million are dependent upon it. Your friendly numismatic broker-dealers, I suppose, among them. For many developing countries, mining is the most important economic endeavor.

The discovery of gold in North Carolina brought prosperity to the region. The discovery of gold in Georgia and later in Alabama prompted Congress to act. Transportation, cumbersome as it was, made long trips to Philadelphia impractical, if not downright dangerous. It made more sense to bring minting facilities to the gold rather than the other way around.

In 1835, branch mints in Charlotte, N.C., Dahlonega, Ga. and New Orleans, La. were authorized and by 1838 all three were in production. New Orleans is the only southern branch mint that coined silver and gold.

As you might expect, original branch mint coins are highly popular in the South. In the old days, you might have been able to pick up southern branch mint pieces at bargain prices outside the region, but since the advent of the Internet there's little advantage to be had with venue location.

Coins from New Orleans, with an O mintmark, are generally thought to have weak business strikes in comparison to C and D mintmarks, but that doesn't necessarily translate to higher prices for the same grade. Be aware that a weak strike is not the same thing as wear when it comes to grading.

Collectors don't ordinarily single out a favorite branch, but if you're wondering what sort of ensemble to put together, might I suggest a Year set. A Year set would be thinking outside the box a little bit, but I think it makes a lot of sense. Be sure to pick a year that you can reasonably hope to accomplish, because many years have a Legacy half eagle or three dollar or some other denomination that is extremely difficult to find.

The Civil War closed down the southern branch mints, but the Confederates conscripted the New Orleans facility to mint a few cents and half dollars. The 14 known Confederate cents were hand stamped samples designed and engraved by Robert Lovett, Jr. of Philadelphia, who feared he'd be branded a traitor and hid the samples and dies in his cellar. These samples are called "originals." Fourteen are known to exist and I guess I don't have to tell you that they're each worth a small fortune.

The dies were sold to New York coin dealer J.W. Scott, who made about 500 restrikes and another 500 for a token before he sold the dies to a fellow named Captain John Haseltine, who made 55 in copper, seven in gold and 12 in silver. He in turn sold it to an opportunistic numismatist named Robert Bashlow. Bashlow had a transfer die made in 1960's, from which he minted and marketed about 30,000 more restrikes.

The Confederate cent is a curious case in which planchets stamped from the same or identical dies may go for $150 or $30,000 or $250,000. If there was ever a perfect example of how a collectible's backstory affects value, this is it.

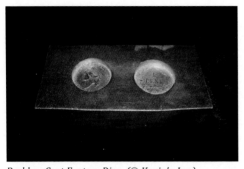

Bashlow Cent Fantasy Dies. (© Kagin's, Inc.)

Strictly speaking, the Bashlow cent is garbage. Fairly or unfairly, Bashlow's brazen attempt to alter the history books for personal profit drew a collective snub from the numismatic community.

I've got to admit it, though—I sort of admire Bashlow's chutzpah. Not quite on par with the genius of the Pet Rock, but those guys probably drink from the same watering hole. Bashlow cents are somewhat thicker than Scott and Haseltine's, but otherwise this is the only way a collector of modest means can own a coveted Confederate coin. I'm pretty sure I still have a few of them.

In addition to the 1861 Confederate one cent and half dollar coins, there are an equally small number of CSA half dimes, Jefferson Davis half dimes, which were minted in Paris, France, CSA Beauregard dimes and the notable Wealth of the South tokens—all of which are highly collectible.

The vast majority of the $1.7 billion in Confederate currency was in banknotes. CSA collectors generally focus their attention on the 72 different types in seven different series that were printed from 1861 to 1864. Of particular interest are the first series "Montgomery Notes," especially the $500 and $1000 denominations. Paper money issued by private banks on both sides of the Mason-Dixon are popular, especially those specimens with Civil War dates.

CSA collectors cherish the historical period for a thousand reasons, none of which hint to an advocacy of slavery. If I'm honest, though, I find it hard to completely disassociate the South's cause célèbre from its artifacts. As a consequence, my personal Civil War collection has an imbalance of Union paraphernalia. But there's no reason why you should feel the same way.

Perhaps you desire to own a Scott one cent restrike simply because Gobrecht's Seated Liberty obverse is replaced with Lovett's French Liberty Head—Minerva, the Roman goddess of wisdom. That's sound and reasonable logic by my way of thinking. Collectors cannot live on Gobrecht alone!

Christian Gobrecht was a brilliant designer and engraver. He made beautiful coins, no question. My one complaint with U.S. rarities aesthetics is that there isn't more diversity. Numismatics function like Egyptian hieroglyphics—coin designs are opportunities to celebrate the country's values and achievements.

For all the coin types and denominations, there were basically only a handful of unique design concepts. Gilbert Stuart and Robert Scot designed coins that spanned the end of the 18th century into the early years of the next. Draped Busts look a lot like Flowing Hair pieces. After that we have Christian Gobrecht, John Reich and William Kneass. Classic Heads look a lot like Capped Heads, which look a lot like Capped Busts, which look a lot like Draped Busts. Liberty Heads were the face of U.S. gold coins for almost 70 years.

True, there are many varieties—a different number of stars on this denomination or an oddly placed date on that, the type of nuances that keep fussy numismatists glued to their loupes and magnifiers. Naturally, I enjoy keeping track of arrows and rays as much as the next coin nerd, but if I had been the director of the Mint in the 1800s, I would have commissioned at least another dozen obverses and reverses for us modern collectors to fawn over.

Listing the bullet points of accomplishments of those who shaped U.S. coinage gives an impression they were hyper aware of their work as important historical documentation of the times—as if employees' exit interviews included a formal report summarizing their achievements for a future museum curator to evaluate. But, in reading selected memoirs, I'm reminded they were only partially motivated by how they'd be remembered in the history books.

Mint superintendents were known to have kept using dated dies into the following year. If its strikes are still good, why wouldn't we keep using it? Employees at the New Orleans Mint worked with the windows closed so that silver and gold filings wouldn't blow away. To say mint employees, usually women for the job of shaving coins down to their proper weights, worked in a sweat shop would be a huge understatement. An exclamation mark to the story is that this government sweat shop job was considered to be a plum position.

Tiny vignettes like those above breathe life into the coinage they left behind. Rather than a simple object of the times, rare coins are a pathway toward connecting with our ancestors, and, when the time comes for us, leaving a bridge for future generations to do the same. Some collectibles do a good job of painting the big picture, like the British Crown Jewels, while others do a good job of cutting out a slice-of-life vignettes, like the Batman #1 comic book. Numismatics is unique in that it does both with equal aplomb.

U.S. rare coins embody the events that took the nation from its infancy to adolescence, foreshadowing the superpower the country would become; U.S. rarities also embody the individual stories of the men and women upon whose shoulders the country was built.

As an investor, it's immaterial whether old currency tugs on your heartstrings the way it does on avid collectors. What is important is knowing that this is where historic coins and banknotes derive their value. At its core, numismatics is a romantic pursuit. The better you grasp the psychology of it, the better your price forecasting will be.

Go West, Young Man

America's Founding Fathers successfully merged philosopher John Locke's (Two Treatises of Government) vision of republicanism with Thomas Paine's (Common Sense) liberalism. Devil's in the details, though, and it's estimated that there were more people than circulating coins as late as the 1830s.

Half a century after the Revolution, the country's economy was hampered by an inadequate medium of exchange. The situation out West, before and after the Civil War, was in particularly dire shape. The shortage of a reliable currency was a frustrating fact of life.

In 1830, a man named Templeton Reid had a novel idea. A jeweler and gunsmith by trade, Reid surmised that he could fill this void with privately minted coins. After all, gold is gold is gold. For an instant, it looked as though he had come upon his own pot of gold.

1830 $10 Templeton Reid The 1st privately issued Pioneer Gold coin. (© Kagin's, Inc.)

Articles in a local newspaper criticizing Reid's efforts had the effect of the New York Times panning an off-Broadway stage production. He was attacked for inaccurate weights and assays. As the first editorial appeared only three weeks after Templeton Reid had opened its doors, it's unlikely the author was able to have the U.S. Mint in Philadelphia report their findings as was claimed in his piece. Regardless, the assay was off, residents lost faith, and the country's first private mint closed as quickly as it had opened.

Private or pioneer (often incorrectly referred to as "territorial") gold pieces are typically scarce or rare in all grades. Templeton Reid gold is extremely rare. The first privately issued gold coins from our nation's first gold rush in 1830 was from Templeton Reid. Of the estimated 1,600 coins made, only a handful survive in each of three denominations, and $10 coins in EF or AU reside comfortably in the million-dollar neighborhood.

I love these coins for their history and romance. One great mystery is what became of a unique 1849 Templeton California $25 gold piece. It was stolen from inside a U.S. Mint office in 1858 and not been seen since. Suffice to say, should it ever find its way back into the public domain, I'd pull out all the stops to be the winning bid.

A year after Templeton Reid had ceased production, Christopher Bechtler and family opened a private mint in North Carolina, which was in operation until 1852. Bechtler gold is scarce but not rare and prices tend to fall around the $5,000 to $20,000 range.

It is a little known fact that Bechtler minted the first one dollar gold piece in 1831, which preceded the U.S. Mint's version by 18 years. My personal collection only has a dozen or so coins that I'd categorize as sentimental favorites. An 1831-Bechtler North Carolina (No Star) gold dollar is one of them. I keep thinking this is easy money bar trivia, but so far I haven't found an opportune time in which to thrill and amaze my buddies down at the pub with this fun fact.

Yes, that's right, save it for a day when I've forgotten my wallet at home.

Claim Jumpers

There have been a few gold rushes, but there's really been only one—only one that changed the face of the nation. The California Gold Rush turned a sleepy Yerba Buena (later to be known as San Francisco) settlement of 800 into a population of over 36,000 in six years. It is estimated that there were about 90,000 forty-niners, but all said and done there were hundreds of thousands—almost half of which traveled from a foreign land—that came to live the California Dream of instant wealth.

In 1848 California was part of Mexico, but by 1850 it'd become the 31st State in the Union. California Indians were pushed aside and/or murdered by the thousands. Forty-eighters retrieved gold by the pound, forty-niners made an average living, and later prospectors fell on hard times. A Mormon named Samuel Brannan is said to have made the most amount of money during the California Gold Rush. He was a newspaper publisher and a merchant who sold supplies to the gold hunters. Never spent a day of his life panning for gold.

Commerce in the Old West was arcane. After a successful day, a prospector would mosey up to the bar of the local town's saloon and hold out a pouch, known as a poke, of gold dust for a shot of whiskey. Saloon bartenders took a pinch as payment. Owners hired big, burly barkeeps with no qualms about greasing their fat fingers before settling the tab. Wise to the saloons' chicanery, prospectors cut their gold dust with metal filings. Neither side were happy with the arrangement.

Pioneer gold originates from about 40 or so private mints, most of which were located in and around San Francisco, but there were notable gold-smelting, assaying and coining companies in Oregon, Utah and as far away as Colorado during its early mining days.

Norris, Gregg & Norris were the first in California. Six months after gold was discovered at Sutter's Mill, the company manufactured $5 gold from its facility in Benicia City, although the coins have a SAN FRANCISCO imprint.

It's convenient that the same qualities that make for an astute numismatic trader are the same as for a dedicated amateur historian. There is no single volume of work that tells the whole story of the Old West. It's only from researching a multitude of historical accounts that an interested party is able to cull an accurate big picture of the times.

Numismatists were caught unaware by gold coins with N.G.&N. (small caps) imprints for years. They were suspected to be Pioneer gold, but nobody knew for sure. It wasn't until the collection of U.S. Assayer Augustus Humbert was sold in 1902 that numismatic historians were able to track down and identify their origin. The Smithsonian's collection includes a unique 1850 N.G. & N. half eagle with a Stockton imprint. Words fail me.

But what if we tried. If not words, let's say putting a price tag on it. N.G. & N. $5 coins made in 1849 are scarce but not rare. This 1850 piece has got more sex appeal than a Hollywood starlet, a truly magnificent coin—but how would we come up with a maximum bid? A *Red Book* isn't going to be of any help.

Uncirculated 1849 specimens run about $30,000. Is this unique 1850 half eagle worth a million dollars? I'd say yes; it's unique and if you want a complete set.... If it had been Moffat & Co., the most prominent of California's private mints, it might be worth double that. But Norris, Gregg & Norris doesn't carry the same cache with collectors as Moffat & Co. or Templeton Reid, and its price I'd expect to be downgraded accordingly.

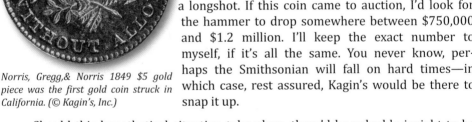

On the other hand, a one-of-a-kind Norris, Gregg & Norris 1850 half eagle is no slouch, not by a longshot. If this coin came to auction, I'd look for the hammer to drop somewhere between $750,000 and $1.2 million. I'll keep the exact number to myself, if it's all the same. You never know, perhaps the Smithsonian will fall on hard times—in which case, rest assured, Kagin's would be there to snap it up.

Norris, Gregg,& Norris 1849 $5 gold piece was the first gold coin struck in California. (© Kagin's, Inc.)

Should this hypothetical situation take place, there'd be valuable insight to be assimilated. If the hammer price surprised me, ran above $2 million, I'd interpret that as positive sign for Pioneer gold as a whole. If I had a Pioneer piece I wanted to unload, it'd be a good time to sell.

Is that counterintuitive?

Sell into strength. Train yourself to think this way. Conversely, on the buy side, I'd figure it may be a month or two before enthusiasm waned enough for there to be an attractive opportunity to come along. That's how you jump into a bull market. Buy into short-term weakness.

Now, let's say the hammer dropped on a price under $600,000. Well sir, in that case, I'd invite you to check it out at Kagins.com, give us a call, and a trusted associate will be happy to give you the lowdown on why, plus Kagin's few percent, it's still an incredible bargain.

The California Gold Rush produced 12 million ounces in its first five years. In today's money, that's about $16 billion. With the invention of more sophisticated mining techniques, such as hydraulic and dredging, by the 1890s that number would be closer to 20 million ounces. Meanwhile, business and citizen groups clamored for an adequate supply of reliable currency.

Proponents of a California branch mint met with stiff resistance in Congress. If California should have a mint, why not New York, and if New York, what does that mean for the southern branch mints? In 1850, California miners were producing 250,000 ounces a month, half of which was sent abroad at a $2 discount to the U.S. Mint's $18 an ounce standard. A compromise bill was passed.

One California private mint, Moffat & Co., received special treatment. How the company managed it is up for speculation, but in a letter to the federal government, Moffat & Co. claimed to be the only California private mint in operation. The most probable explanation is that then-Treasury Secretary Thomas Corwin bought Moffat & Co.'s assertion or Moffat bought his support.

Corwin had a reputation of being a sharp wit, but he also preferred to avoid making waves. At least that's my impression of the man. He opposed the Mexican-American War and sponsored legislation that would have allowed the 15 southern states to hold onto slavery. It's difficult to pinpoint Corwin's motivation for choosing Moffat & Co. other than their excellent reputation.

In 1849, Moffat & Co. made crude ingots—small rectangular gold bars with random weights and values imprinted seemingly as an afterthought. Strange considering John Moffat was an expert metallurgist.

Only three denominations of ingots survive, two of which are unique. Moffat & Co. ingots are unremarkable, simple, and practical if not beautiful works of art. The Smithsonian has the priceless $9.43 and $14.25 ingots in its collection, too. The $16 variety is the only type that remains available to the public sector—not that it hap-

Dr. Donald Kagin as the oldest living pioneer. (© Kagin's Inc.)

pens very often. More of a once in a blue moon kind of thing. As such they often set record prices and have been a terrific investment.

At present, I don't have one for my personal collection, but several have passed through Kagin's coffers. Those clients, they report, are uniformly pleased with the ingots' ROI. Top-tier grades of Pioneer gold have performed extraordinarily well in recent years, fast becoming a favored area of interest for serious collectors with serious money at their disposal.

In lieu of a California branch mint, the 1850 compromise bill allowed for an official United States Assay Office, from which its coinage would be granted semi-official status—sanctioned by the federal government in every way short of the magic words, "legal tender."

California delegates were assured a branch mint was just around the corner and agreed to it. Augustus Humbert, a New York watchcase maker, was appointed chief assayer. Moffat & Co. received the contract and in a semi-official capacity issued an octagonal-shaped coin officially known as an ingot but what was and is commonly referred to as a "slug."

This is the granddaddy piece of the era—it's the coin the pops into everyone's mind at the mention of California gold. The spiral reverse resembled a pocket watch—people loved or hated it and no in-between. For me, it's a feature that sets it apart—love it or hate it, regardless—it's worth the extra money to obtain a quality piece with well-defined rims. Nice reeded-edge varieties with a Target reverse run about $100,000, while the 50 reverse in Uncirculated commands closer to $250,000.

There is so much demand for this iconic type of coin that I've rarely seen these slugs drop in value. They have been one of the best performers of all numismatic coins. Demand seems to constantly outstrip supply.

Humbert's United States Assay Office teamed with Moffat & Co., stacking the deck in their favor, and they eventually eliminated their competition, before they were put out of business with the advent of the San Francisco Mint in 1854, which took over their building space and equipment.

There are other notable short-lived California private mints—all of them, as a matter of fact. A prominent San Francisco judge and businessman operated Schultz & Company brass foundry. They made a $5 gold piece in 1851. On the reverse, Schultz is misspelled "Shultz," which no doubt explains why there wasn't an 1852 issue. Coins from the Pacific Company are thought to have been forged by hand, with a sledgehammer—more or less the same way blacksmiths have been doing it since the Iron Age some 3,000 years ago.

This $10 Baldwin 1850 gold coin displays the iconic vaquero or cowboy design (© Kagin's, Inc.)

Credibility was a concern for all private mints, but California ones in particular. Miners' Bank, Baldwin and Pacific Company, among others, were effectively put out of business by newspaper accusations of spurious coin values.

In order to instill confidence, most types present some version of Miss Liberty on the obverse. Moffat 1849 and 1850 $5 and $10 round coins reads MOFFAT & CO. on her coronet, which I've always thought was a cheeky gesture. Every time I think of it, I'm forced to suppress a chuckle. It's like watching news clip footage of half the Los Angeles Police department trailing O.J. Simpson's Bronco down the freeway. It never gets old.

My personal favorites are coins original design obverses, such as Baldwin & Co.'s Vaquero Horseman, Oregon Exchange Company's beaver and Colorado firm of Clark, Gruber & Co.'s Pike's Peak (on the reverse of their 1860 eagles and double eagles), which bears no resemblance whatsoever to its geographical namesake. I'm telling you, you can't make this stuff up!

I'm not alone with a bias toward Pioneer's with unusual engravings. They tend to be rare, but there is a premium to be paid on top of that. I would look for a time when the average spread between the private Liberty Heads and Pioneer's with unique motifs closes and use that as a buying opportunity.

Early Moffat $5 and $10 pieces are scarce but not rare and may be a good place to get started building a Pioneer gold collection. In today's market, the larger denomination coins are the sought-after pieces, and I'd expect them to continue to lead the way. Nevertheless, one area I definitely think offers Hidden Value opportunities is small-denomination California gold. As popularity for Pioneer gold continues to increase, look for a spillover effect to give prices a boost.

It's estimated there are only 35,000 small-denomination Pioneer specimens. Many varieties are obtainable in Uncirculated for about $1,000. The *Red Book* estimates approximately 570 varieties, but I believe there are now a few more. Either way, more than enough to keep busy for a while.

$10 1852 Moffat & Co. Moffat enjoyed an an excellent reputation among California gold rush coiners. (© Kagins, Inc.)

Kagin's is selectively active here, but mum's the word—that's just between you, me and the lamppost. Or, possibly, it's not that big of a secret. What I'm looking for is Pioneer pieces with good original luster and color A Morgan silver dollar went for $161,000 a few years back, and the toning of that rare high grade 1879 Washlady, I'd grant you, surely added to the hammer price. But with old U.S. gold coins, I want the color to be as close to the original as possible.

When I'm making an investment decision on a coin, this is the first question I want answered: Is it rare? I hope the buyer of the aforementioned 1879 Washlady is happy with his purchase, truly. But I can tell you this—I wouldn't have paid nearly that amount. It's not a fundamentally rare coin.

Pioneer gold, which is fundamentally rare, is less susceptible to that Morgan dollar flavor-of-the-month price volatility. This category of coins has had a fairly dependable, straight line 10% to 13% annualized return over the last decade.

The Bland-Allison Act of 1878 authorized the resumption of silver dollars, and here marks a significant demarcation for U.S. coins from a numismatic point of view. Coins before this time are typically rare in all grades, while coins afterward are usually rare only in top grades. There are exceptions—there are always exceptions!—but no question I lean toward specimens minted before 1879.

I'm immediately tempted to launch into an equally lengthy discourse on Pattern coins—experimental pieces with equally fascinating backstories—but I think this covers the gist of it. Hopefully, the chapter has broadened your understanding of how rare coins and collectibles are priced.

Chapter VIII

Assembling and Managing Your Numismatic Portfolio

Although the main objective here is to give you a solid foundation from which to improve your buying and selling habits, you'll notice I've emphasized the value of consulting a numismatic professional. They will help you avoid mistakes, but perhaps as crucially a wizened coin dealer will be able to point you in the right direction locating the specific numismatic pieces you're interested in.

Advanced collectors and sharp investors are not shy about asking for a second opinion. As long as the dealers' commissions, or "spreads" as they're called in the trade, are within industry standards or better, it is money well spent. Not only do I consult with my associates before a big sale, but we usually formulate a game plan of if-then scenarios. It's not always possible to cover every contingency, because I can think of plenty of exceptions in which we were forced to improvise our tactics, but generally speaking I'd discourage you from making decisions on the fly.

Once there's a handshake, it's a done deal—you own it. Consulting with a trained numismatist can assist you formulating a game plan so that the vast majority of the time, your results turn out for the better.

Of course, I understand there is an element of fun and excitement pursuing your own path. It's what prompted me to write this book. From my perspective, after a lifetime of owning some of the finest numismatic specimens known, the most memorable part of it has been the chase. In this chapter and the next, we'll discuss those things that separate the pros from everyone else.

If we've done our homework and are unafraid to call in an expert if and when need-be, we should be able to minimize the possibility of acquiring a poorly graded or overpriced coin. But before we get to that, let's examine the factors to consider when constructing and managing your numismatic portfolio.

Determining Your Goals

I figure it's a fair assumption that you already have an investment portfolio. If this is not the case, the presumption is that you will someday soon, and the advice in this book will still prove to be valuable. But, let me remind everybody, precious metals and numismatic investments are moderately speculative, that's there's no way of getting around that, and I'm not advising anyone to dip into the rent envelope.

I am not an expert on other sectors of the financial marketplace, but today's options appear limited. Bond rates for instance are about as close to zero as they can get, so for wealth protection, let alone asset appreciation, bonds don't seem the way to go. The stock market is at an all-time high. History is pretty clear on the subject. Buying at the high or near the high is not a sound strategy.

Nevertheless, without getting too bogged down commenting on areas outside of gold and rare coins, it is understood that your investment portfolio will not consist entirely of hard asset vehicles. How you go about dividing your portfolio is largely based upon your overall goals and convictions with the various sectors' risk/reward numbers and your personal tolerance for risk.

As you can imagine, I'm quite comfortable trading gold and rare coins. In fact, I'd probably rather trade gold from the short side in a bear market than speculate with shares of stock. But even I don't have all my eggs in one basket—not even the one basket I know really well.

Push comes to shove, I'd say you want to consider in the neighborhood of 10% to 15% of your money in precious metals and coins at the low end of the numismatic cycle (Stage One/Seven), and 5% to 10% at the high end (Stage Four/Five). A young person or someone with an aggressive nature may wish to bump those numbers up, say, upwards of 20% to 30%. A couple nearing retirement or someone who's conservative with their investment capital may go the other way and tone it down a notch.

We'll talk more about how to select a numismatic strategy that fits your temperament in a moment. But in the here and now, let me make it clear that your previous education regarding the risk levels associated with certain types of investments may be wrong. I'll say again, even bonds usually considered a "safe" investment seem destined for poor returns.

All right, so we know we're in the early stages of what appears to be the making of a gigantic bull market. And now you've determined how much of your portfolio you wish to devote to hard assets, or to what degree you wish to modify the numismatic portfolio you already have. OK, now what?

The first and most important piece of advice on the subject I can give you is this: Never fall in love. I'm proud of my personal collection, but not one of those pieces are on par with my wife or kids or even the dog. For my family, I'd walk over hot coals or bid to my last cent. Rare coins, on the other hand, come and go. I'm never desperate to own one specimen in particular no matter how cool and desirable it is.

Desperation breeds poor decision making. I never fall in love with an investment idea to the extent that I don't have a plan to get the heck out of it if I'm wrong. I'm not wrong often, but when it happens, I'm keen to cut my losses as soon as humanly possible. Dump the losers and hold onto the winners—that's the ticket.

We discourage it, but if you're looking for quick appreciation, speculating in bullion coins or common, lower grade pre-1933 U.S. gold coins may be the way to go. A moderate, more prudent time frame of three to five years targets appreciation and wealth preservation. Popular high grade 18th- 19th- and early 20th-century coins and currency are excellent examples of the type of material that hold their value, especially in times of economic uncertainty and higher inflation.

If you're looking for the highest possible rate of return on a relatively decent budget and you're willing to wait five or more years, purchasing proven rarities that are currently out of vogue is a good option. They include Colonial, Pattern and Pioneer coins, the latter of which includes privately-issued gold and the U.S. Assay Office gold issued during the California Gold Rush.

For those with the longest time frame and the ability to finance large purchases, as we've mentioned, Legacy coins have proven to be the best long-term performers. By now you're already familiar with 1804 silver dollars and Brasher Doubloons. Add to that an 1890 "Watermelon" $100 Treasury note, and the sort of specimens you'll see in books like *The 100 Greatest U.S. Coins* and *The 100 Greatest American Currency Notes* (Whitman Publishing).

This unique read seal 1890 $1000 grand watermelon treasury note is considered to be the most valuable U.S. banknote. (© Heritage Auctions, Inc.)

It's not quite as simplistic as to say buy the most expensive coin(s) you can afford. I'll give you an example: Say you have a million dollars to invest and you put it all into one magnificent piece. Just because most pieces in this category moved like gangbusters, it doesn't necessarily mean yours will be one of them. It all goes back to the not-all-your-eggs-in-one-basket theory.

How you break it down is dependent on several things. How confident are you with your eye for a winner? I know I wouldn't feel comfortable with less than a handful of properties. So say between a half dozen and a dozen coins is a good target range. If you're a collector who happens to enjoy series or multiple type-set collecting, you may own a few dozen specimens to complete a set. Though, of course, if I were your advisor, I may nudge you in the direction of limiting your scope and aiming for investment-quality coins and notes, but this is largely a battle of the investor in you versus the collector. How you balance the two is a personal preference as much as anything.

Coin collecting is a lot of fun, and if you have to compromise certain rigid investment smarts to satisfy your inner-coin collector, then I won't argue with that. Or, perhaps you want a coin that completes a set, but it doesn't come at the best price. These are the kind of decisions that you'll struggle with, like everybody, but as long as you keep your emotions in check you should be all right.

Also, I recommend that you keep something in the kitty. You never know when an extraordinary offer will come along, what I like to call "opportunity coins." No doubt, there are bargains to be had.

Stick around long enough and you'll come across someone who will be desperate to sell you a real beauty at a price you cannot believe. If he's a good friend maybe you pull him aside, but otherwise just try not to rip the guy's arm off with a handshake before he changes his mind. So for this contingency, I wouldn't be 100% invested.

As a corollary to this idea, there will inevitably be a buyer who comes along and offers you an exorbitant sum for a prized possession. For me, this is almost always an easy decision. When it comes to the sell side, my investor mentality usually trumps my collector, and I take the money and run. I've probably already got my eye on another piece—one that in another five or six years will hopefully break my heart and pad my bank account, just like this one did. For you, it's another judgment call, and how you decide one time may not be how it goes the next.

Cheat Sheets & Pricing Transparency

Once you've decided what type of coins or paper you wish to acquire, it's time to get familiar with current values and investigate pricing history. Current price guides are broken down into two main categories: retail and wholesale. Of the price guides we've mentioned, knowing full well prices are in flux, you may ask why bother with the once annual *Red* and *Blue Books*. Why not just go with some combination of PCGS. com, NGC.com or *Coin World* weekly magazine for, say, your retail guides? Pricing information, after all, has been gathered in a much more timely fashion. Auction sites like Heritage and Stack's Bowers post recent realized sales, so do we really need to get a *Red Book*?

It could be partially that I have a fondness for the *Red Book*—I don't think I've ever not had one. But what you'll notice is there are price discrepancies between the different publications. Sometimes pretty big discrepancies.

Remember, rare coins are not the same as interchangeable stock certificates. It could be that similar coins are changing hands at relatively wide margins, at the same coin show, an aisle apart and both end up being good deals for the buyers. Although I tend to want to be the guy on the aisle paying the lower amount, there's no telling if whatever accounted for the price differential becomes an even wider margin, months or years down the road, when it becomes time to sell.

What I'm driving at is these price guides provide more of a range, and sort of knowing what that range is, the *Red Book* is as good as any from which to give me a quick frame of reference. My eyes are trained to move across the page quickly. But it all depends. These days, I'm just as apt to log onto one of my grading-service accounts for a ballpark price, because that's really all it is, a ballpark number.

I don't know that it's necessary to consult with every price guide, but I certainly like to know what the range of prices are for each main category, both retail and wholesale. If I'm buying at the high end of the range, I better have a darn good reason. The coin better shine like the Sahara sun!

The next thing you might notice is that there's an awfully big discrepancy between *Red Book* and *Blue Book* prices. The wholesale price on mid-range priced coins are up to 50% cheaper on the identical coins—meaning both price guides are edited by the same people, Kenneth Bressett and Jeff Garrett.

"How do I get a dealer's license?" you might ask, perhaps kidding on the square. As it turns out, you don't need a license, and with so-called vest pocket dealers, it's something of a gray area, anyway. I don't know that you'll be able to pass yourself off as a dealer, though. It's a small community and we know whose brokering deals and who's buying for his coin club.

Be that as it may, it's not that easy of a question to answer. What you'll also notice is that the commission's gap begins to really close as you move up the scale. You and I very well may be at the same auction, competing for the same coin, but the gavel always falls on the top bid and it doesn't care about anyone's credentials.

Just about anyone can obtain an online subscription to the dealer's network on the Certified Coin Exchange. I know I don't like paying retail for a common-date Peace dollar. No reason why you should either.

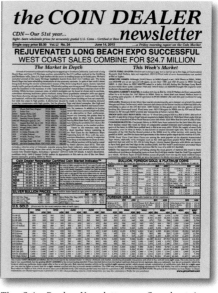

I'd also suggest you get a subscription to the *Greysheet*. (Or its companions, *Bluesheet* and *Greensheet*, if those are the markets you prefer.) The prices you see running across the CCE screen are numbers dealers post based on their regurgitation of *Greysheet* info. Practically every dealer in the country subscribes.

In truth, *Greysheet* prices are hardly top secret, but I'll tell you why it is particularly important. Although my firm tends to work with high-end pieces, it's the semi-numismatic prices that jump out at you each week. A very active segment of the market, and, better yet, prices are pegged pretty close to spot on. From that I'm able to gain a sense of that elusive ebb and flow of price movement that I was talking about earlier. Easier than, say, the rare numismatics that Kagin's typically brokers—ones that may only post a new price once a year or not at all.

The Coin Dealer Newsletter or Greysheet is a standard pricing guide. (© CDN, Inc.)

If I didn't have a sense of how the multitude at the bottom half of the numismatic triangle were shifting, it'd be rather difficult to gauge pricing for the top-tiered bunch.

If you're looking at a *Greysheet* now, and it still looks like a jumbled mess of numbers, you perhaps haven't narrowed your interests down well enough. If you've told yourself you're going to be looking at Mint State $20 St.-Gaudens, $10 Indian Heads and some particular key-date Morgan, gaining an expectation of the figures that will arrive next week will get easier. This is how you begin to hone your powers to anticipate relatively short-term price fluctuations.

Give yourself some time. Some of this is a matter of experience. If this is your first time up, let's say you'll pass the bid on Faberge eggs, but, by all means, roll up your sleeves and get in there! That's the way you're going to get experience.

You can also attend coin shows where many transactions occur among coin dealers as well as with collectors and dealers. I overheard a man explaining to his wife how the buying and selling process worked. He likened it to many forums where buyers and sellers haggle over a desired item. Your brain is already trained for price comparison shopping. You watch a few active coin markets and pretty soon you'll have your own sense of what's happening in the overall marketplace.

Now, when you're reading *Coin World* or *Numismatic News* articles or newsletters from your favorite numismatist prognosticator, you'll have a different take. You'll be an active participant in the discussion. It's the difference between walking into an anatomy class by mistake and being one of the students in the classroom taking notes.

Or, if you don't feel as if you've reached numismatic grad school yet, let's say pricing coins and banknotes isn't complete voodoo anymore. Hopefully. You're going to get there. But before we move on, there are a couple more pricing guides that deserve a mention.

I don't know about you, but I find the artwork on 19th-century U.S. banknotes much more fascinating than many types of coins. The neo-classical imagery is astounding in their detail. So, for currency, I find Track and Price to be a valuable Internet source to research auction records.

There is also a new interactive website for banknotes called *The National Bank Note Census*, and from what I can see, it's extremely comprehensive. The $100 membership fee is tax deductible, so that's nice, too.

The whole of this book goes to pricing, but the last thing I want to say on the subject of picking prices to jump into or out of a market with is to trust yourself a little bit. Go into negotiations with confidence. If you're the investor who's been nodding along, who gets it, you're going to do fine, I promise.

Auctions are an excellent avenue for obtaining the best specimens. The Kagin Americana Auctions, are one of the largest source in the industry for quality numismatic Western Americana and associated ephemera as well as offering U.S. coins and currency. (© Kagin's, Inc.)

Follow the Yellow Brick Road

You can obtain numismatic objects from a number of different sources, each with their pros and cons. I've had practical experience with each of them, and I don't know that I'd say I have a big preference for any one over another. Then again, I'm an old dog and I suppose I enjoy the intimacy of private sales and traditional in-person auctions. But I'll try to give you a sense of what each is like.

Often the best items are found at traditional auctions. Maybe that's another reason I like them. Although most museum-worthy pieces are sold certified by PCGS or NGC an item may go for $700,000, or it may go for $1.7 million. This is where the big boys play and it doesn't get better than this.

For the collector who's honed his coin grading skills, trusts his pricing method, and has a handle on the adrenaline meter, I say, bring it on! More the merrier. On the other hand, you may want to keep your hand down when it comes to items you are not totally prepared to bid on, because you can be sure that your competition is.

This is one reason why even accomplished collectors will bring in a sharpshooter for this kind of setting. It's likely the item has no price history whatsoever—none worth considering at least. It's complicated and rather difficult to gather price expectations close to the mark. But if you're ready for it, don't let me dissuade you from going it alone. Many of the most familiar faces are private collectors, and for the most part, they're formidable opponents.

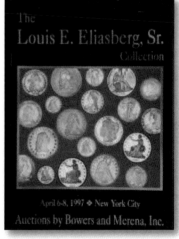

I'll add that I think it's nice a large percentage of Legacy items are still sold through traditional auction settings. I can't go over every nuance I might process, but being able to see the other main players gives you a certain vibe, like everyone is going to open their wallets tonight.

It could be you like how there's broad support under what looks to be an opportunity for you to capture the winning bid that presses you on. Or, it could be that you don't like how two bidders have run so far from the pack. The price is still within your range, but now you decide to withhold the bid. The room finds a way to give you a vibe.

One of the catalogs of the Louis Eliasberg collection — the only complete collection formed of U.S. coins (© Stack's Bowers, Inc.)

My dad was amazing in these situations. Sure, I know my way around numismatics, but my dad was a magician. One time he came into an auction room, rechecked the lot numbers we were interested in, took another look around the room and told us to up our maximum bid numbers by 15%. A pretty healthy jump for ole dad. We nabbed about 75% of what we were going for. Otherwise, without dad's re-appraisal, we'd have probably only gotten about 25% of the items we were after, maybe less. Those choice pieces from the Eliasberg collection have appreciated by such an outrageous amount, I'm almost embarrassed to say.

If you do decide to hire a professional, you have to make sure that you insist on a non-compete agreement. I know, it seems as if this should be obvious. If your dealer has an interest in a certain piece, and he discloses this upfront, and you have a lot of other pieces in which he intends to represent you with the high bid, and you're OK with it, then I don't see a problem for this situation. What I'm trying to say is that if a dealer is representing you, but instead of presenting the item at his cost plus a prede-termined commission, he keeps the item for himself and then turns around and offers it to you for your maximum bid? Well, in that case, I'd find myself another dealer.

But, as far as I know, there's no law against it. So go into an agreement with a clear understanding. At the major futures exchanges, the big commercials and trading houses run teams of floor brokers, some are buying and some are selling, in order to disguise what they're really doing. The only people that should be allowed to take a peek at your maximum bid sheet at an auction are people you trust.

The overwhelming majority of coins sold through these auctions are certified so we don't need to be grading experts to join the action. It could be you'll still want to hire a professional to assist you if, say, you wanted to develop your instincts with fun-damentally sound tactics. For the same reason I hired a golf pro when I took up the game. Hit from behind the ball to get out of sand traps, that sort of thing.

It could be an item you want that's going under the gavel at a private estate sale in Atlanta and you need somebody on an airplane, like, right now. Yes, then by all means, call your guy.

But otherwise, you've got all the tools you need. Auctions can get tense, but it's not exactly running with the bulls in Pamplona. Just about every professional numis-matist I know will happily give you a free hour tutorial, subject of your choice, if you offer to buy him lunch. Take advantage of that. Come with a plan and he'll buy you lunch.

The big change in the present era, of course, is the advent of the Internet. Now we have online auctions. In the early days, it really only made sense to trade com-mon coins in this fashion. The screen resolution wasn't very good. And at first only semi-numismatics traded this way—not exactly sight unseen but too close to make a difference, which is why no one would dare trade investment-grade or above in this manner.

I can't peg when it was precisely, but not too few years ago, screen resolutions improved to near television quality. Books like *Numismatic Photography* (Zyrus Press) gave everyone the know-how to take crisp, clear pictures. New computers and giant monitors and slick Internet providers are able to easily download large high-resolution images for our viewing pleasure. In some ways, it feels better than spying through my trusty Zeiss—it's that good. Not one of the coins I've won through Herit-age or Stack's Bowers online auctions have disappointed me upon receiving it.

For both the buyer and the seller, the online auction is a no fuss no muss solution. It very well may become the predominant venue for numismatics one day—but, to tell you the truth, on a day to day basis, what you tend to find here is a lot of junk. Coins that dealers were unable to sell through other channels.

I think of online auctions in the same way I think of shopping at Ross. No doubt they've got some bargains, but you have to rummage through 40 yards of tightly packed garments to find the one decent polo shirt. Excluding special event online auctions, ones in conjunction with live-setting participants, this is not the first place I'd think of to offer my clients' best coins, nor is it a place I'd expect to find those same pieces for sale.

All the same, I find myself scrolling through coins offered online slightly more often than our receptionist shops for shoes on Amazon.

Before I divulge where the best coins tend to be, let me address a segment of the online auction market I've avoided to this point. I fibbed earlier. Technically I have never bought or sold a coin through eBay. I know it's popular, I know several Kagin's associates have made eBay transactions—so I took credit by proxy. You've heard the stories: eBay is fraught with counterfeits and so forth. It seemed like a place where you have a bunch of dealers swapping the same Chinese Pandas back 'n forth in a weird zero-sum vacuum. I still have no idea how they make money.

But the more I looked into it, the more attractive this option has become. It brings everybody into the mix. If you're going to PayPal some guy in China you've never heard of, with a name you can't pronounce, $10,000 for a rare American coin, well sir, you probably deserve what you're going to get.

Do I really need to tell you that you don't have a long-lost $10 million bank account in Nigeria? Do I really need to tell you not to buy and sell rare coins through your local pawn shop?

Fifteen seconds of due diligence to make sure you're conducting business with a reputable dealer or collector is about all it takes. Google Earth will confirm brick-and-mortar stores, or pick up the phone and call the guy—it's that simple.

Since working with PNG members—and the Industry Counsel for Tangible Assets has our back, too—counterfeits and shaky sellers rarely become issues on eBay and Amazon internet sites.

Online auctions and website storefronts are a great way to meet people and get contacts. These are the dealers that are interested in the same type of items that you're interested in. Down the road, naturally, you'll be looking for a particular piece. Who do you think you might give a call? Yes, that's right, don't be shy about asking for business cards from your online trading partners. They know their clients' collections—coins that may one day end up being in your collection.

Indeed, I've become so enamored with eBay-style numismatic trading that when Kagin's secured the Saddle Ridge Hoard Treasure deal…that we went to Amazon with it. Not that eBay wasn't a good option, but offering scores of the same coin to hundreds of thousands of fresh buyers was the more compelling option.

As I put the finishing touches on this manuscript, by all accounts, Kagin's partnership with Amazon is going swimmingly well. Over half the coins were sold in the first week alone; two thirds by a month and a half. There have been no security issues. The coins are beautiful, customers are happy, and it looks to be a huge coup for us.

PCGS and NGC have made changes to their holders that make it very difficult to counterfeit a graded slab. If you're still concerned about counterfeits, you can buy books like *Numismatic Forgery* (Zyrus Press) to really know what to look for. For the most part, it's much ado about nothing.

The author auctioning the first Saddle Ridge Hoard Treasure coin—a $20 1874-S—for the benefit of the Old San Francisco Mint renovation project. (© Kagin's, Inc.)

If a reputable dealer, one like Kagin's, ever let a counterfeit slip past, they'd make good on it. It's a black eye for the industry, but, thankfully, the security measures in place are quite good, and fraud is far more the exception than the rule.

I've kept you in suspense long enough. So where do we find the best coins? Well, they're exactly where you'd expect them to be. If you're looking for Harry Winston jewellery, there's a good bet you'll find a store on Rodeo Drive or 5th Avenue. Unfortunately, the Harry Winstons of the numismatic trade don't often have brick-and-mortar establishments. How do we find them?

They're in the inventories of the dealers listed on those business cards you picked up at the auction. You can Google the name of the coin you're looking for and voilà you've got your contacts. Google is your friend. I know many with an interest in numismatics are woefully slow about joining the Internet revolution, and if that's the case, I don't know what to tell you. Go to more coin shows.

These days, coin dealers of all shapes and sizes use their websites to showcase their wares. Like every business does. Dealers purchase the coins they think their customers will want to buy. As resellers, dealers buy at one price, mark it up and hold it out for resale. Let's talk about that for a minute.

Say a coin you're interested in is listed on a dealer's website for $21,000. You've done your homework, you like the coin. You note on *Coin World Trends* and the CU (Collector's Universe) Price Guide that the retail range is a hefty $17,000 to $22,000. Probably means the price is in heavy flux, and you like that too. But you were really hoping to pick it up toward the low end of the range. In this case, you decide you're going to have to budge on price. You pick up the phone and make an offer for it at $19,500. That makes reasonable sense.

You have made what is called a counteroffer. The law says your counteroffer is good for a reasonable length of time—whatever that is—and it becomes null if the seller makes a counteroffer of his own. In the meantime, you leave yourself open to another buyer stepping in and meeting the seller's original price. There's no, "Oh, wait a minute, I would have paid $22,000!" If a buyer comes in at the seller's price, boom, it's a done deal, it's over. But as long as you're aware of that, I would feel perfectly comfortable haggling with a dealer over price.

Kagin's Collectors and Kagin's Advisors websites offer access to selected inventory, as well as a resource for market news and numismatic education. Many high-end dealers exhibit all or part of their inventory online, but due to the rarity and associated costs they usually require purchases to be done directly with one of the company's numismatic experts. (© Kagin's, Inc.)

Which is the perfect segue to talk about coin shows. This is where you get to see everybody's tent pitched. I love coin shows because this is the heart and soul of the business. I could easily send associates, but I still go to a lot of coin shows. It's not impossible to imagine a successful numismatic trader doing it all from the comfort of his office chair, but that's not me. I love everything about them.

I should hasten to mention that as a dealer my company has particularly strong motivation to attend, especially the bigger shows, like Long Beach, FUN and the ANA shows. If you've ever walked through one of the large shows, what you'll notice is that there is a good number of unattended stalls. You know they paid a handsome price for the space, so where are they?

Probably on an airplane home. Before the big shows open, they'll have a day for the dealers to set up. This is when most of the money exchanging hands at a coin show takes place. Dealers buying and selling amongst themselves, adjusting their inventories. I have a client that I know would love a certain piece—so I buy it, add Kagin's few percent and present it to him.

Most of the high-end dealers don't expect to conclude big money deals on the spot. I don't see too many public patrons carrying attaché cases full of money, and I'm not too keen to transport a multi-million dollar inventory around the country. Still, a significant amount of our business originates out of the people I've met from coin shows, so I hang around. At your next one, please feel free to stop by Kagin's and say hello.

But, for a lot of my brethren, they wrap up their dealer-to-dealer business and they're gone.

Coins shows are terrific places to hone your grading skills. In my early days, I'd spend hours upon hours combing through dealers' inventories. My dad was a big shot, so even as a poor teenager the other dealers would put up with me. Pretty soon, not only did I develop a sharp eye for nailing the Sheldon scale, but later, following the advent of PCGS and NGC, I'd scour the bins for poorly graded slabs and have them regraded. Not that I do it very often anymore, but, as I recall, I had a pretty good batting average, especially for those coins in my area of expertise.

If you put in the time, you could learn the skill, too. You look at enough coins, you'll begin to see the nuances that separate the grades. I don't find it to be a skill that I rely on quite as much as I once did—as I say, PCGS and NGC have our backs on this— and my numismatists, David McCarthy and Meredith Hilton, have younger and better eyes than I do. Still, it's there when I need it. Either way, accomplished grader or neophyte, or anywhere in-between, I highly recommend that you attend. If coin shows do for you half as much as they've done for me, they'll be well worth your time and effort.

Continuing Education

For those investors who wish to learn more about the industry there are many resources. Some of them are:

- The American Numismatic Association is a congressionally chartered, non-profit educational organization and is the largest coin club in the world with about 28,000 members. Its overarching mission is to educate anyone wishing to learn about the various aspects of numismatics. The ANA hosts several seminars, shows, exhibits and publications to further their efforts. Money.org

- The American Numismatic Society is another educational association which advances numismatic scholarship, especially in ancient, foreign and early American specimens. Numismatics.org

- The University of Rare Coins provides online curriculum with a comprehensive study of numismatic topics, including several devoted to vocational training. Through special arrangement with the author—that's me, Don Kagin—you can access some of these courses for free by going online. UniversityRareCoins.com

- The Professional Numismatist Guild is the largest and most prestigious association of professional numismatists. In conjunction with the University of Rare Coins, they offer a fully funded internship program for aspiring professional numismatists. PNGdealers.com

Additionally, there are many coin clubs throughout the United States and abroad. There are specialized coin clubs, such as the Society of Private and Pioneer Numismatists, the Society of Paper Money Collectors, and the Liberty Seated Collectors Club. For a complete list of clubs and associations, please contact the ANA at Money.org.

Numismatic investors may wish to follow specialized newsletters in the field. Two of the better ones I have followed are:

- *Rosen Numismatic Advisory*—Maurice Rosen, editor
- *The Forecaster*—John V. Kamin, editor

Chapter IX

Liquidating Your Portfolio

A quick glance to my resume of extracurricular activities betrays my devotion to the industry. Still, I'd have to admit, as a whole, the numismatic profession has had a bad case of myopia.

You wouldn't have to tell a stock or bond trader the buy side is only half the equation. Exiting a position is every bit as important as getting in. Unfortunately, it's an element of investing the average dealer isn't used to giving much thought to other than putting out a WE BUY COINS sign at coin shows.

To be fair, it was the nature of the business. The Hobby of Kings was an upper crust, gentlemen's endeavour. They assembled their collections with love and care and no real desire or expectation to sell. If their coins appreciated in value, terrific, but otherwise, they still owned a magnificent slice of art and history.

Indeed, most of the best pieces in numismatics still find their way back into the public domain through estate sales, or other ways in which notable, significant collections, for various reasons, are liquidated in one fell swoop. For many, collecting is simply a passion.

If your numismatic education follows a path anywhere similar to my own, there will be a pink cloud moment. Every coin you look at will present its beauty in full force. For me it was in my first year of post-graduate numismatic studies.

Until that time, Dad had nurtured my interest. He'd basically given me free reign to buy and sell coins on Kagin's behalf, albeit lower grade, lower priced ones, and had even given me a sort of allowance to begin my own collection. I still have the first coin I bought with that money; I was nine years old. A 1909 V.D.B. cent (no, there was no S mintmark—that came many years later along with another story for another book).

Then there were the 1936 to 1942 proof sets. Bought those with my bar mitzvah money in the late 1960s. They were beautiful and the dealer told me how they would only go up in value. I wanted to impress my father with how I was such an astute buyer. Little did I know, proof sets in a game of Hearts are a handful of spades without the Queen of Spades to rescue the trick.

It took about six months of watching prices sink that it dawned on me prices were never coming back. My investment had dropped significantly.

This part I remember clear as day, like it was yesterday.

It felt as if Dad had grabbed me by the scruff of the neck, slapped my cheek and threw a bucket of cold water in my face. He said, "Son, we're in the collector-investment business. We're not here for wild speculation. We're not here to gamble—none of that.

"Numismatics is emblematic of world history—yes, very fascinating, and that's all well and good. At Kagin's, however, we're in the business of making money. Not all pretty coins are destined for significant price appreciation. We're in the business of finding coins with hidden value. We're in the business of picking winners. Everything else, Donnie m'boy...everything else is window dressing."

The coins in company inventory may stay there for weeks or months at a time. Commissions on trades put money into company coffers, yes, but if the choice of rarities we elect to purchase for our inventory are losers—decline in value before they're sold—Kagin's would have been out of business a long time ago.

There are only a handful of companies of our size and scope. Kagin's success is a tribute to my father's vision and acumen, and I remain cognizant of that fact. Company transactions revolve around two things: providing clients with exceptional service and offering numismatic objets de vertu with tremendous appreciation potential.

Coins with hidden value, coins destined for higher ground will perform for our clients or will perform while idle in our inventory. Either way is good for us. (Any other way is not good for us.)

It is not enough to consider at what wonderful lofty numbers we'd be willing to take profit on our individual properties. Our exit strategy ought to cover each of three basic possibilities: what to do if we're right, what to do if we're wrong, and how long we're willing to sit and watch it do nothing before we call it quits.

Of course, Kagin's clientele includes those old-school collectors. Funny, nobody seems to mind the part in which we make every effort to buy low! But, yes, these old-school fellas usually have no real intention of ever selling. That's OK, too. Who wouldn't want to leave their progeny a lot of money? So, we'll look at passing your collection on to your heirs in two chapters still ahead.

Most people, I expect, will have a foot in each camp. There are coins in my personal collection, like that Lincoln cent, like certain sentimental Pioneer pieces, like the superstar Saddle Ridge specimen I picked out before they went to market—those are coins I'll never part with. But for the majority of them, let's say more of an investment vehicle. Let's say more like Dad's No.1 objective—picking winners and cashing in!—is applicable HERE.

Ways & Means

Although the individual coins that make up the market basically move in tandem, coins are just like stocks in the sense that on a daily basis some are moving up and some are moving down. In earlier chapters, we mentioned the various transaction platforms without going into too much detail pro versus con. It makes sense to tackle it from the seller's point of view, too.

As a buyer you don't have any control over the matter. Say, a coin you want is being sold through a dealer's consignment, private sale, public auction or wherever. Guess where you have to go to get it?

Sure, coins are brought back into public trading venues at the pleasure of the seller.

For clients with top-tier coins to sell and not in a big rush to receive payment, which could be up to six months, I lean toward putting it into a well-publicized auction. An open forum environment brings together dozens possibly thousands of active participants vying for each item. It is typically in an auction environment where we see record sales get posted.

At a minimum, you won't wake up the next morning with that agonizing feeling you may have sold too easily.

One instance in which I wouldn't want to take a Legacy coin to auction is in the midst of a big bear market slide. Auction prices, which represent a broad public sampling, often lead the way up. But, surely, auction prices lead the way down.

In such a bear environment, I'd rather take my chances brokering a private transaction rather than not meeting a reserve or some other huge disappointment. I wouldn't want my client to be the first to find out the market's taken another 5% hit. Conversely, as a buyer, when prices are in the midst of a short-term slide, this is exactly when I prefer auctions to the other options.

Since most pieces go into an auction without reserves, what you tend to find is that there are some real bargains, a few sales that will bring a raised eyebrow, but for the most part, coins trade hands at prices you pretty much had expected.

Those fancy auction catalogs, which go out to thousands of prospective buyers, don't come cheaply. Commissions the auction houses charge, factoring in dealer fees, is on the expensive side. Which is another reason why auctions are not a happy place to find out your coin isn't worth what you thought it was.

Auction houses disguise their fees to the buyer by charging the bulk to the consignment seller—but we can do the math. In recent times, there's been a move to assign fees on a more judicious basis, but this is mostly a feel-good gesture as the total commission payouts on auction transactions remains about the same. Six one way, half dozen the other.

As a seller, you're looking at zero to 10%, and on the other side, you're looking at a 15% to 20% buyer's fee—but, as I say, it really doesn't matter how the fees are split from your perspective. If the hammer price on one of your coins drops at $10,000, you'll receive around $8,000, maybe a little more, and then it will take some time for the administrator, up to 45 days, to cut you a check. Strictly speaking, how the $2,000 in commissions is divvied up is immaterial to both the buyer and seller, you see.

Using a dealer for an auction sale isn't necessarily more expensive than going direct. Kagin's, as it happens, has agreements in place with the major auction houses at favorable rates since we do so much business with them. Our fees are nearly absorbed by the savings. It is a courtesy Kagin's provides dealers when bringing their wares to one of our auctions. Which, to be honest, isn't so much a feather in our cap, as it is standard-operating-procedure in the industry.

The spotlight on big auctions shines the brightest on the best pieces, which may have all come from one notable collector, or originate from the same period in history, such that the event takes on a sort of theme. Say, an Ancients & Roman auction, for instance.

Ideally, if you're a seller, you want your property to fit under that themed umbrella. An auction that highlights Ancient and Roman coins in its marketing literature and so forth will naturally bring out buyers who are interested in those categories.

On the flip side, auction houses don't discriminate, and there could very well be an oddball Pioneer gold piece lost among all those generic U.S. gold coins. This is when an otherwise beautiful specimen might slip through the cracks, and, if it does, you'll want to be there. Pick it up for a song, that's the ticket.

In public auctions, coin lots are made available for viewing a day or two in advance of the auction. Major houses are in the habit of making their entire catalog, with vivid photographs, available online a few weeks before the action starts.

At a predetermined, well-publicized time the bidding begins. The auctioneer might kick off the festivities 5% above the second-highest mail bid.

The one thing I want to say about mail bids is that people are predisposed to be non-aggressive with them. If a coin you're watching goes to a low-range mail bid, uhm, let's say, it's usually not a good sign.

Unless you're hoping that coin price is going to fall further—in which case, it's a terrific sign. Few months down the road, perhaps at the next big auction, with otherwise bullish long-term prospects in place, if another one comes along, a price dip like this may be a good time to throw out a lowball offer of your own.

In a live setting, you lift your hand or a numbered paddle to bid. Auctioneers tend to advance the action in 5% increments. Their 90-mile-an-hour cadence reflects the speeds at which auctions move. Price for an item may go from $200 to $1,000 in 15 seconds; over 200 lot numbers can sweep past in an hour—so, you've really got to be on your toes.

Don't worry about making the sort of gaff that you might see on a TV sitcom. Scratching your nose at an auction will not result in an accidental purchase, I can assure you. By the same token, don't expect an auctioneer to recognize that tugging on your earlobe is an indication to bid.

Nobody enjoys that sort of ambiguity—you've got yourself confused with a James Bond villain. Make your signals clear and concise, just as outlined in the auction house's Procedures & Guidelines manual.

Auction Is Not Always The Answer

A couple of chapters back, I mentioned some of the things I look for in the faces of auction competitors—saving one of the better ones for now. Dealers purchase with the mindset they'll be able to add their few percent and then resell it to their usual clientele.

For the night following the drama of a hotly contested auction piece, it ought to ease your mind considerably if you've won the lot against an industry professional who calculated the retail price to be 5% or 10% above his final bid.

No one bull-bear indicator we've talked about is infallible. When you analyze any random investment vehicle what you'll find is a mixed bag of signals. It's when you determine that you have a preponderance of evidence, one way or the other, that you ought to be prepared to act.

Holabird-Kagin Americana live auction. (© Kagin's, Inc.)

If I have you convinced that auctions are the way to go, perhaps I've oversold the argument. For most pieces, most of the time—most people prefer the expediency of dealer transactions. When I tell clients they may have to wait five or six months to get their money, they'll give me a quizzical look, as if I misunderstood the question. What, we're not talking about selling the house!

A firm like Kagin's will advance up to 50% of a conservative estimate for auction items, but in the fine print, it reads like a loan. Persons looking to sell usually hope to be putting cash in their pocket today. OK, tomorrow. Maybe a couple of weeks from now the very latest.

Definitely not six months.

With a dealer there are two basic options. Of those, both consignment and immediate cash sales entail more or less what you'd expect. However, there are a few matters worth highlighting.

The ask on a consignment is a mutually agreed upon price. While it is in everybody's interest to get as much for the coin as possible—commissions typically run in 5% to 10% range—the dealer will lean toward lowering it to a competitive offer. Every business's shelf space is valuable. It's a reasonable enough thing to do, true.

It's also an area of potential conflict of interest. Be on your guard, perhaps standing firm with your original, higher estimate.

It's hard to say how long you might expect to wait for a consignment piece to sell. A lot depends on what the dealer feels comfortable as a turnover rate, and how aggressive you wish to be from your side. Just to throw out a frame of reference, I think you'd hope for a sale within six to eight weeks after hanging a price tag on it.

For instance, that $21,000 coin from the other chapter, only now the roles are reversed, and you're the seller—if it had been sitting for four months, and we got an offer for it at $19,500, I might advise you to take it. Whether I advise taking the money or not, I'd bring you the proposal, and it would be your decision.

Although there may be some line-item in the consignment agreement, it is basically an at-will arrangement and either party can bow out of it whenever they like.

Though I've painted this scenario as rife with potential trouble spots, the reality of it is that most dealers are in fact trustworthy, and they're smart enough to know where their bread gets buttered. A good dealer is looking out for his client first and foremost. They rely on referrals and repeat business, naturally. It would be awfully shortsighted if an advisor burned a valuable client for a quick, instant commission.

In any event, we are not usually programmed to think of short-term anything. For my money, a consignment sale is your best option if you're OK to wait two or three months to collect on the proceeds. If you're willing to get somewhat more aggressive with price, the item may sell in half the time—could be a few days or a fortnight—so a consignment could go off much quicker than I had previously outlined. Hard to tell, sometimes.

One thing dealers don't like to do with consignments is keep bumping the price down. It casts a shadow of desperation, scaring off potential buyers instead of enticing them. I'm not saying you can't adjust your price periodically, but better to be thoughtful about it from the get-go.

Somebody's liable to think your coin dealer also sells Lady Diana dinner-plate commemoratives.

A Little Help from My Friends

For all the nifty ways we look to buy and sell, one method remains dominate. Numismatics has always been and, I suppose, always will be cash and carry. For the most part, numismatic investing means: Cash on the barrelhead transactions strongly preferred.

Americans invented the Mexican flea market. Of course, this is how we do it.

We've already talked about how to negotiate with a dealer in an adversarial position, but there are a few things I'd like to add. First and foremost, it need not be adversarial at all negotiating various agreements. It could be he's a trusted advisor, with a history of offering you good numbers for the pieces you've brought to him in the past. It may not be necessary to hunt too much for outside quotes.

Of course, I'm the type who likes a second opinion. Trusting your guy is one thing, but let's keep in mind that pricing numismatics is a subjective art. It is unlikely any one dealer would come in with the top bid or low offer across the board for your coins.

Here's a couple more things you should know. You're not likely to realize *Red Book* prices for items you've brought to your dealer. You know that, though—this shouldn't come as a shock.

Dealers don't have an unlimited sense of humor when it comes to a client shopping them around. If you're going to call four dealers every time you go to sell one of your coins, I'd know my chances are slim. Who's got time for that? This is one of those times in which, as a dealer, I might invoke the legalese reasonable-length-of-time clause. Withdraw my bid.

You've upset me. I've probably made a mental note to avoid doing business with you in the future. I can't speak for you, of course, but I don't suppose you'd want to lose a valuable dealer contact, like myself, in this way. It's not worth it. So, to a degree, you're better off sticking with a couple-few of your favorite dealers.

If you're talking to the right dealers, quotes from two or three of them should suffice. It will get you pretty close to the top bid you would have had not bothering the other 37 guys and gals on your list. We'd appreciate it.

That way you won't bring the entire numismatic and collectibles industry to a grinding halt. And, you won't have to spend the next four days sifting through your email inbox comparing proposals and typing out laborious clarifications to all those dealers who were never going to buy, regardless.

A win-win for everybody.

All the Marbles

To this point, we have not discussed how to juggle the various coins and banknotes in your numismatic portfolio. Now would be a good time for it.

In the chapter that covered numismatic cycles, we mentioned the idea of scaling into a full position—hopefully, near the end of Stage Seven slash the beginning of Stage One. To continue the discussion on managing your inventory, it again makes sense to do it in conjunction with cycles.

Buy low, sell high. Sounds great, how do we do that? Nobody's crystal ball is that picture perfect clear. It's a game of probabilities, and we manage our risk/reward with that in mind. The reality of finding cycle lows and highs is that it's a hit and miss affair, which is why we use a method closely related to the schema of Las Vegas blackjack card-counters.

What those blackjack players do is keep a simple low-high tally of cards left in the deck. When there are more face cards, the player has the advantage. This is when they pad their bets. When there are more numbered cards in the deck, a disadvantage. This is when they lighten their bets.

We don't know our placement in the numismatic cycle precisely. It may be many years from now when we can pinpoint precisely where we are on our theoretical price-movement map. The good news is that we can say with a much higher degree of probably if we're in the approximate vicinity of a low. This is when we pad our bets.

The approximate vicinity of a low. This is when we go small.

The reason I've kept this subject for the chapter on liquidation is because, for most people, it's a more difficult proposition from the sell side.

If you knew the precise day the market was to hit a low, you'd still have difficulty assembling a full numismatic position simply because the sort of pieces you'd wish to collect won't be available at reasonable prices on this precise day.

It'd be difficult not to scale into your buy side. But, as we know, it's no trick at all to sell our portfolio in a single shot, and the freedom that comes with a winning position makes getting out all the more an open-ended proposition. Then, of course, life has a habit of throwing us curve balls. It could be that we're in a temporary pinch, and we can't wait until the top of the cycle to cash out—we need to look for a price spike in. Or, conversely, we receive a cash windfall in the middle of the bull cycle, and we'll want to use a stage dip to bring our numismatic percentages up to snuff.

The kinds of coins you'll prefer trading in the mid-stages are semi-numismatics up to investment-grade. You'll want to avoid actively trying to manage Legacy coins, period. The air is thinner up there—it could take months to find a suitable buyer for a truly exquisite piece.

If you need to liquidate a portion of your portfolio prematurely, it's better to see if you can tide over your cash flow situation with semi-numismatics. Perhaps investment-grade pieces in the $20,000 range and below. Kagin's account executives advise clients to have a portion of their portfolio in semi-numismatics for precisely this possibility.

At the top of the cycle, when you're aiming to liquidate the bulk of your investment numismatics, it's more a pedestrian affair—if not hampered too badly by the increased price volatility usually present at this stage. You'll want to plan ahead to schedule an approximate date of liquidation for higher-end pieces, and stick with that approximate time and date come hell or high water.

The sale of a short-lived Legacy property will bring out the sharks. They'll know you're desperate.

In the final stage of a bull market, the pattern of sales we want to make ideally will cast a net over the whole price-peak timeframe.

With this in mind, it is not terribly troubling if in hindsight I'm able to look back and see the last two or three pieces of a liquidated collection were not sold until the early stage of sliding into the new bear market. The better you are with your long-term forecasting, the smaller the net you'll need to capture the peak.

One of the ways in which you can do this is by using a "trailing stop" method. Numismatics, of course, does not have the kind of transaction orders found on stock exchanges. But we can still borrow the tactic. Stock and futures traders try to squeeze everything they can out of a winning long position by employing a trailing stop.

A sell stop in the financials is when price comes back down through a threshold. Then it becomes a market order and executed at the best available price. What the stock boys will do is tighten a trailing stop as the price move closer to their pie-in-the-sky number.

You can't hand your coin advisor an order like that, though, perhaps with his assistance, you can monitor prices in the same mindset. If a coin reaches your dream profit margin, or slides back down through a certain threshold—say, by monitoring *Greysheet* or *Coin World* quotes—you'll execute your plan to liquidate.

If you don't capture the high in the market, chances are you got pretty close.

Great Expectations

One of the hardest things for any of us to do is to be patient. Whether we're sitting in the same spot for long periods on a trip, or waiting for our numismatic property to appreciate with enough profit margin to justify the risk.

At a minimum, even for fast-moving sectors of the coin market, I think you're looking at a three-year commitment—and that's if you nail a pretty decent sized move over that timeframe.

Most of my ideal winning coin trades take place over five-to-seven year period. Not coincidentally, about the length of time a coin-cycle bull market.

Getting out of a winning coin trade is one of those hardships none of your friends will want to hear about.

On the downside, I certainly would not want to be caught watching an investment property to drop by half. It's hard to put an exact number on how far I'd let a bad idea play out, because I'm generally inclined to give things a fair measure of latitude and I'm usually right. Still, I know I'd be awfully nervous if a coin had lost 30% of its value.

If it comes down to it, be prepared to bite the bullet. It bears repeating: Dump the losers and hold on to the winners—the same as any savvy stock or futures trader will tell you.

The new concept we introduce is the notion of a time stop. I was originally thinking of the poor souls who bought silver bullion in the late 1980s with the entirely reasonable presumption that $5 an ounce was cheap.

Didn't move, however, for almost 20 years. It's only now, another 10 years down the line, that silver has paid its big dividends. That's no good. We want to keep our money in the areas posting the most positive results. Be the guy who was buying silver in the late '90s.

In more practical terms, the reason you might wish to get out of a coin property after only, say, three years is because it has underperformed relative to the other coins in your portfolio. You think that investment capital is best utilized in some other area. If you use a time stop in this fashion, however, I think you'd want to be confident this other coin group was in the midst of a healthy upswing—no sense moving your money, racking up commission charges. Not for just a different sideways market.

Easy Street

Most people have difficulty with the patience required in order to sell at the last possible moment before the tide turns. For me, following divesting from company and personal portfolios, looking to get back in two, three, four years on is when the waiting becomes difficult.

Surviving a bear market is tough enough without the agony of monitoring dismal price action day after day. I'm dying to get back in there! As the Kagin's company principal trader, when I preside over an unusually small inventory, it cuts into my pride. It appears as if the cupboards are bare.

I know a fellow who's a New York Stock Exchange specialist. Now, a specialist is like a guy who gets to walk around and look at everybody's cards during a poker tournament—the one thing that really bugs me about the NYSE—but even stacked-deck specialists have their bad days. What this guy would do is splash cold water on his face, then treat himself to the most expensive steak dinner in Manhattan.

I was with him on one such occasion. After a couple glasses of wine, a grotesque amount of fine foods, a liberal dose of good conversation this guy's shaken demeanor began to turn strong again. It was no time at all till he was back to his usual obnoxious, self-entitled self again. Family, what're y'gonna do!

Point is, I use a similar tactic to assuage grief. When I'm feeling as empty as Kagin's coffers, I turn my attention to other collectible areas that interest me. It was during one of these occasions I had the bright idea to expand Kagin's into those areas. Over the years, I've been fortunate to see many spectacular Americana coins, antiques and miscellaneous collectibles pass through.

Numismatics is my first love, but I've got room in my life for more than just pretty coins. I aim to make the most of it. Hope you do the same.

I don't know what your patience trick will be. You may have to tie a string around your finger. You may have the discipline to mark key dates on your calendar, set an alarm clock and forget about it. I don't know what yours will be, but it'll probably have to be something. Maybe it's waterskiing, who knows?

Long-term investing inevitably comes with long periods of inactivity—both, invested or on the sidelines. Maybe you don't need any trick at all to manage the times when your patience is stretched thin. Maybe. Kind of doubt it.

For those times, what I'd like to do is remind you of your game plan.

You have a game plan!

The market can't fool you anymore. If you've had a bad day, a bad trade, a bad 2017 this too shall pass and the law of averages will see you through to Easy Street. Or, at least to that same neighborhood. Which, all things considered, isn't a bad place to be.

INVESTOR MAKES GOOD DURING HARD TIMES

With millions invested in a diversified portfolio, an investor purchased almost $2 million in rare coins over the span of three years, starting in 2005 through mid 2008. Feeling the burn of the September 2008 financial markets crash, this investor was caught short of cash. Needless to say his various financial obligations didn't disappear along with his revenue stream: He had less than two weeks to raise the funds needed to meet those obligations, amounting to an additional $500k. Since most of his portfolio could not easily be sold and/or would represent substantial losses (60% or more) if liquidated, our investor turned to his rare coin portfolio, which was the only asset in position to provide the liquidity he needed. He contacted his numismatic investment advisor with the following email: *" I am in a jam with this market fluctuating so wildly. I need to raise an additional $500k quickly. I hate to do this but help me Obi Wan Kenobi...you are my only hope..."* In response, the advisor wired him $500k well in advance of the two week deadline. How did he do it? Although this collection contained several excellent rarities that had increased in value, inevitably, there were a few underperformers. The advisor strategized the liquidation by packaging some of the better performing pieces with those which had not financially matured, minimizing loss to approximately 9%. As a result the investor was able to acquire $500k and meet his obligations with minimal sacrifice to his portfolio.

Kagin Newsletter relating actual financial emergency transaction we conducted in 2008. (© Kagin's, Inc.)

Chapter X

Choosing the Right Investment Advisor

As I've alluded, Kagin's, Inc. was founded by my father, Art Kagin. Way back in 1933. Prior to that, he was selling *Colliers* magazine subscriptions door to door. A customer paid him with an 1883 "no cents" nickel and kindly pointed out the Mint's error. He was hooked instantly.

A short time later, he started the family business.

You could say I have numismatics in my blood. I grew up with it. Between my dad, the associates around the office, and my own burgeoning interest that began at an early age, it would be easy for me to take for granted the knowledge I've acquired along the way.

My experience with trading gold is not quite so inbred. There's a connection between gold and numismatics, naturally, but, frankly, the inelasticity of high-end coins to its underlying bullion make it two distinct trading vehicles.

As a company, Kagin's does much more with semi-numismatics and bullion than we used to, but our primary line of business is still with the high-end properties. My education on gold trading, I suppose, came about the same as you, the same as anybody. I bought a few books on the subject.

During his life and now posthumously, A.M. "Art" Kagin, is one of the most revered numismatists of all time. Dubbed the "Dean of Numismatics," Art's reputation and longevity in the industry is unsurpassed. He devoted 70 years to numismatics. (© Kagin's, Inc.)

Whereas I don't have to travel too far to be updated with the inside scoop on numismatics, the large precious metals trading houses are in London, New York and

Los Angeles. We prefer San Francisco, but I'll save the civic pride speech for another occasion and cut to the chase. Kagin's now does a fair amount of business with those trading houses.

We buy in scale, so we can present it to our clients at the best prices, but back to my point. Through those business relationships, I've cultivated invaluable personal relationships with a few double-sharp gold traders.

It's in conjunction with their council, bouncing my thoughts off them and vice-versa, my perception of the investment environment gets shaped and funnelled into my decision-making process of buy, hold or sell.

They're pretty sharp, maybe I think I'm pretty sharp, and when we're all in agree-ment—sometimes when I'm happy with a majority vote—and I pull the trigger, it's been my good fortune to have an enviable track record to show for it.

It may be arrogant, but my thought is this: I know how much I rely on expert advice...it might not be such a bad idea for you, too.

As I say, you're perfectly free to go it solo. You have the good fortune of having leafed through this book—I'd say your chances are better than average!

I've already mentioned how I regularly arrange pow wows with company associ-ates and partners, but the reason I mention my friends in the bullion trade is because in hindsight I now see how valuable it is to have the inside scoop on how big player, member firms operate.

It's given me an added advantage for knowing bullion prices, which goes into how I prioritize and collate elements of the big picture. Which, in turn, is how I narrow it down to individual offers to buy or sell those small but extraordinary historical objects.

Watching a parade of pundits chatter on the financial news channel is nothing at all like having a confidant's ear and advice you can take to the bank.

In a sense, this chapter is especially for someone who intends on going it alone. Dealers are the people you'll be working with whether you employ them as advisors or not. They hold the inventory of the coins you'll want to buy, and this is where you'll come when you want to sell an item.

I mean, I guess you could do everything through auctions, and then forgo using a dealer—but you're still paying the vig to an auction house and you better know how to grade. Unfortunately, there's no way of getting around paying somebody's commis-sion. Kagin's can't get around it and you can't either.

Regardless, you should know what dealers do.

There are duties a numismatic advisor performs on behalf of his clients that I've glossed over. If you intend on flying solo, perhaps it's only minor administrative things, but, nevertheless, you should know what they are—especially since you'll be performing those tasks, now.

Besides the obvious, there is perhaps one other reason I'd like to lobby on behalf of the numismatic community. Also in my self-interest, as luck would have it.

Although I have my circle of pros in the business that I work with and rely on, I actually get a surprising amount of good ideas from my clients. I am sometimes astounded by the creativity they've shown, and, for this reason, too, I wish you would consider the idea. But, yes, sure, you can go it alone.

This is not most people. Most people develop relationships, not unlike my own. The natural place to begin the discussion in earnest then is how to pick one. I don't think it's enough to say "reputation" alone, because the natural leap from there is "track record."

I was introduced to the chief trader of a big precious metals house—I think he flies into work every morning, literally—but I just couldn't establish a rapport with the guy. He very well may be a genius, but every time I spoke with him, he sounded drunk. Helicopter taxi service, indeed! Complete gibberish.

A good track record is important, obviously, but let's backup a step first.

Report Cards

A good place to begin your hunt for a numismatic partner, or partners, is by contacting the American Numismatic Association. The ANA, located in Colorado Springs, can give you a list of member dealers in your area.

Knowledge. Integrity. Responsibility.

Not that being in the same proximity is necessarily an overriding factor—much of my inner-circle call home well outside the 415-area code. But, for most people, I think having an advisor you can meet in person is a good thing, someone who goes to the same coin shows you do.

At the very least, your advisor should have a membership with the ANA. They should probably be members of PCGS and NGC. I don't know that it's necessary to be a member of the more prestigious Professional Numismatic Guild—I do business with non-PNG members all the time. But besides being in business for a long time and having strong financial resources, all PNG members subject themselves to

The Professional Numismatists Guild is a non-profit organization composed of the world's top rare coin, paper money and precious metals dealers and experts. Web address www.pngdealers.com is your go-to source for finding reputable, expert numismatic dealers. PNG members must follow a strict code of ethics when conducting business. (Photo courtesy PNG. © All rights reserved.)

compulsory arbitration for any credible complaints against them. In other words, one always has recourse when dealing with a PNG dealer.

It's not so bad if you're working with a newbie dealer from an adversarial position. Newbies tend to overprice or underprice their wares, which theoretically means you'll get a bargain half the time.

In practice, it doesn't go down that way too often. Dealer firms of note don't let new associates price the best pieces in their inventories.

This newbie may well turn out to be a fine numismatist and financial advisor one day, but better to let him learn the ropes on someone else's dime.

We're not talking about the dealer across the table. In your advisor's role, we want the fellow with a few trophies on his shelf. I say it's not imperitive to be a member of PNG, but, in the same breath, I'd have to admit these are the men and women I know on a first-name basis. They are the dealers that I regularly conduct business, the dealers who understand a handshake is a binding agreement.

They are the dealers of whom I know will uphold all the tenants of the PNG honor code.

On the other hand, as soon as I say that, I'm tempted to take it back. Maybe we are talking about the dealer across the table? At one coin show, browsing the aisles, I stopped at one dealer's booth. It was manned by a sharp, eloquent young associate. I don't know if he knew who I was or not, but he had sure done his homework. He presented a smooth and compelling appraisal of the piece.

I let the coin go but tried to hire the kid on the spot. Don't confuse gray hair with talent and experience—it's not always the same thing.

Don Kagin on the set of Good Morning America with Joan Lunden in 1981. (© Kagin's, Inc.)

It's not such a bad idea to consider a dealer from across the table to represent you in future dealings if you like him. You got to where you are in life, to one degree or another, by trusting the feelings in your gut. If you're at a coin show or an auction, and, after speaking with a particular advisor, you're radiating positive energy—it could be that dealer is a good fit for you.

The one thing I want to caution you about going with your gut is that many dealers are former collectors who have turned to coin dealing as a way to support their habit—if you'll forgive the allusion.

I've geared this book for the investor—so let me make this clear—the collector-cum-dealer who can dazzle you with history or grading tips isn't necessarily the same guy who can guide you toward realizing profitable transactions. Which, by my way of thinking, is really the most important part.

OK, you've met an advisor candidate you like, now what?

Yes, by all means, you'll want to check out his track record. Does he have a history of successful purchases in your areas of interest? If you've met any of his other clients, do they appear fiercely loyal? And so on.

I'm not necessarily trying to steer you away from brokers or vest pocket dealers. For all I know, your independent dealer is brilliant. But, if I were you, I think I'd want at least one contact tied into one of the big firms. Either way, it's worth examining the machine of a full-service numismatic dealer.

First off, using a full-service coin dealer isn't the equivalent of choosing Merrill Lynch over one of the discount stockbrokerages, like eTrade or ScottTrade. The big houses, yes, like Kagin's, are kept in the loop. It's a small loop.

If you're not in the loop, you're not in the loop.

There are no ScottTrades or eTrades in numismatics. However, as I say, as you move up the price scale, the industry kind of polices itself. For us, commissions rarely become sticking points with clients.

I do feel obligated to address it, though. I know for Kagin's clients who do a fair amount of business with us that they may receive additional discounts on their spreads.

Let's go back a chapter. Remember the story of Atlanta, of how you know of a private sale, and that's when you call-in your hired gun, your numismatic sharpshooter? Yes, well, that's not how it typically works. How it works in real life is that we call you not vice versa. We let you know about the private sale in Atlanta.

A good dealer is going to have contacts up and down the country-side, North, South, East and West, from left to right and right to left such that when something new and exciting comes down the pike, you'll have your crack at it.

"John, you know that 1907 Rounded Edge $10 Indian Head in Choice Uncirculated you've been looking for? I just spoke with an estate administrator in Atlanta who's got one, and it doesn't sound as if he knows the difference between Wire

A typical numismatic investment portfolio. (© Kagin's, Inc.)

Rim and Rounded Rim. We may be able to get a Rounded Rim for a Wire Rim price. If that's the case, we'll see about passing along some of our savings. Family is in a hurry for the dough. We're going to send someone down there. Hopefully pick up the entire collection. Shall I keep you abreast?"

That's more likely how that conversation plays out.

Your broker or vest pocket dealer or president of your coin club could be a brilliant numismatic advisor and strategist. He may have been the one who turned you on to investment-grade Indian Head eagles—no question, a fine choice—but if he's not in the loop, he's not in the loop. You may have to wait a few years for another shot to buy one at a reasonable price.

Don Kagin on the 700 Club set with host, Pat Robertson, circa 1982. (© Kagin's, Inc.)

The nice thing about large numismatic houses is that they have specialists. Should you suddenly develop an urge to collect Colonial coinage, there's probably a specialist on-hand for you to talk to. Follow-up educational materials in the mail.

You may be surprised by how many nooks and crannies there are with numismatics—so, it's a nice perk.

My colleagues and I typically took the dusty library-book path toward becoming qualified numismatists. And, I understand, you're an investor who simply wishes to profit from rare coins and gold as quickly and as efficiently as possible.

Near instant access to a team of professionals that can hand you the Cliff's Notes version seems to make sense for someone standing in your shoes. Point me to the part where it says, 'This is what you should be looking for.' An experienced staff of specialists can do that.

Let me get down to brass tacks, though. I'll tell you the biggest reason why I prefer working with large dealers. What makes a dealer large is having an expansive inventory of numismatics or other collectibles. I like the idea of a dealer who puts his money where his mouth is.

Dealers and companies, both.

A thorough vetting of due diligence issues will go a long way toward finding a numismatic investment counselor best suited for you and your ultimate investment success. You may be working with a young associate and that could be fine and dandy. As long as I knew the names on the masthead had weathered a few storms, prospered in good times, I'd feel comfortable doing business with a rare coin brokerage holding those credentials.

Chapter XI

Financial and Tax Characteristics

One of the great myths perpetuated by financial writers is how complicated the U.S. tax system is. In reality, it's not that much more difficult than being able to read a bus schedule. The IRS simply has an incredibly thick bus schedule.

In college, there was a physics professor who allowed her students to bring in a cheat sheet for exams. She reasoned the important part of her class was learning how to solve problems. The library was a two minute walk, and, inside, a person could find just about every formula that's been put onto papyrus, chalkboard or laptop. Her thought was to make exam questions extremely challenging. Let's test the students to see if they know what formula to use when. If they can't remember F=ma, they'll have it, but let's see if they can apply what they've learned to real world problem-solving.

There are only a handful of reg's with implications that are vital to investors. If you've read other books on investing or numismatics, the noteworthy talking points on taxes those authors highlighted are undoubtedly the same in these last two chapters.

The four million words that comprise U.S. tax regulations is an unprintable tome—a monument to politicians' willingness to be seduced by lobbyists and other special interest groups. Granted, there's no way to get a fraction of those words on one of my old physic prof's half sheets of paper, but the reason I went through all this is to try and take the power out of the Evil Empire some of us know as the IRS.

The tax code is scary, the IRS is scary, and a natural reaction is to throw up your hands and say forget this junk. But, I'm telling you, there are a couple of key things here, that's it. Not an Evil Empire, nor too terribly scary. Soon we'll get back to gold and rare coins.

Get through the next few pages in this chapter and the next and you're home free. Turbo Tax knows the formulas, and Turbo Tax can take it from there. I'm serious.

Cheaters Never Prosper

For these two chapters on taxes and estate planning, I enlisted the expertise of my friend, Dr. D. Larry Crumbley (dcrumbl@lsu.edu), author of *Forensic and Investigative Accounting* (Commerce Clearing House), in order to be sure the accounting information we're passing along is up-to-date and presented in a logical fashion.

I see some of you scratching your heads. Didn't Kagin just say taxes were a piece of cake? Yes, that's true, but did you also see the part where I mentioned the U.S. tax code has four million words to it? It's so massive there are only theoretical estimates of how many pages a book like that would entail. Somewhere between 20,000 and 80,000 appears to be the range of best guesstimates.

In addition to thanking Larry for his generosity, I'd like to apologize in advance for any inaccuracies that may have occurred inadvertently during the editorial process. It should be noted that while Larry did all the heavy lifting in these two chapters, in several instances, I was unable to resist the temptation to insert miscellaneous commentary and opinion. The views expressed are mine and not necessarily that of Dr. Crumbley's.

Consider also that our tax code changes costume faster than a Las Vegas showgirl backstage between numbers—the IRS releases supplements practically on a daily basis. For these reasons, the information presented here should be used for general guideline purposes only. For advice regarding your specific circumstance, I suggest you consult with a qualified CPA or tax attorney directly.

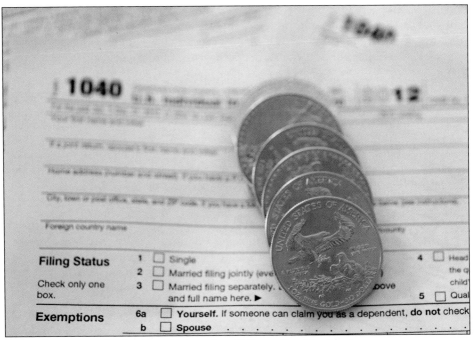

Many bullion coins can be placed in retirement plans. (© Dreamstime, Steveheap)

Nevertheless, this is not an area of investing you'll want to farm out to a consultant without having at least a rudimentary grasp of how it all fits together. The old jokes goes, "What's the difference between tax avoidance and tax evasion?"

"Five years and a $10,000 fine."

It's funny because tax avoidance and tax evasion are called from the same playbook—easy to get your signals crossed. Google "famous tax scandals" and witness former vice presidents, world champion boxers, opera singers, hoteliers, mobsters and civil-rights leaders. A former IRS commissioner is on the list, which is laugh-out-loud funny.

If it can happen to Credit Suisse to the tune of $2.6 billion, it can happen to you. As the first bank of its size and stature to plead guilty to criminal wrongdoing in two decades, it could be a fluke—an audacious conspiracy so egregious that law enforcement couldn't possibly ignore it. But my sense is that the winds have shifted. In May 2014, Credit Suisse was the latest in a series of high profile corporation misconduct prosecutions. The IRS and Justice Department, it seems, are taking a more aggressive posture with S&P 500 companies that play fast and loose with the rules.

A moot point for the likes of us, the average citizen. Federal law enforcement has never felt a compunction to look the other way for individuals caught with their hand in the cookie jar. Numismatics, the IRS is well aware, is a tailor-made for tax shenanigans. Open a coin shop inside a cash-only restaurant and the IRS will have their man camped out on the sidewalk before the dinner rush.

There are probably a number of dealers who might not report a $35 profit from a common Morgan dollar sale, and the IRS seems OK with this. Skip reporting a five-, six- or seven-figure profit? That's another story altogether, and, I'd have to say, I don't like your prospects for happily-ever-after. Your choice of non-extradition countries, I'd bet, isn't everything you'd like it to be. Otherwise, the only thing Club Fed and Club Med have in common is that they rhyme.

Commit the same crime over and over and no matter how slick you think you are you're going to get caught. Just don't do it.

Since the IRS doesn't provide a strict, bottom-line number for realized profits that must be reported, I can't either. Technically, a $35 profit is supposed to be there. Other than using hypothetical numbers at opposite ends of the profit scale, I'd be foolish to guess at a number in print. My feeling is that there are enough legit loopholes to exploit to keep my taxes down rather than risk finding out I'd pushed things too far.

Though our main focus will not be on criminal matters—mind you, I'm no expert on the subject—I reckon the serious answer to the old industry joke above is one of intent. If you made a mistake, an honest mistake, the IRS likely will punish you with the usual bureaucratic hoops before a settlement can be reached.

If they can prove intent—uh oh, that's different—suddenly the joke isn't funny anymore. Federal judges are known to hand out generous chunks of time with a smile, as if they're doing you a favor. If there's been a crime—even the almost harmless, theoretically victimless white-collar kind—you really don't want to have the same face as the mug shot the Feds pin it on.

Our objective with this chapter is to identify those areas of the tax code that are pertinent to collectors and investors of numismatic properties and highlight tax avoidance tips of the legal variety.

What's in a Name?

The place to start is with how the IRS labels your activities within the numismatic community. Throughout our discussion, I've used "collector" and "investor" in an almost interchangeable way, the difference vaguely determined by one's emotional attachment to his coin portfolio.

The IRS uses similar language, but by April 15 it's choose one or the other. Your classification has important tax implications. Of the two, investor is favorable because you can deduct related expenses and trading losses, so we'll look at the criteria you'd need to meet in order to claim investor status.

The third category the IRS uses for numismatics is for dealers, which entails generally favorable business treatment. However, other than mentioning that it exists, it's not something we need to spend too much time discussing.

The critical determining factor that separates an investor from a collector is a clearly established profit motive. As with most tax matters, if the IRS calls into question a claim of investor status, it is up to the taxpayer to provide supporting evidence. For this reason, it is highly recommended that you keep organized business records.

Factors considered by the IRS for numismatic investor status:

- The manner in which an activity is conducted.
- Expertise of the taxpayer or his advisors.
- Amount of time and effort expended.
- Expectation that assets may appreciate in value.
- Success of taxpayer in carrying on other activities.
- History of income or loss with respect to such activity.
- Financial status of the taxpayer.
- Elements of personal pleasure or recreation.

If your numismatic activity shows a net profit in any two out of five consecutive years, you have the option to call yourself an investor—your expenses and losses are now tax deductible. Auction receipts or dealer account summaries suffice as proof. If you cannot show a net profit in two out of five consecutive years, numismatic deductions are disallowed, what the IRS calls "hobby losses."

Say you're just starting out, filing for the first time as an investor. You wonder if your normal deductions, like mortgage interest, is still deductible. The answer is yes. Your status as either a numismatic investor or collector is independent of the other sections on your tax forms.

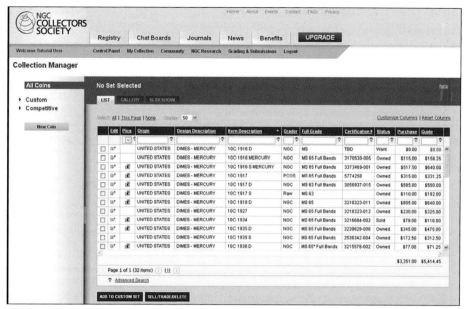

Online collection services are offered by many companies, including this one by the grading firm NGC. This service allows users to record and track their collection in a secure environment. (© NGC)

The following practices are helpful toward satisfying the IRS's investor guidelines:

- Keep detailed records of all transactions, the same as if you were investing in stocks, bonds or real estate. A separate bank account dedicated to numismatic trading is also advisable.

- If you attempt to deduct numismatic literature, be sure at least some of it is investor-oriented.

- Keep a trading journal, or make notes of your conversations with your dealer, in particular coins he envisions has strong upside potential.

- Keep your coin and banknote investments in separate safe-deposit boxes, deducting the expenditures as business expenses.

- Contribute regularly to a specific investment program.

By following these guidelines, you can be reasonably assured of your investor status, qualifying you for capital gains treatment and other tax advantages.

Trading Places

One of my father's good friends was a very successful stockbroker who lived in the same neighborhood. His clothes, I remember, had perfect creases. Somehow he was able to get through the workday without a wrinkle. His shoes were always spit-shined to a high gloss that could make a drill sergeant weep with envy.

Periodically, he would whisper to dad a hot stock, even though he never played the stock market (gambling is someone else's game). Dad told me his tips were so good that he could probably get a bank to accept them as collateral on a loan. It is one of those things this stockbroker would repeat that I think is the perfect way to open a discussion on capital gains.

He'd say, "A short-term profit is always better than a long-term loss."

The reason I led this section off with this stockbroker's witticism is to remind everyone to keep tax considerations into perspective. You may delay a coin sale a couple of weeks in order to capture a tax credit, but, rule of thumb, you're going to buy when you think the price is going higher, and you're going to sell when you think the price is going lower—and not much else needs to go into that formula.

Honestly, the stockbroker's tax credo doesn't often come into play with rarities. The big deal about capital gains comes from holding an investment for 12 months, but, as you know, it is only in the most unusual of circumstances that you'll be liquidating a top-tier Legacy piece so soon.

With gold bullion and related cash market precious metals, there may be times when you contrive fiscally sound reasons for buys or sells based on XYZ tax motivation or loophole. For stocks and bonds, a so-called wash sale might make sense, liquidating an underwater position in December and buying it back again in January—if the IRS didn't have a 30-day wait rule, which tends to screw up that plan 10 ways from Sunday. It almost never makes sense for rare coins, though. What I'm saying is that 96% of the time, you just really shouldn't do it.

Instead, I would think of tax treatments as possibilities to consider after the fact, after you've liquidated.

Nevertheless, with regard to investment-related tax issues we'll continue to discuss below, there could be times when you see a tax advantage as the impetus for a move. This is almost certainly a bad idea. The transaction commission is going to swallow the envisioned profits before you even get started. On the other hand, if you're backed into a corner, you're backed into a corner—you gotta do what you gotta do.

I've made a special effort here to question an investor's motivation to sell based on a tax incentive. I worry that a psychologist's diagnosis would include some immediate gratification angle. In the mortgage industry, there is a whole dedicated branch that seeks to get VA home loans refinanced. VA homeowners, who are often scratching to stay afloat, are sold on the idea of a lower rate and skipping the first month's payment. The reality of it is that those VA homeowners will put $14,000 or more onto their loan, and instead of 12 years to go, will start back at 30. No way the sweet taste of a carrot will mitigate the sting of that stick.

There are exceptions. It could be that you're squeezed and forced into reducing your income tax liability, or you risk defaulting on some other, bigger commitment. So say you've made the tough decision, you're going to borrow from Peter to pay Paul, just this one time. You have to, you've got no choice.

Your plan is to sell several of your worst performing coins at a loss in order to take a tax deduction—one that ultimately saves your top priority investment. In this situation, where it seems as if you're aware of your risky surroundings, but feel compelled to move forward anyway... In this narrow circumstance, were I your advisor, I'd go along with it.

I'm your advisor not your legal guardian, though—you don't need my blessing to have me execute a transaction on your behalf. Then again, in this hypothetical, I am your advisor, so before we did that, I'd implore you to sit down and take stock. Let's see if we can't find a more suitable pocket from which to pull funds.

During the course of our conversation, it could be we solve your temporary cash flow issue with a low interest loan using another collectible as collateral. Could be that that Old West handgun you inherited and thought was rusty turns out to be a Very Fine 1847 Colt Walker. Instead of a few thousand, the new estimate I give you is $550,000 to $675,000. After I set the gun down and I'm able to breathe again, I'd helpfully remind you that your wife hates firearms.

Point is, there's probably an alternative to avoid taking a proactive measure in coins or gold because of a tax advantage. The tax code is always going to be there, which you'll employ to better results if you don't use it to artificially affect your usual buying and selling habits.

A Capital Idea

Once you do sell, the investment transaction will show either a profit or loss; the IRS expects to be informed of this development on the next report you file. If you were in position for 12 months, the net result qualifies for favorable treatment. For proponents, capital gains and capital losses are positive motivation for the man on the street to take charge of his retirement needs. For critics, it is how old-money looks after its own, how old-money stays old-money. Truth is, of course, it is both.

I have no trouble with people making decisions in their own best interest. That said, the superrich ought to be just as concerned about the growing divide in income as the folks in the lower brackets. From the other side I'd say, the millions of middle class that benefit is worth letting a few Mitt Romneys off the hook. A country that rewards hard work and invention necessarily penalizes the flip-side group.

The middle class is what has made America great. The middle class, another great American invention, is the reason life in the 18th century didn't simply meander along, as things had the previous 2,000 years, into the present day.

America's vow to provide a level playing field, that anyone can make it, is what separates this country from every other. It is why China will never catch us, and why God really is on our side. For all the jaundiced observations I've made throughout this book, I hope this is the one slice of optimism that resonates.

The ironic thorn in our present-day Washington D.C. rose garden is that politicians are too committed to their ideals. For a company CEO, you want the rugged individualist. Ayn Rand's Howard Roark. Or, if we're thinking of literary characters, for me, Philip Marlowe or Lew Archer. Trouble is, we need our government representatives to be a bit more on the sleazy side. Howard Roark may be the perfect architect to design a proposed freeway bridge, but if politicians can't come together with a compromise of interests, it will never get built.

All of which has what to do with taxes? Right.

If you're an old hand with stocks and bonds, you'll anticipate reading 23.8% as the number. Unfortunately, Congress bumped the rate for antiques and collectibles. If you fall into one of the top two brackets, collectible capital gains is 28%, plus, as of 2013, an additional 3.8% surtax.

The calculation is different if capital losses exceed capital gains. As an individual taxpayer, a Short-Term Capital Loss or Long-Term Capital Loss means you can deduct a maximum of $3,000 from any other income. Any STCL or LTCL in excess of $3,000 may be carried over indefinitely and used for future tax years until it is gone. Another reason why maintaining organized business records is so important.

With the proper planning and maintenance of records, your numismatic-related expenses can be turned into valuable tax savings. If you fall within the 33% tax bracket, an extra $1,000 of deductions is worth approximately $330 when you file your federal income tax return. Keep track of your expenses for items like coin folders and tubes, sales taxes, interest expenses, safe-deposit box rental, postage, stationery— and you'd be surprised at how much you can save.

A number of expenses besides the obvious ones above also may be deductible. An investor can typically deduct accounting and legal advisor services, professional numismatic advice, financial planning consultation and, should you be lucky enough, a personal assistant's salary.

Be cautious in claiming deductions that are attributable to coin collecting as a hobby rather than an investment. If an IRS agent questions a deduction, you will be required to prove its relationship to the preservation of your investment. For instance, if you took your family to Las Vegas, where you happened to purchase several coins, still, I think you'd be pushing it to try and deduct your vacations expenses.

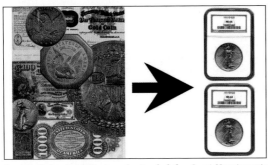

Legacy Coin portfolios can be traded for easily liquidated coins through tax-free "Section 1031" like-kind exchanges. (© Kagin's Inc.)

Gladly Pay You Tuesday, For a Rare Coin Today

The tax laws postpone gains on certain coins or currency trades as long as they involve like-kind property. Theoretically, you can constantly trade up and defer capital gains' tax indefinitely. Of course, if and when you finally sell your previously Semi-Numismatic traded items, your income tax gain is based on the cost of the first items purchased. However, by trading you can postpone the tax burden until later when tax dollars are worth less. Think of postponing your tax liability as an interest-free loan from the federal government.

The IRS has ruled that like-kind—of the same nature and character—exchanges qualify for non-recognition of gain. This includes bullion-related coins for other bullion-related coins—Krugerrands for Austrian-100 Coronas, or rare silver coins for rare gold coins.

The IRS offers a number of other examples of like-kind exchanges, but essentially the main distinction is that a semi-numismatic coin is priced within 15% of its melt value; otherwise, it falls into the collectible category. For instance, rare coins for bullion is not a like-kind exchange (for non-dealers) and will result in capital gains tax.

The tax law defers gains from trades as long as they meet the following like-kind exchange requirements:

- There is an exchange of property held for productive use in a trade or business or for investment purposes.
- Both properties must be like-kind.
- If cash or other property is received (called "boot") in addition to the like-kind property, the fair market value of the boot is taxed to the extent of any actual gain on the transaction.

To give you an example, say Sam exchanges $25,000 fair market value (FMV) of bullion Mexican 50-Peso gold coins (cost basis of $12,000) for $22,000 FMV of bullion Austrian 100-Corona gold coins and $3,000 cash (boot). Sam must pay a tax on $3,000 of the $13,000 realized gain ($25,000-$12,000). However, $10,000 of the gain is deferred ($13,000-$3,000).

The exchange of numismatic currency for other numismatic currency also should qualify for like-kind exchange treatment, but there have been no definitive rulings on this.

The Taxman Cometh and Cometh Again

There are no property taxes levied on coin collections as there are in real estate. Some states charge a sales or use tax for retail (non-dealer) sales of rare coins. Cities, counties and transit authorities also charge sales and use taxes. Five states do not charge sales tax: Alaska, Delaware, Montana, Oregon and New Hampshire. Interstate sales are not taxed. If you purchase your coins by mail from an out-of-state investment house, you will pay no sales tax, but some states require residents to declare out-of-state purchases. Failure to pay the out-of-state tax can be illegal.

If you purchase coins through an auction and have them sent to you, you might find the cost of shipping much less than the taxes you would have incurred if you took delivery at the place of the auction sale. But, in this case, a use tax may be due.

If you are living within the same state as your investment firm, you might be tempted to have your coins shipped to a relative or friend out of state and then delivered to you. A compensating use tax is due on this transaction, though it is rarely collected. This practice probably constitutes fraud and can be detected by a sales tax audit. If the seller ships an empty box, this strategy is probably illegal to the seller.

In some states, like California, you can avoid sales tax on your rare coins by purchasing bullion, gold or silver worth $1,500 or a like-amount of foreign coinage, with every purchase of rare coins. You should check with your tax advisor or state board of equalization for your state's policy.

Do It for the Kids

The vast majority of every purchase or sale you make in numismatics will involve a relatively quick, one-time cash transaction. While we do accept payment plans for extraordinary purchases from buyers, it doesn't occur that often. However, my friend Dr. Crumbley assures me it happens often enough to include a word on the Installment Tax Method.

Suppose you decide to sell your coin collection and/or one or more coins. If you are not a dealer in rare coins, the installment tax method may create a tax savings. If the buyer pays you at least one payment in a different tax year after the year of sale, you automatically qualify for the installment contract treatment. It's important to note that an installment contract must contain a minimum annual interest in order to avoid having the IRS impute an interest income amount for a transaction.

To understand the advantage of this installment contract election, you'll need to know how to compute the taxable income in one year. Use this formula:

INSTALLMENT TAX FORMULA

$$\frac{\text{Selling price less costs and basis}}{\text{Contract Price}} \quad x \quad \text{Payments during the year}$$

For example, suppose on December 2, 2013, you sold for $1,500, a roll of coins which cost you $250 in 1985. If you received a down payment of $180 in December 2012, $480 in 2014, and the remainder in the next year, you would recognize the following taxable gain in the respective years (see Table 14.1 below).

As this example illustrates, any gain from the sale of the coins is spread over a three-year period. Spreading gains over a number of years will normally result in a net tax saving if for no other reason than the time value of money. If a coin sale results in a loss, the installment method should not be used.

TABLE 14.1

$$\frac{\text{TOTAL GAIN}}{\text{CONTRACT PRICE}} \quad x \text{ CASH RECEIVED} = \frac{\text{TAXABLE}}{\text{INCOME}}$$

2012 $\frac{\$1,250}{\$1,500}$ $180 = \$150$

2013 $\frac{\$1,250}{\$1,500}$ x $480 = \$450$

2014 $\frac{\$1,250}{\$1,500}$ x $840 = \$700$

But, as I say, this situation will not likely come up too often. The reason I've kept this section off the cutting room floor is there is one aspect of the tax installment methods you'll want to know about. It involves sales to related parties.

In general, a related party includes spouses, children, grandchildren and parents.

The IRS are no fools and tax code rules now make it difficult to sell securities to a related party in which everyone knows will be followed by a forgiveness of the debt. But, as of now, you can still pass along real estate, rare coins and collectibles using this technique.

Here is how a coin collector or investor could transfer his or her coin collection to heirs and avoid any estate or gift taxes, which could be as high as 40%. Suppose a parent sells his collection to his two children for $600,000 on July 3, 2013. The collection has a basis of $50,000 and was held as an investment. The parent will receive non-interest-bearing notes payable at $14,000 per year ($28,000 if parents are married). As each payment becomes due, the parent forgives the note.

Good planning can lead to financial secuirty. (© Dreamstime, Wavebreakmedia, Ltd)

There are some valuable advantages of this installment sales-gift. First, this technique spreads the gifts over a number of years in order to take advantage of the $14,000 gift per person exclusion to avoid any gift tax. A person can give $14,000 away each year to a relative or anyone without incurring a gift tax.

Second, the children are vested immediately with absolute ownership. Thus, any subsequent appreciation in the coin collection is not included in the parent's estate. Third, the children receive a step-up in basis equal to the selling price. Fourth, any gain on the coin collection is spread over the duration of the pay-off to the children.

An alternative strategy is to sell the collection to the children with a balloon payment many years later, say, 25 years down the road. Due to inflation, the children will pay off the liability with cheaper dollars. This strategy allows assets to be transferred from one generation to the next generation with less estate tax payable.

Under the law, any gain to be reported under the installment method is accelerated whenever a related party resells property within two years of the initial installment sale.

Nice Guys Should Never Finish Last

I don't know if it translates into good karma—what comes around goes around—or what it is exactly, but on some level it seems clear that giving something to charity is just the right thing to do. At least for us, my wife and I have been fortunate. One of Candace's and my favorite charities is the American Cancer Society. For every dollar we donate, about 90 cents of it goes to actual charity work, which is better than outstanding.

Although I encourage it, it's not something I'd likely bring up first with a client. It's a free country, after all. But, fortunately, many of Kagin's clients do feel the same way about charitable contributions, and they'll broach the subject. After applauding their decision, I slip back into my professional advisor's role and go over the tax code's charitable deduction guidelines. Obviously.

Under the tax laws, an individual is allowed, in general, a charitable deduction equal to the extent of the fair market value of any contributed coins. One of the factors in that situation is to get a reasonable idea of what the material could be sold for between a reasonable buyer and a reasonable seller within a reasonable period of time.

If you contribute any property to a charitable organization and pay an appraisal fee to someone in order to determine the fair market value, these appraisal expenses are deducted from adjusted gross income. But there is no deduction for the contribution of one's services to a qualified charitable organization. There is no deduction for gifting coins to individuals or rental value of property used by a charitable organization.

A person does have to be careful about selecting an appropriate charity for receiving tangible personal property. In order to qualify for the full fair market value deduction, the utilization of the contribution by the charity must be directly related to the exempt function of the charity. If not directly related to the exempt function of the charity, then the taxpayer's deduction is limited to its cost.

For example, a rare coin has a cost basis of $2,500 and a fair market value of $4,000. The coin was held three years and then given to a church, which sells it in order to use the proceeds. Since the rare coin is not directly related to the exempt function of the church, the deduction to the donor would be limited to the cost of $2,500, which is called the adjusted basis. However, if the rare coin is donated to an appropriate museum to be used for display purposes, the donor would be entitled to the larger $4,000 deduction.

When the fair market value of the coins is less than the cost basis, the fair market value is the deduction. Suppose in the previous example the coin has decreased to $2,300 (from its cost basis of $2,500). Here only $2,300 would be deductible if given to either the museum or the church. Do not contribute loss assets; sell them and take your deductible loss.

Thus, whether a contribution is for an "unrelated use" or "directly related use" to a charity is important to a taxpayer. The term "unrelated use" means a use which is unrelated to the purpose or function constituting the basis of the charitable organization's tax exemption. For example, if a coin collection contributed to an educational institution is used by that institution for educational purposes by being placed in its library for display and study by the students, the use is not an unrelated one.

But if the collection is immediately sold and the proceeds are used by the organization for educational purposes, the use of the property is an "unrelated use." If a collection is contributed to a charitable organization or governmental unit, the use of the collection is not an "unrelated use" if the recipient sells or otherwise disposes of only an insubstantial portion of the collection.

In some situations, if the recipient organization disposes of the property within three years of the contribution, the donor may be required to recapture the appreciation element, which amounts to having put it back into his reportable income.

What proof of use should a taxpayer maintain? Regulations state that you may establish that the contributed property is not in fact put to an unrelated use by the charity or that at the time of the contribution it is reasonable to anticipate

The Kagin Collection of Pioneer Coins was the finest and most complete collection ever assembled. This collection was loaned to the Old San Francisco Mint for exhibition purposes. Some items have been donated to the museum and Kagin's received a charitable tax deduction. (© Kagin's, Inc.)

that the property will not be put to an unrelated use by the charity. For example, in the case of a gift of a coin collection to a museum, if the donated coins are of a general type normally retained by such museum, it is reasonable for the taxpayer to anticipate (unless he or she has actual knowledge to the contrary) that the coins will be put to a related use by the museum, whether or not the coins are later sold or exchanged by the charity.

If a taxpayer makes a charitable contribution of appreciated property and claims a deduction in excess of $250, he or she should attach to their tax return the following information:

- Name and address of the organization to which the contribution was made.
- The date of the actual contribution.
- A detailed description of the property along with the conditions of the property.
- The manner of acquisition. (For example, purchase, gift, inheritance, etc.)
- The fair market value of the property along with the method utilized in determining the fair market value (if there was an appraiser).
- The cost or adjusted basis of the property.
- Where the deduction is reduced by any of the appreciation, the reduced amount.

- Any agreement or understanding between the taxpayer and the charity.
- The total amount claimed as a deduction for the next year.
- A statement from the charity that documents the property's use.

Say that Last Part Once More

OK, it is possible I misled you with regard to the complexity of the U.S. tax code. For me, things start getting complicated when I have different groups of coins on different installment plans going back X, Y or Z number of years. For the sheer number of transactions Kagin's makes, we do it the old-fashioned way—we hire a reputable accounting firm to do it for us.

I don't know if I were you that I'd be brave enough to do my personal income taxes, much less the company's, without a professional tax advisor. But even if you're stubborn about hiring outside help, from what I understand, Turbo Tax does a pretty darn good job. You basically go through it answering multiple choice questions. It's got to be better than going back and forth between a dozen IRS reference guides, so it's probably well worth the $100.

Listed below are some of the important areas we've talked about, and mark the unfamiliar topics, because those are the ones we'll be talking about in Chapter 12:

1. Gifting: Current laws (2014) allow an annual gifting of $14,000 to any number of individuals ($28,000 per married couple). You are also allowed a one-time $5.25 million ($12.5 million for a married couple) lifetime gift exception. These exemptions allow you to avoid substantial estate taxes.

2. Estate taxes: There is a federal estate tax on the fair market value of all assets when a person dies. The estate tax law exemption for 2014 is $5.34 million (inflation adjusted). However, anything over this amount is subject to a 40% tax rate. If any monies are due, they must be paid within nine months of a death (plus a six month extension). Proper planning is essential and can be accomplished through some planned asset sale or insurance.

3. Capital gains taxes: Virtually all the investments you own, including rare coins and currency, are considered capital assets (unless you are a dealer). If they are owned for over one year, they are considered long-term versus short-term for items held less than one year.

    While long-term capital gains (the difference between what you paid including commissions and what you sell the investment for) are taxed at 0/15%/20/23.8% for stocks and securities, there is a flat 28% plus 3.8% rate for collectibles, including coins and currency.

4. Like-kind exchanges (Section 1031): A significant way to defer the 28% (or 31.8%) tax rate on numismatic gains is by conducting a tax-free, like-kind exchange. Under current IRS rules, collectible coins are distinguished from bullion related coins if their numismatic (or collectable) premium is at least 15% above the bullion (melt) value due to their rarity. If a coin collection was

traded through a qualified intermediary (coin dealer) for an equal or lesser value of other numismatic coins such as fungible U.S. $20 gold coins (graded MS-64 or higher), then the investor can defer capital gains taxes.

5. Trusts: This technique is an increasingly popular and cost-effective way of transferring your coin or currency portfolio while avoiding expensive probate proceedings. A living trust allows you to be in control of your assets and instructs your designated trustee(s) to proceed with your desired directions and execute your trust upon your death. But there are no tax advantages of living trusts.

   There are other trusts that address spousal and family strategies which take maximum advantage of tax exemptions. (See Chapter 12).

6. Charitable gifting: Another way to take full benefit of the appreciated fair market value of your numismatic portfolio is to donate it to qualified Section 501(c) (3) non-profit organizations. Making lifetime gifts to charities provide a double tax benefit: an income tax deduction and a reduction in one's estate. Presuming the organization accepts and has use for your collection, you can deduct the entire amount of the fair market value (which can be determined by a qualified coin dealer). Other strategies include donating partial interest per year in a collection, with the entire amount donated over a 10-year period.

   There are some limitations with this scenario, and they are explained in detail on our website, Goldandrarecoins.net.

Another charitable contribution vehicle is a Charitable Reminder Trust which allows you to get both a tax deduction and a steady stream of income and ensures estate tax avoidance. There are limitations to this scenario, and a qualified advisor is necessary when incorporating this scenario into your strategy.

Chapter XII

Estate Planning

Nothing is certain but death and taxes. I wonder how many times a person hears this phrase in a lifetime. Yet, it's astonishing how often it comes as a shock to people when they learn the federal government has an estate tax. Of course, they're going to want to get you one last time!

It's our job to see that that doesn't happen.

Back in 1984, California passed Proposition 37, The Lottery Act. I'd just finished up my post-grad studies. It's embarrassing to admit, but my college

(© Dreamstime, Karen Roach)

chums and I would spend an inordinate amount of time thinking of clever and cynical things to say about the way my father's generation were running the world. I'd like to think I'm more sympathetic these days—glass houses, you understand—but getting back to the old lottery debate, the running gag was "the lottery is a tax on people who are poor at math."

In that same way, the federal estate tax rate—which in 2013 was bumped from 35% to 40%—is a tax on people who are poor at finance. Thirty years later, the gag has a new setup but the same punch-line—only it doesn't seem as funny as it once had. It doesn't take a sociologist to deduce which groups are destined to draw the short straw.

Be that as it may.

Sympathetic or not, I know that I've got my family covered. I suggest you do the same. This is not an area of personal finance exclusive to the wealthy. I would argue that it's more important for the man or woman of modest means. If you haven't begun planning your estate, the aftermath of your demise, now is the time. Don't procrastinate. If you leave it to Uncle Sam to unravel, it is your heirs who'll pay the price, both in terms of money and aggravation.

Of course, we've been talking about estate planning right along. Building wealth from smartly allocating your investment dollars is the real trick, and we've spent a good deal of time discussing how gold and rare coins can be utilized to meet your financial goals.

Before you reach those goals, perhaps when you become within shouting distance, you'll want to make sure the fruits of your labor aren't wiped out in probate court. Anyone with income, property or investments should be concerned with estate planning.

It's beyond the scope of this book to begin talking about annuities and life insurance products. My workday revolves around identifying specific investment opportunities, so it shouldn't come as a complete surprise that my investment capital is divided between those vehicles I've identified with favorable risk/reward, and Johnny-on-the-spot cash instruments, such as gold bullion.

I Knew You Were Trouble

Your circumstance is likely to be quite different. You're a doctor, a lawyer, or you own a string of dry cleaners; you're a clever IT tech, a doting grandpa or grandma, you own a few hospitals, or perhaps you're the athletic club's superstar tennis pro—in which case, you don't have the same kind of time that I do for investment analysis. As such, a good portion of your investment portfolio resides in mutual funds that you don't have to think too much about.

Perfectly understandable.

It's the reason why many of you will hire someone like me—to mind the store while you're away doing other things. I'd simply like to take a moment, this one last time, to remind everybody to take care with whom you invite to watch over the store. Or, with whom you invite to watch over your mutual funds, watch over your collectibles, watch over your kids on date night, as the case may be. These are the important choices of your life.

Meanwhile, learn as much as you possibly can, then go ahead and trust your gut to steer you in the right direction from there. As President Reagan used to say, "trust but verify".

Yeah, go ahead, write that down. Post it on your refrigerator.

Learn as much as you possibly can about given situational conundrum, then trust your gut to steer you in the right direction.

At any given price, a commodity can move higher or lower. As investors, it's been our job to place the odds in our favor. To sift the silt from the gold dust, as it were. Perhaps you'll attribute your success to some oddity you've picked up along the way. Silver tends to rise on a full moon, tends to fall on a new moon—and no, it doesn't matter why it works, it just does. Regardless, however you've managed to do it, you're in charge of a pretty sweet nest egg.

Warren Buffett, the Berkshire Hathaway billionaire, believes the right amount to leave children is "enough money so that they would feel they could do anything, but not so much they could do nothing."

If that is the sort of problem you have, you worry about leaving your kids too much money, my hat is off to you. For the rest of us, it's a matter of transferring the wealth we've accumulated to the next generation in your family line as expeditiously and tax-free as possible.

The federal government imposes a transfer tax on the fair market value of all assets (less liabilities) held by an individual when he or she dies. The taxable estate includes such assets as coins, stock, life insurance proceeds (even though paid to someone else) and property owned jointly with someone else.

The IRS finally officially answered the question as to what valuation is placed upon a numismatic collection on the date of death. In Revenue Ruling 78-360, the IRS indicated that coins and paper currency are included in the decedent's gross estate at their fair market value, whether or not the decedent is a dealer in coins or currency or as an investor or collector.

We mentioned in the last chapter how a person could use a tax-exempt gift to minimize any estate taxes that may be looming, and it's worth taking another look. A person can give up to $14,000 per child per year (in 2013), or $28,000 (if both parents jointly agree), without tax consequences. Coins are ideal for such gifts. An excellent strategy is to space the gift over a number of years.

Keep in mind that there is a federal gift tax to the donor, but the $14,000 exclusion and the lifetime exemption of $5,250,000 in 2013 (inflation adjusted) allows a married couple to pass a huge amount onto their children tax-free.

For example, a family with three children could give away tax-free in one year, $10,584,000, calculated as follows using 2013 laws:

$28,000 x 3 =	$84,000
2 lifetime exemption	$10,500,000
	$10,584,000

If you use up this exemption giving gift, there will be no lifetime exemption available at death, however.

It could be you decide to do nothing. When you inherit property, you receive a step-up in basis to the fair market value on the date of the decedent's death. You can avoid income taxes altogether by merely saving your collectibles until your death.

Then your heirs receive a step-up in basis to the coins' fair market value at the date of death.

For example, suppose you bought a coin for $4,000; on the date of your death the coin is worth $14,000. The $10,000 ($14,000 less $4,000) gain escaped income taxes when you died since your heirs received a basis of $14,000 in the coin. Thus, you may wish to retain until death, any coins which have increased significantly in value (especially in the case of an elderly taxpayer) so that your heirs receive this step-up basis. There is no step-up in basis when you make a gift. The $14,000 will be included in your gross estate.

Although there are differences amongst investors' objectives, attitudes, temperaments, and net assets, the process of estate planning should always include five basic steps:

1. Gathering the facts.

2. Evaluating the obstacles of estate impairment.

3. Designing the plan.

4. Implementing the plan.

5. Reviewing the plan.

For details on each step, visit our website at Goldandrarecoins.net.

See You on the Other Side

By the time most people hear the phrase fixed income, they are already nearing retirement—but by then it could be too late. Few individuals manage to set aside sufficient assets on a regular basis to live out their golden years comfortably. Social Security and union pension plans alone are usually not enough. What little there is becomes less and less, as those income streams become weakened by inflation.

That's if you can count on those institutions to be there when you need them. Unions are cutting deals with their corporate sponsors in order to keep businesses solvent. Experts agree that Social Security will need a shot in the arm soon, too. With a tremendous number of Baby Boomers moving into their 60s, privatization measures notwithstanding, the only alternatives are higher taxes, reduced benefits or some combination of the two.

To be fair to FDR's New Deal, Social Security was never intended to be the country's retirement plan. It was envisioned as a safety net, but through various socioeconomic factors has become the primary source of income for a large percentage of our retired population.

The surpluses that went into the program during the height of the Baby Boomers working careers were spent by other government agencies and now it has been hung out to dry. As threats go, it's Titanic heading into a chilly fog. Understandably, no politician wants to be standing on poop deck when that ship goes down.

In the meantime, the federal government has tried to encourage individuals to create retirement plans in order to prevent our older population from becoming wards of the state. By allowing tax breaks for workers who enroll in plans such as IRAs, Keoghs and qualified pension plans, the government helps ensure the financial independence of the elderly. Also, since retirees are normally spenders not savers, any additional income they receive will go into the economy and stimulate it.

The earlier you begin to plan for retirement, the more you can solidify your financial position. You'll need a solid nest egg of retirement investments, like gold bullion and rare coins, to allow you to grow old in the lifestyle you're accustom.

As a starting point, assume that you will need about 80% of your regular income to live comfortably in your later years. Although some of your expenses, such as taxes, will lessen, other expenses, such as medical expenses, will likely increase.

The Future is Now

Employees not covered by another qualified plan can establish a tax-deductible Individual Retirement Account. For 2013, the contribution ceiling is the smaller of $5,500 ($11,000 for spousal IRAs) or 100% of compensation. This contribution ceiling applies to both traditional non-deductible IRAs and Roth IRAs. Contributions to Roth IRAs are not deductible, but all earnings inside a qualified Roth IRA are not taxable. Also, all qualified distributions from a Roth IRA are not taxable. The catchup contribution available for those age 50 or over is $1,000.

Neither the taxpayer nor spouse may be active participants in any other qualified plan to benefit fully. If an employee is an active participant in a qualified plan, the traditional IRA deduction limitation is phased out proportionately between certain adjusted gross income ranges.

IRA ACCUMULATIONS

TOTAL GAIN BASED ON $10,000 ANNUAL CONTRIBUTION

Years Contributed	6%	8%	10%
10	$131,810	$144,870	$159,370
20	$367,860	$457,620	$572,750
30	$790,580	$1,132,830	$1,644,940
40	$1,547,620	$2,590,570	$4,425,930
45	$2,127,440	$3,865,060	$7,189,050

(© Kagin's, Inc.)

The amounts accumulated in an IRA can be substantial. For example, during a period of 45 years, a total of $2,127,440 can be accumulated in a couple's IRAs at an annual compounding rate of 6%. Notice how much more can be accumulated by increasing the compounding rate ($2,127,440 at 6% versus $7,189,050 at 10%). The earning power of compound interest in a tax-deferred retirement account is formidable.

Since 1982, most collectibles have been prohibited from being invested in IRAs. If a traditional IRA invests in collectibles, the amount invested is considered distributed to you in the year invested. The taxpayer may have to pay a 10% additional penalty tax on early distributions.

Any amounts that were considered to be distributed when the investment in the collectibles was made, and which were included as income at that time, are not included as income when the collectibles are actually distributed from the IRA.

The term collectible includes the following:

- Artworks
- Rugs
- Antiques
- Metals
- Gems
- Stamps
- Coins
- Alcoholic beverages
- Certain other tangible personal property

There are some exceptions to this prohibition in IRC § 408(m)(3). For example, an IRA can invest in one, one-half, one-quarter, or one-tenth ounce U.S. gold eagles, or one-ounce silver eagles. An IRA also can invest in certain other types of precious metals forms.

BULLION ITEMS ALLOWED IN IRAS

COINS

Gold	Platinum
American Eagle (proof & uncirculated)	American Eagle (proof & uncirculated)
Australian Kangaroo	Australian Koala
Australian Nugget	Canadian Maple Leaf
Austrian Philharmonic	Isle of Man Cat
Canadian Maple Leaf	Isle of Man Noble
Various Perth Mint coins	
American Buffalo	

Silver	Palladium
American Eagle (proof & uncirculated)	Canadian Maple Leaf
Australian Kookaburra	
Canadian Maple Leaf	
Mexican Libertad	
Austrian Philharmonic	

No proof versions of these coins are accepted WITH THE EXCEPTION OF gold, silver, and platinum American Eagle proof coins.

BARS

Gold, Silver, Platinum, and Palladium bars must be fabricated by refiners approved by The New York Mercantile Exchange/The Commodities Exchange (NYMEX/COMEX).* Minimum fineness required:

Gold	.995+
Silver	.999+
Platinum	.9995+
Palladium	.9995+

* These NYMEX/COMEX approved refiners change from time to time. Current lists are available upon request from the public relations office of NYMEX. Updated May 2009.

There are several types of retirement plans designed to meet specific needs. For detailed information, please visit our Retirement Planning section online atgoldandrarecoins.net

This Isn't Goodbye

Since the time of our death is uncertain, everyone, young or old, should plan for the contingency of death. Even with the great advances in modern medicine, not every one is lucky enough to grow old gracefully. Why build an estate and allow much of it to go to the Federal and State governments through estate taxes? Yes, most states have death taxes too. So although taxation is not the only factor to consider in developing an estate plan, taxation is still an important consideration.

You have several tax alternatives when disposing of a rare coin collection. I mention some that you might discuss with your tax advisor:

1. Sell the collection gradually, risking being classified as a dealer (with ordinary income).

2. Sell it all at one time and use the installment method to defer the overall capital gains tax.

3. Sell it to a relative in return for a private annuity.

4. Transfer the collection to a non-profit organization, using a charitable remainder annuity trust.

5. Receive an annuity issued by a charitable organization for your coin collection (a gift annuity).

I have tried to outline most of the more important points concerning numismatics retirement and estate planning. Let me reiterate that you should consult your accountant or attorney before making any important decisions along these lines.

I don't think I thought of planning an estate as a real priority until my father passed away. Yes, it was in my job description, it's something I'd been helping clients prepare for years, but it wasn't until Kagin's was passed over to me that I realized the import of a smooth transition—a few signatures on a few forms. It allowed my family to grieve for our loss instead of facing the daunting prospect an endless back and forth with the federal government.

That's how I keep Dad's spirit alive and vibrant in my daily life, with all the wonderful lessons that he taught me over the years.

Art Kagin was a confident man. He trusted his eye for a winner and that allowed him to be more aggressive with his bidding. With a wink, he'd say, "Mistakes are usually ones of omission not commission."

By all accounts, I should probably give Dad a posthumous writing credit. Much of what we've talked about here are his guiding principles. But perhaps his greatest gift to me was passing along an insatiable curiosity to know more. We can always learn more.

If I've helped pass along the bug, my work is done!

It is my hope that after reading this book you'll have the same added confidence that Dad's lessons have given me. I wish all of you good hunting and good fortune with your adventures in gold and rare coins.

Chapter XIII

Saddle Ridge Hoard Treasure
The Greatest Buried Treasure Find in U.S. History

It was surely one of *those* days. A day unlike any other. Must have been something in the air, too. Something magical.

It was chilly, as springtime in Northern California often is, on this day unlike any other that a young couple took their dog out for a walk, gaining familiarity with their rural property. Then, poof, there it was. Just like that, a mysterious shiny object piercing the surface of the ground.

Buried beneath an old oak tree, they unearthed an unusual metal can. It was heavy, and they thought it might be full of paint. A real chore to get it home. Using a screwdriver to

Saddle Ridge Hoard Treasure, "Pot of Gold." (© Kagin's, Inc.)

pry off the lid, they could hardly believe their eyes. Who stumbles across a pot of gold? *It's too farfetched to contemplate!*

After a long moment of bewilderment and concern for their safety, they went back to the spot that likely marks X on a hastily drawn map that's yet to turn up where they found many more.

Straight Flush

Eight metal cans housed, rather well as it happens, 1,427 rare U. S. gold coins. It is interesting to note to my dismay: no Pioneer slugs among them. The Treasure consists of 50 eagles, four half-eagles and 1,373 double-eagles, ranging 71 different dates and mintmarks from 1847-1894. Predictably, the majority were coined in San Francisco, but other mints of the era, including Philadelphia, Carson City, New Orleans, and even as far away as Dahlonega, Georgia are represented.

For Old West history buffs, it's entertaining to spitball its circumstance. Who buried the loot and why? Face value was a terrific amount in the late-1800s. My mind leaps immediately toward fanciful incidents of skullduggery. The booty culled from daring and dashing Wild Bunch train robberies? Could be, but the truth is probably more benign.

The nation's banking system could best be described as fledgling at best. Many people, especially in the West, were leery of banks. Mattresses and burial sites were common ways for people to guard their money. For all we know, the Saddle Ridge coins were the town dentist's life savings. But more likely from someone in the mining industry where bonus compensation sometimes comes periodically. It's certainly interesting to speculate.

The pioneers brought civilization to hostile territory, overcoming the elements with hard work and grit. Their sweat and blood fermenting into a new, uniquely American spirit. The accomplishments of the men, women, dentists and children too numerous, too far-flung to sum up in a single sentence. But if I tried, it'd look like this:

A breed apart.

Still, $27,980 would have been an awful lot of money for the average 19th-century dentist or merchant. Forgive me if you and I are chatting on it at a cocktail party, and my mind wanders back to Butch and Sundance!

Not Bad Work If You Can Find It

The new owners of the greatest buried treasure find enlisted the help of a couple of lawyer friends who researched who might best assist them in conserving, marketing and selling their new find. A couple of numismatic firms were approached but they soon settled on our firm here in the San Francisco Bay area. I assume their choice may have had something to do with our credentials, reputation and years of experience in marketing U.S. gold coins.

When the coins were scheduled to be brought to Kagin's, you can imagine our anticipation. We were like orphaned beggar children experiencing Christmas for the first time. Kagin's office space includes two conference rooms, though it nonetheless difficult securing enough table space to have the whole collection laid out.

Issue resolved, what a magnificent sight it was! It was the treasure revealed in countless Hollywood movies. The office felt to expand preternaturally, a warm golden glow emanating from the center tables.

I recall being handed that first coin from senior numismatist David McCarthy. "This is amazing," I said. "They all are." David fully agreed. *This is as good as it gets.* He was given carte blanche restoring them to their original luster, and after several months accomplished just that.

For a company like Kagin's, prepping and cataloging coins is a relatively straight-forward process. Collectors don't appreciate anything bordering on a doctored coin, so we used a combination of a number of solutions including a mild, professional-grade solvents to remove the copious amounts of grime, rust and debris that had collected while buried beneath the old oak tree for over 120 years. The process took several months of painstaking work for David.

The surprising part was that although several of the cans had rusted-through breaches, several of the coins were in remarkably good condition before we had even touched them. It was soon clear that most were Mint State, and eventually we determined that over a dozen represent specific dates and mintmarks as the finest examples known.

Once the coins were returned from PCGS with grade assignments, that's when the hard part came. This is when we earned our commissions. Planning the sale. As representative for the seller—in this case a friendly, formerly struggling young family who still may be pinching themselves—it's our job to obtain the most amount of money we can on their behalf.

The tricky part about pricing the coins was trying to balance two opposing forces. On the one hand, Saddle Ridge represents a tremendous boost in supply, which we know is bearish. It'd be like finding another Prudhoe Bay oil field on oil prices. But we've also learned not to underestimate the value of a good backstory to collectors.

The romantic lore of the Treasure is a huge selling point. Which was our reasoning when, in opposition of basic economic theory, we priced the cheapest coins with generous backstory premiums.

Both the owners and we at Kagin's wanted as many people as possible to be able to acquire one of these artifacts from this unique story. Even though we knew we could sell out the cheapest pieces for 50% more, we felt the pricing of even the no-grade pieces (due mainly to unprofessional cleaning prior to us receiving the coins) at $2,575 including shipping was the right price for everyone. The coins will most likely appreciate from here, I think, so I feel good about the buyers' prospects, but as to the matter of collecting the most amount of money we can on our clients' behalf, thus far we've done well. This is one of those rare times when it looks as if everybody will come out a winner.

As this manuscript goes to press, we're about four months into the Saddle Ridge sale, and I'd have to say I'm rather encouraged and pleased with the results so far. Over two-thirds of the coins have sold. If the entire collection had been swooped up quickly, I'd know we had priced things too low. On the other side, the consequence of none of the coins selling is, well, too horrific to consider on an empty stomach—then or now. That was never going to happen.

Of course, in show business it's all about your opening box office numbers. *Better believe we care.* We were sweating those first 24 hours! But the reports coming back were fantastic. In the first day, we'd sold almost half of the almost 1,400 coins up for sale.

All in all, this is just about how we planned the Saddle Ridge sale to go.

Under the Big Top

Over the years, I've been lucky enough to be involved in some way or another with several Old World treasure finds, most of which originated from shipwrecks. In 1999, I represented the State of California's interests with the $15 million gold found on the *S.S. Brother Jonathan.* I was Odyssey Marine's chief numismatist on the $50 million silver and gold found aboard the *S.S. Republic.* There have been others.

The way these things go is that you want to kick off your marketing campaign with a big splash. For the Saddle Ridge Treasure, Kagin's pulled out all the stops.

A pet project of mine is tending to the restoration of the Old Mint, the "Granite Lady" as we San Franciscans are apt to call the impressive stone building. Our goal is to establish a state-of-the-art American Money & Gold Rush Museum on the vault floor. We plan a complete renovation of the San Francisco History Museum on the first, second and attic floors.

The first year the Old Mint went into production was in 1874. A lot of little things need a facelift. To date, we've raised over $14 million, including $4.75 million of it coming from the proceeds of a congressionally-approved commemorative that celebrates the 100th anniversary of the great San Francisco earthquake. And that the Granite Lady survived it.

Dr. Kagin auctioning the first coin from the Saddle Ridge Hoard Treasure –an AU $20 1874-S which brought an astonishing $15,000. (© Kagin's Inc.)

Our idea was to formally announce the Saddle Ridge Treasure in conjunction with a charity exhibition and fundraiser for the Old Mint.

It was a swanky affair, with the City's high society in attendance. All manner of business and entertainment media covering the event. Everybody anxious to take a peek at the Treasure close-up. Oh gosh, I had a marvelous time.

I've been to this type of shindig before, and I'm always keen to see how people who are not necessarily into numismatics react to the collection being presented. For the Old Mint charity event, Kagin's brought 60 Saddle Ridge coins to show off. It was heartening to see how the folks in attendance lingered over them. There was a high level of enthusiasm, which sort of fits in with how I see the popularity of our "hobby" growing.

Our former financially strapped young family were in generous spirits, donating an 1874-S double-eagle. It was expected to bring in something slightly over its $4,500 price tag. Nobody expected the $20 gold piece to bring in $15,000—a welcome and handsome contribution to the charity. It seemed, at the time, to be a good omen.

Validation for Diversifying into Semi-Numismatic Gold

While the face value of the Saddle Ridge Hoard Treasure is $27,980; its value today will approach $11 million. A calculation of the internal rate of return over that time is approximately 6.1% annually (see graph below)! That's a period that includes several wars and depressions and recessions. During this same period the value of the U.S. dollar has decreased 96%.

I could not have contrived a better scenario to confirm the wisdom of long-term diversification of one's assets into U.S. gold coins!

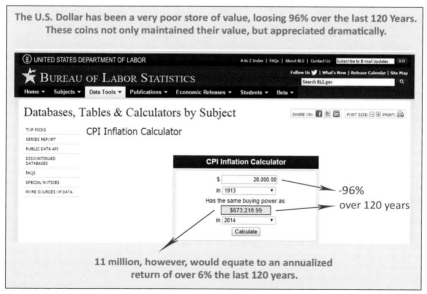

Department of Labor, Bureau of Labor Statistics (Courtesy of Santiago Capital)

The Paparazzi

The publicity generated by the Saddle Ridge story is estimated to have reached over a billion people. Virtually every major newspaper and news organization, and, I'm told, 1.65 million websites from around the world carried the story. For 11 straight days David and I participated in scores of interviews including late night and early morning live shows in Australia, Great Britain, France and Germany to mention a few.

In terms of exposure, Saddle Ridge is right up there with if not surpassing the $130 million *S.S. Central America* treasure. Of course, some of the credit for this needs to go to Kagin's partnership with Amazon.

Kagin's page on Amazon.com.

The Amazon deal was something in the works months before the Saddle Ridge Treasure. It was a convenient alignment of the stars that we were able to launch Amazon's new look for its Collectibles & Fine Art department with the Saddle Ridge coins.

We've been up to Amazon's headquarters in Seattle a couple of times, and Amazon executives say they're as thrilled as we are with the way things are shaping up. It feels as if we're making some cutting-edge inroads toward bringing numismatics to a whole gigantic, untapped audience of collectors and investors, and that's very exciting.

In an effort to expose this wonderful numismatic story to a new generation of potential collectors, I was able to get Mary Burleson, president of Whitman Publishing Company to donate a new *Red Book* to every buyer and Steven Roach, Executive Editor of *Coin World* to offer them one month subscriptions. Kagin's donated a one year virtual membership in the American Numismatic Association as well as a copy of this book to each of the buyers who purchase Saddle Ridge coins. Hopefully this initiative will lead to new collectors and investors of this fun and potentially lucrative hobby.

The whole Saddle Ridge affair has been very exciting—it's put a real spring in my step. On the dawn of an impending long term bull market, it seems as if future generations of numismatists will mark the period with important events like this one.

If you are fortunate enough to purchase one or more of the coins, I invite you to let us know how your shopping experience went.

I'd like to take a final moment to thank everybody involved, from our friendly, formerly struggling young couple to our new friends at Amazon. My entire staff at Kagin's—a handpicked staff of professionals who showed why they're the best in the business. Finally, I wish to thank all the savvy collectors who snapped up valuable slices of Old West history. It has been truly a once in a lifetime experience.

For a free booklet on the Saddle Ridge Hoard while they last contact info@goldandrarecoins.net.

Conclusion:

The Immediate Future of Numismatic Investing

It's literally been decades since the prospects for substantial appreciation in rare coin and currency products has been so good. While the circumstances are certainly not exactly the same as in 1978, a combination of several positive developments elaborated throughout this book have created a wonderful opportunity for the advanced investor to substantially benefit from what will surely be a long-sustained numismatic bull market.

Whether it is wealth preservation or asset appreciation, the timing to acquire the best coins and currency could not be better. By working with an experienced numismatic advisor, you can significantly increase your success in meeting your goals while reducing your risks. Now is the time to take advantage of this perfect storm of opportunity.

This Book is Only the Beginning

As a unique benefit to our readers, we have established a dedicated web site that provides more in depth information on various related topics not essential to numismatic investing. Additionally, it will provide updates on market conditions while providing commentary and timely buy/sell recommendations and strategies for rare coins and precious metals. The first year's subscription fee is included with the purchase of this book.

Topics will include:

- Silver Bullion Coin Investing
- Numismatic Collecting
- A History of Numismatic Investing

- Guarding Against Forgeries & Counterfeits
- More Suggestions for Managing your Portfolio
- Retirement Planning using Keogh's and 401k's
- Qualified Pensions & Profit Sharing Plans
- Estate Planning
- Wills and Trusts

Please feel free to leave questions, comments, or suggestions at info@goldandrarecoins.net. I make every effort to respond to inquiries personally. Good luck and successful investing!

Donald H. Kagin Ph. D.

Appendix I

Investment Case Studies

Anyone can select an investment portfolio on an ex-post facto basis to demonstrate virtually any yield. However, the coins in these first two portfolios publically offered by Kagin's, Inc. in the last decade contained very rare investment-grade numismatic coins, that were actually sold via auction and price lists. On an average, portfolios of this caliber have been increasing in value at an average annual rate of 10-12% during the past fourteen years. As a matter of fact, over 99% of all Gem-quality coins have appreciated in the last 10 years.

Case Study I

Classic Gold Rarities Portfolio

In October of 1982 Don Kagin and his father Art attended the Louis Eliasberg Gold Auction. Mr. Eliasberg had accomplished what no one else had done, assembled a complete set of U.S. Coins. Like a number of dealers there that night, they had prepared bids for nearly every auction lot for these great coins. After about 20 lots the Kagins, and virtually every other dealer, had not purchased a single coin. Art turned to his son and said, "The market has changed, we have to raise our bids by 10%." On the spot they did and became the single largest dealer buyer at that sale.

From this purchase, Kagin's produced the Classic Gold Rarities portfolio, which included most of the coins from the Eliasberg collection, plus some key specimens already in inventory. Art & Don's prognostication was accurate; the market was advancing and the portfolio sold out within 45 days.

Case Study I (cont.)

More than 30 years later, the firm assessed the performance of this portfolio. The conclusion was amazing: The entire portfolio increased by over $5.8 million dollars! With an average appreciation of 346% for thirty years, annualized appreciation averaged at about 11%.

Description	Grade	1983 Value*	2013 Value*	Growth $	Growth (%)	Avg. Annual Growth (%)
EXCEPTIONAL 1852-C GOLD DOLLAR	MS-63	$5,250	$20,000	$14,750	281%	10%
CHOICE PROOF 1858 GOLD DOLLAR	PF-65	$15,000	$37,500	$22,500	150%	6%
CHOICE PROOF 1861 GOLD DOLLAR	PF-65	$9,000	$15,000	$6,000	67%	2%
RARE PROOFLIKE 1875 GOLD DOLLAR	MS-60	$11,500	$17,500	$6,000	52%	2%
RARE 1798 QUARTER EAGLE	AU-50	$11,750	$40,000	$28,250	240%	9%
EXCEEDINGLY RARE PROOF 1829 QUARTER EAGLE	PF-63	$37,500	$200,000	$162,500	433%	16%
EXCEEDINGLY RARE PROOF 1831 QUARTER EAGLE	PF-63	$50,000	$85,000	$35,000	70%	3%
MAGNIFICENT PROOF 1833 QUARTER EAGLE	PF-65	$70,000	$175,000	$105,000	150%	6%
CHOICE PROOF 1881 QUARTER EAGLE	PF-65	$12,500	$40,000	$27,500	220%	8%
CHOICE PROOF 1885 QUARTER EAGLE	PF-65	$12,500	$27,500	$15,000	120%	4%
CHOICE 1854-D $3 GOLD	EF-45	$18,000	$50,000	$32,000	178%	7%
CHOICE PROOF 1862 $3 GOLD	PF-63/65	$17,500	$40,000	$22,500	129%	5%
CHOICE PROOF 1888 $3 GOLD	PF-63	$12,500	$17,500	$5,000	40%	1%
POPULAR PROOF 1879 FLOWING HAIR $4 GOLD STELLA	PF-60	$26,500	$115,000	$88,500	334%	12%
SELECT UNCIRCULATED 1800 HALF EAGLE	MS-63	$17,500	$35,000	$17,500	100%	4%
SUPERB AND VERY RARE 1825/1 HALF EAGLE	MS-65	$75,000	$300,000	$225,000	300%	11%
1825 OVER 4 U.S. HALF EAGLE ONE OF ONLY TWO PIECES KNOWN	VF-25obv EF-45rev	$200,000	$850,000	$650,000	325%	12%
SUPERB FINEST KNOWN 1831 LARGE D HALF EAGLE	MS-67	$65,000	$300,000	$235,000	362%	13%
ATTRACTIVE 1834 NO MOTTO HALF EAGLE	MS-60/63	$4,995	$7,500	$2,505	50%	2%
POSSIBLY FINEST KNOWN 1843-O HALF EAGLE	MS-63	$8,500	$65,000	$56,500	665%	25%
CHOICE PROOF 1862 HALF EAGLE	PF-63	$17,500	$65,000	$47,500	271%	10%
CHOICE PROOF 1863 HALF EAGLE	PF-63	$20,000	$75,000	$55,000	275%	10%
PROOF 1870 HALF EAGLE	PF-63	$15,000	$50,000	$35,000	233%	9%
CHOICE PROOF 1893 HALF EAGLE	PF-65	$12,500	$75,000	$62,500	500%	19%
GEM PROOF 1915 HALF EAGLE	PF-67	$16,000	$75,000	$59,000	369%	14%
EXCEPTIONAL UNCIRCULATED 1795 EAGLE	MS-63	$55,000	$350,000	$295,000	536%	20%
CHOICE UNCIRCULATED 1799 EAGLE	MS-63/65	$24,000	$50,000	$26,000	108%	4%
MINT STATE 1799 EAGLE	MS-60	$14,500	$45,000	$30,500	210%	8%
BEAUTIFUL CHOICE 1800 EAGLE	MS-63/65	$32,500	$165,000	$132,500	408%	15%
PROOFLIKE 1801 EAGLE	MS-63	$28,000	$140,000	$112,000	400%	15%
CHOICE UNCIRCULATED 1803 EAGLE	MS-63/65	$37,500	$80,000	$42,500	113%	4%
EXCEEDINGLY RARE PROOF 1846 EAGLE	PR-63	$62,500	$350,000	$287,500	460%	17%
GEM MATTE PROOF 1912 EAGLE	PR-67	$27,500	$100,000	$72,500	264%	10%
EXCEEDINGLY RARE CHOICE PROOF 1861 DOUBLE EAGLE	PR-63/65	$72,500	$150,000	$77,500	107%	4%
CHOICE PROOF 1866 DOUBLE EAGLE WITH MOTTO VARIETY	PR-63	$36,000	$75,000	$39,000	108%	4%
CHOICE PROOF 1878 DOUBLE EAGLE	PR-63/65	$36,000	$65,000	$29,000	81%	3%
CHOICE PROOF 1881 DOUBLE EAGLE	PR-63/65	$40,000	$65,000	$25,000	63%	2%
CHOICE PROOF 1882 DOUBLE EAGLE	PR-63	$45,000	$65,000	$20,000	44%	2%
FAMOUS 1883 DOUBLE EAGLE CHOICE PROOF	PR-65	$90,000	$250,000	$160,000	178%	7%
SELECT PROOF 1886 DOUBLE EAGLE	PR-63	$37,500	$60,000	$22,500	60%	2%
EXTREMELY RARE MCMVII (1907) $20 GOLD "ULTRA HIGH RELIEF" BY AUGUSTUS ST. GAUDENS "AMERICA'S MOST BEAUTIFUL COIN"	PR-67	$240,000	$2,500,000	$2,260,000	942%	59%
CHOICE UNCIRCULATED MCMVII HIGH RELIEF ST. GAUDENS DOUBLE EAGLE	MS-65	$25,000	$57,500	$32,500	130%	5%
MCMVII (1907) HIGH RELIEF SAINT-GAUDENS DOUBLE EAGLE GEM PROOF WITH LETTER FROM THE WHITE HOUSE	PF-67	$55,000	$275,000	$220,000	400%	15%
CHOICE MATTE PROOF 1908 DOUBLE EAGLE	PF-65	$37,500	$86,000	$48,500	129%	5%
GEM PROOF 1909 DOUBLE EAGLE	PF-67	$42,500	$200,000	$157,500	371%	14%
CHOICE PROOF 1912 DOUBLE EAGLE	PF-65	$32,500	$80,000	$47,500	146%	5%
THE FABULOUS 1927-D DOUBLE EAGLE CHOICE BRILLIANT UNCIRCULATED PROBABLY THE FINEST KNOWN SPECIMEN	MS-65	$250,000	$1,900,000	$1,650,000	660%	24%
RARE 1929 DOUBLE EAGLE	AU-55	$8,500	$27,500	$19,000	224%	8%
ELUSIVE 1931-D DOUBLE EAGLE	AU-55	$15,000	$35,000	$20,000	133%	5%
ATTRACTIVE $5 1849 NORRIS, GREG, NORRIS	EF-40	$5,500	$17,500	$12,000	218%	8%
$10 1849 MINERS BANK	AU-50	$16,000	$65,000	$49,000	306%	11%
POPULAR $50 1851 R.E. HUMBERT "SLUG"	AU-55	$32,500	$100,000	$67,500	208%	8%
1855 KELLOGG & CO. $50 GOLD PIECE	PR-63	$225,000	$550,000	$325,000	144%	5%
POPULAR WASS, MOLITOR & CO. $50	F-15	$15,000	$30,000	$15,000	100%	4%
TOTAL		**$2,399,995**	**$10,711,000**	**$5,811,005**	**346%**	**11%**

A complete list of Kagin's Inc. Classic Gold Rarities Offering (Chart created by Kagin's Inc., with data and permission from Coin Dealer Newsletter, and The Guide Book of United States Coins)

Case Study II

Eleven Piece Pioneer Type Set

The Eleven Piece Pioneer Type Set was assembled in the year 2000 by Donald Kagin, Ph.D., the leading expert in Pioneer Gold coins and patterns, who selected eleven coins for the portfolio. The request was that of authors Les and Sue Fox, for their collecting guide, *The U.S. Rare Coin Handbook*, to be an example of the kind of collection that could be assembled for those interested in collecting Pioneer Gold coins. Being that the book was targeted to all types of collectors, the grades of the coins were good, average even, for what was available. Dr. Kagin purposefully chose these grades to keep initial investment costs at a level that would be attainable to most collectors and investors.

At the same time, Dr. Kagin recorded values for a portfolio of the same coins, but in higher grades. This portfolio would represent a collection worthy of the firm's clientele. Fourteen years later, the portfolio in more common grades impressively appreciated by 138%. Even more astounding, the portfolio in higher grades had appreciated 165%!

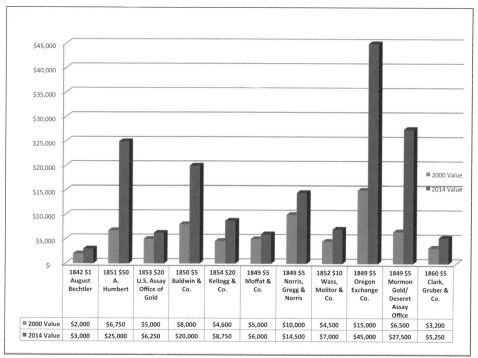

	1842 $1 August Bechtler	1851 $50 A. Humbert	1853 $20 U.S. Assay Office of Gold	1850 $5 Baldwin & Co.	1854 $20 Kellogg & Co.	1849 $5 Moffat & Co.	1849 $5 Norris, Gregg & Norris	1852 $10 Wass, Molitor & Co.	1849 $5 Oregon Exchange Co.	1849 $5 Mormon Gold/ Deseret Assay Office	1860 $5 Clark, Gruber & Co.
2000 Value	$2,000	$6,750	$5,000	$8,000	$4,600	$5,000	$10,000	$4,500	$15,000	$6,500	$3,200
2014 Value	$3,000	$25,000	$6,250	$20,000	$8,750	$6,000	$14,500	$7,000	$45,000	$27,500	$5,250

Numismatic investment has passed the test of time. The track record is clear. (Chart created by Kagin's Inc., with data and permission from The Guide Book of United States Coins, 67th Edition.)

Case Study III

The First and Finest U.S. Silver Dollar

In January 2013, Stack's Bowers sold the finest example of the first U.S. Silver Dollar, the 1794 Flowing Hair PCGS Specimen 66 - seen above - for a record $10,016,875 (including buyer's fee). The following is a 68-year sales record for this Legacy coin:

Year Sold	Sale Price	Rate of Return
1945	$900	
1947	$1,250	17.85%
1984	$264,000	15.57%
1986	$209,000*	-11.02%
1988	$375,000	33.95%
1991	$506,000	16.16%
2010	$7,850,000	15.52%
2013	$10,016,875	8.46%

The dip in rate of return from 1984 to 1986 directly coincides with the gold market crash I often refer to throughout my book(s). Source of data: David Ganz, Numismatic News.

Legacy coins have proven profitable over the years; however, as you can see from the chart above, this Legacy coin was easily attainable in 1945 at $900 but at over $10 million today, less people are able to acquire this type of coin which, if available, would be an outstanding investment.

Case Study IV

The Unique 1783 Nova Constellatio Quint

The unique 1783 Nova Constellatio Silver Pattern Quint is considered to be the first American coin having been struck soon after the Revolutionary War. It was sold in auction in 1979 for $55,000.00. In April 2013 this iconic numismatic specimen brought $1,175,000.00; an appreciation of 2,000% or 59% on an annual basis. Perhaps the single highest appreciation for a numismatic item in over 34 years!

Case Study V

Legacy Currency

In 2008, at the peak of the coin/currency and financial market, a hedge fund manager, a.k.a. "Greensboro", purchased a number of high-quality and very rare bank notes as part of his attempt to complete a set of all the different currency variations. Most, but not all, of these notes, while high quality, were not unique nor considered great rarities. When it was clear to "Mr. Greensboro" that the collection was as complete as could reasonably be expected, he sold it in auction. Four of the notes were unique, semi-unique (2 known) or classic rarities.

In April 2013 the non-classic notes, while having recovered somewhat from the crash of 2008, brought from 60%-80% of their peak value. Yet the classic notes brought record prices with the four notes bringing more than 20% over what he paid.

	2008	**2013**
1890 $5 Treasury Note FR360	$161,000	$282,000

The following three certificates/notes listed were purchased privately in 2008 for a total sum of approximately $5,000,000.

1891 $1,000 Treasury Note F-379c		$2,585,000
1890 $1,000 Treasury Note F-379a	$5,000,000	$1,527,500
1878 $100 Gold Certificate F-1166c	_____	$2,115,000
	$5,161,000	**$6,509,500**

Appendix II

Selected Bibliography

NEWSLETTERS

Gold and Energy Advisor, 925 S. Federal Highway, Suite 500, Boca Raton, FL 33432

Hadrian Brief, Dillon Gage Group and Hadrian Partners, Ltd., 1500 Broadway, 14th Floor, New York, NY 10036, Nick Kalives, author

Rosen Numismatic Advisory, P.O. Box 38, Plainview, NY 11803, Maurice Rosen, publisher/editor

The Dines Letter, P.O. Box 22, Belvedere, CA 94920, James Dines, editor

The Forecaster, 19623 Ventura Boulevard, Tarzana, CA 91356, John V. Kamin, editor

NUMISMATIC TAX AND ESTATE PLANNING

Crumbley and Crumbley, *Financial Management of Your Coin/Stamp Estate*, Information Services, Baton Rouge, LA

Crumbley and Curtis; *Donate Less to the IRS*; Vestal Press, Vestal, NY

Crumbley, et al., *Forensic and Investigative Accounting, 5th Edition*, Commerce Clearing House, 2012

Hoffman, et al., *Federal Taxation: Corporations, Partnerships, Estates, and Trusts*, Centgage, 2013

ECONOMIC AND GOLD REPORTS

Eligius Investments, LLC: Gary Knaus, Investment Performance Research, Rates and Returns of Sharpe Ratios, Various Investment Portfolios Including Rare Gold and Silver, 3333 Warrenville Road, Suite 200, Lisle, IL 60532

GE Private Asset Management, Inc.; Raymond E. Lombra: Rare Gold Coins Enhance Your Portfolio, 1600 Summer Street, Stamford, CT 06905

Santiago Capital, References from presentation, "The Gold Bubble": Brent Johnson, Santiago Capital, 301 Battery Street, 2nd Floor, San Francisco, CA 94111

ONLINE RESOURCES

One of the advantages to investing in gold is that gold metal does not degrade or perish and always retains the value of the alloy. Visit Goldandrarecoins.net to learn more about the history of gold and how it became the choice element to be used as money.

GUIDE BOOKS

Friedberg, Robert: *Paper Money of the United States, 19th Edition.* New York, The Coin and Currency Institute, Inc.

Ganz, David L.: *The World of Coins and Coin Collecting, 3rd Revised Edition.* New York, Scribners

Garrett, Jeff and Bowers, Q. David: *Gold: Everything You Need to Know to Buy and Sell Today*, Whitman Publishing, LLC, Georgia

Kagin, Donald H.: *Private Gold Coins and Patterns of the United States.* New York, Arco Publishing, Inc.

Mercanti, John M.: *American Silver Eagles: A Guide to the U.S. Bullion Coin Program.* Whitman Publishing, LLC, Georgia

Travers, Scott: *The Insider's Guide to U.S. Coin Values 2010*, Del Publishing, New York

Yeoman, R.S.: *A Guide Book of United States Coins, 66th Edition*, Racine, Wisconsin, Western Publishing Company, Inc.

NUMISMATIC INVESTMENT ORIENTED BOOKS

Bowers, Q. David: *High Profits From Rare Coin Investments, 12th Edition.* Los Angeles, Bowes & Ruddy Galleries, Inc.

Ganz, David: *The Essential Guide to Investing in Precious Metals: How to Begin, Build and Maintain a Properly Diversified Portfolio* . Krause Publications. Wisconsin

Precious Metal: Investing and Collecting in Today's Silver, Gold and Platinum Markets. Whitman Publishing, LLC, Georgia

Travers, Scott: *How to Make Money in Coins Right Now, 2nd Edition.* Del Publishing, New York

Travers, Scott: *The Investor's Guide to Coin Trading: Secrets for Profits in Coins and Precious Metals.* Del Publishing, New York

BIBLIOGRAPHY OF INVESTMENT PUBLICATIONS

Non-numismatic periodicals and websites which often contain numismatic articles:

Barron's	*Fortune Magazine*
Bloomberg News	*Money Magazine*
Business Week	*The Economist*
Forbes	*Wall Street Journal*

NUMISMATIC MAGAZINES AND NEWSPAPERS

Bank Note Reporter	*Currency Dealer Newsletter*
COINage	*Numismatic News*
Coin Prices	*Paper Money Magazine*
Coin World	*The Numismatist*

WEB RESOURCES

ANA Money.org	NGC's NumisMedia
Certified Coin Exchange	Numismatic Guaranty Corporation
Coinflation	PCGS Coin Facts
Coin Week	University of Rare Coins

Appendix III

Glossary

Alloy	A combination of two or more metals.
ANA	American Numismatic Association, world's largest association of coin collectors.
ANACS	American Numismatic Association Certification Service; like ANA located in Colorado Springs.
Assay	Test to ascertain fineness, weight, and consistency of metal.
Auction	Favorite method of public or mail-bid sale of numismatic items in which buyers compete for coins consigned for sale.
Authentication	Determination of genuineness of item.
Bag Marks	Small marks acquired by coins in handling in mint bags.
Bank Notes	Paper money issued by banks mainly in the 19th century.
Bit	A Spanish-American 1 reale piece, originally worth 12½ cents in the United States until 1857.
Bourse	Sales room for dealers at coin or stamp shows.
Bullion	Uncoined gold or silver.
Bullion Coin	Modern coins struck and valued solely for gold content and value, such as such as American Eagles, South African Krugerrand, Austrian 100 Corona, Hungarian 100 Korona, Canadian Maple Leaf, Mexican 50 Pesos or Centennario. Numismatic coins are pieces valued for rarity and collectability, rather than precious metal content.
Cabinet Friction	Surface wear on a coin caused by friction between it and its container, such as an old fashioned felt-lined tray.

Certified	Coins that have been graded, assigned a unique ID, and holdered (slabbed) by an independent grading firm.
Clashed Dies	Term used to describe coins struck from obverse and reverse dies which clashed together without a planchet in place. These coins usually show mirror images of the die on the opposite side.
Cob	A Spanish-American silver piece of the 16th-18th centuries, usually irregular and crude.
Commemorative	A coin issued to mark a special event, place, or person.
Common	As relative to numismatic rarity. A rare coin that is easily available.
Continental	Paper money issued by Continental Congress in the American Revolution. Continental Coins are usually called Colonials.
Counterfeit	A coin or note made to look genuine with intent to deceive or defraud, either in commerce or for sale to collectors.
Crown	A general term categorizing silver coins of U.S. dollar size, approximately 1½-inch or 38.1 mm.
Decoration	Metallic award often intended for wearing a military or civil recognition of merit.
Die	A piece of metal engraved with a design and used for stamping coins or other similar pieces.
Die Variety	A coin with the same basic characteristics but with minor alterations.
Disme	One-tenth of a dollar. An early term for a dime used for U.S. Mint 1792 coinage.
Dollar	Large silver coins first struck in Joacimsthal by Bohemian counts of Schlick in 1517 and called talers, daalders and finally dollars in various countries issuing large-size silver pieces.
Doubloon	A large Spanish-American gold coin of 16 escudos struck at several mints from Mexico to Santiago de Chile.
Eagle	A U.S. $10 gold coin.
Encased Postage	Postage stamps encased in brass containers with advertising on back and mica front, issued and circulated during the Civil War after coins had disappeared from circulation.
Error	A numismatic item with a mistake in its manufacture.
Exonumia	Numismatic items not of Government issue, including tokens and medals and encased postage.

Face	The surface of a coin, usually called obverse; the correct term for the front side of a note.
Fantasy	Unauthorized money purporting to be issued by a real or imaginary governing authority as a coin.
Field	The space on a coin not occupied by the design.
Flan	Blank planchet on which a coin is struck.
Fugio Cent	The first official United States coin authorized by Congress and struck by private contractor in 1787.
Gobrecht Dollars	Pattern silver dollars designed by U.S. Mint engraver Christian Gobrecht in 1836 with seated Liberty obverse and flying eagle reverse.
Hairlines	Minute lines on proof coins resulting from handling or cleaning.
Half Eagle	A United States $5 gold coin.
Hard Times Tokens	Copper pieces about the size of cents struck between 1837 and 1841 and unofficially serving as money. The coins bear political or commercial messages recalling the financial depressing following President Andrew Jackson's attack on the Bank of the United States.
Hidden Value	Additional value not easily apparent to the novice.
Holder	The receptacle that coins and notes are put in when they become certified. Includes a tag.
Incuse	Sunken letters or designs stamped into coin or medal.
Inscription	Words, numerals, and abbreviations on coins.
Krugerrand	South African bullion gold coin of one Troy ounce first issued in 1967 portraying President "Oom Paul" Kruger (1825-1904).
Kagin Number	Variety and die numbers assigned to private gold coins and patterns referenced in *Private Gold Coins and Patterns of the United States* by Dr. Donald H. Kagin.
Large Cent	Pure copper 26 to 27 mm cents struck 1793-1857, a favorite series of U.S. collectors.
Legend	Words following the curvature of a coin.
Lettered Edge	An inscription around the narrow edge of a coin.
Leveraging	Borrowing money such as stocks, coins or currency as collateral.
Maple Leaf	Canadian bullion one ounce gold coin first issued 1979.
Matte	A dull frosted surface usually found on proof coins.

Matte Proof	A proof coin with a finely granulated surface produced by the issuing authority.
Maverick	An unidentifiable specimen, such as a token not bearing indication of any place of issue.
Medal	Numismatic item, usually of metal, not intended for circulation as money but commemorative or artistic in nature.
Military Payment Certificate	Paper scrip for use by armed services personnel, created as an anti-black market device protecting the U.S. dollar.
Milled Edge	A thick, raised rim around the coin bearing striations also called reeding.
Mint	Factory striking coins for government.
Mint Luster	The "frost" on the surface of an uncirculated coin.
Mint Mark	Distinctive symbol or letter identifying the place in which a coin was struck. In the modern U.S., P for Philadelphia, D for Denver and S for San Francisco.
Minor Coins	A silver coin of less than crown weight or any coin in base metal.
Misstrike	An error in striking.
Morgan Dollar	U.S. silver coin struck 1878-1921, named for designer, Mint engraver George T. Morgan; replaced by Peace design 1921-1935.
Mule	A coin whose obverse and reverse dies were not originally intended to be used together.
National Bank Note	Paper money issued by nationally chartered banks from 1863 through 1935 and secured with government bonds as collateral.
Nickel Three Cents	Three-cent pieces of copper and nickel alloy coined in the U.S. from 1865 to 1889.
North African Notes	1934 and 1934A U.S. silver certificate with yellow seals used by U.S. armed forces in North Africa and Sicily during World War II, specially printed to prevent use in the U.S. in the event of military setbacks overseas.
Note	A piece of currency.
Numismatic Premium	Added value above the value of the precious metal (intrinsic value).
Numismatics	The science of coins, paper money, medals and tokens.
Numismatist	A deep student or informed professional knowledgeable in numismatics.

Obverse	The face side of a coin, bearing the principal design.
Overdate	A coin made of superimposing one or more numerals on a previously dated die.
Overstrike	A coin produced on a previously struck coin.
Patina	The natural coloring acquired by a coin over time due to oxidation.
Pattern	Trial piece or proposed design for a new coin or denomination, one which may or may not be adopted for regular coinage.
Penny	British copper coin equal to ½ shilling, kept as an American slang term for the cent.
Pieces of Eight	The Spanish-American 8 reales silver coin, legal tender in U.S. until 1857.
Pioneer Gold	Those privately-issued gold coins struck prior to 1864. These include coins struck in Georgia and North Carolina, California, Oregon, Utah and Colorado. They also include government issued coins by the California State Assay Office and the U.S. Assay Office in San Francisco.
Planchet	The blank piece of metal on which a coin is struck.
Plated Coin	A coin with a thin covering of a rare metal over a base metal.
Private Gold Coins	Gold coins struck in what is now the United States by private minters associated with gold rushes of Southern Appalachia and the West; also called Pioneer or Territorial Gold.
Proof	A piece struck for collectors using specially polished dies and coinage blanks frequently struck two or more times to assure maximum detail.
Quarter Eagle	The U.S. two and one-half dollar gold piece.
Re-engraved	A die that has been recut after having been worn from long use.
Reeded Edge	Serrations running across the thickness of a coin edge, an old anti-clipping safeguard.
Restrike	A more modern impression from an original die.
Reverse	"Tails" side of a coin, often carrying the denomination or subordinate design; opposite of obverse.
Relief	Any part of a coin's design raised above the coin's surface.
Recut	Re-engraved.
Rim	The peripheral raised portion of a coin.

Retooling	Engraving or smoothing work on an already struck coin done outside the mint generally intended to restore or strengthen lost detail.
Scrip	Paper money other than government issues, including emergency notes, paper tokens of merchants or local authorities.
Series	A particular design or motif used over a period of time. This can be used for a single denomination, or in some cases, used for several denominations. The Liberty Seated series encompasses five denominations, the Barber series three, etc. Pioneer is a series of coins issued by individual companies during the time of the gold rushes.
Serrated Edge	Toothed edge on a coin.
Slab	The slang word for a hermetically-sealed holder made of hard plastic which typically holds a certified coin.
Slug	Popular name for $50 gold pieces issued by private mints in California from 1851 to 1855, later applied to coin-diameter blanks intended to fraudulently substitute for coins.
Sovereign	An English gold coin of 20 shillings struck by the Royal Mint or its branches.
Specie	"Hard money" of gold and silver. Specie: a coin, usually precious metal.
Stella	A $4 gold pattern coin of the U.S. designed to serve as an international coin.
Store Card	A token bearing a business name and intended as a local medium of exchange and advertisement.
Striations	Raised lines on coin surface caused by harsh die polishing, typical of many 19th century proof and pattern coins.
Tag	The label inside the holder that contains the coin's name, date, denomination, variety, grade, and barcode (unique ID).
Territorial Gold	Popular name for privately issued gold coins from Oregon, Utah, Southern Appalachia, California, and Colorado during gold rushes.
Token	A piece usually struck in base metal and issued by a private individual as a coin substitute.
Tooling	Additional engraving to bring the devices of a coin into higher relief (same as retooling.)
Trade Dollar	Dollar-size silver coins issued for foreign trade, particularly with the Orient.
Trial	A piece struck at any stage in the preparation of regular dies.

Type	A variation in design, size, or metallic content of a specific coin design. Examples include the Small and Heraldic Eagle types of Draped Bust coinage, Large-Size and Small-Size Capped Bust quarters, and the 1943 Lincoln cent struck in zinc-coated steel. Types are within a series.
Type Coins	A representative coin, usually a common date, from a particular issue of a specific design, size, or metallic content.
Trime	Tiny silver three-cent pieces struck in U.S. from 1851-1873.
Uncirculated	A piece in the condition as issued by the mint. Without wear.
Variety	Significant difference within a specific type, such as bold versus delicate lettering on Eisenhower Bicentennial dollars of 1976.
Verdigris	Green coating found on copper coins.
Vignette	A bank note design that shades gradually into the surrounding unprinted paper rather than having sharp outlines or a frame; used in making up the larger format of a bank note.
Wire Edge	Having a sharp rim around the perimeter of a coin.
Whizzed	Harsh wire brushing to simulate mint condition.